The Invisible Hospital
and the
Secret Garden

an insider's commentary on the NHS reforms

JOHN SPIERS

Health Policy Adviser
the Social Market Foundation
London

Formerly, Chairman
Brighton Health Care NHS Trust
and Adviser to the Prime Minister
on the Citizen's and the Patient's Charter

with a Foreword by
Daniel Finkelstein
Director, the Social Market Foundation

Radcliffe Medical Press
Oxford and New York
in association with the
Institute of Health Services Management

© 1995 John Spiers

Radcliffe Medical Press Ltd
18 Marcham Road, Abingdon, Oxon OX14 1AA, UK

Radcliffe Medical Press, Inc.
141 Fifth Avenue, New York, NY 10010, USA

British Library Cataloguing in Publication Data

A catalogue record for this book is available from the British Library.

ISBN 1 857751 26 4

Library of Congress Cataloging-in-Publication Data is available.

Typeset by Marksbury Typesetting Ltd., Midsomer Norton, Bath
Printed and bound by Biddles Ltd, Guildford and King's Lynn

...how men fight and lose the battle, and the thing that they fought for comes about in spite of their defeat, and when it comes turns out not to be what they meant, and other men have to fight for what they meant under another name...

William Morris, *A Dream Of John Ball* (1888)

The relentless chugging, the enclosed space, the weird passengers who are not what they seem and are apt to disappear, the sudden plunges into dark tunnels...

Anon, *'Ticket To Ride – A Trainspotter's Guide',* The Guardian, (Screen Section), London, 17 April 1995

It's wonderful how such a small thing can drag so many carriages after it with such a weight. It's a proof what a strong thing steam is.

Diary Of William Tayler (1837)

And again he said 'Dom-bey and Son,' in exactly the same tone as before. Those three words conveyed the one idea of Mr Dombey's life. The earth was made for Dombey and Son to trade in, and the sun and moon were made to give them light. Rivers and seas were formed to float their ships; rainbows gave them promise of fair weather; winds blew for or against their enterprises; stars and planets circled in their orbits, to preserve inviolate a system of which they were the centre. Common abbreviations took new meanings in his eyes, and had sole reference to them. AD had no concern with anno Domini, but stood for anno Dombei – and Son.

Charles Dickens, *Dombey And Son* (1846–47)

Dedication

For Ruskin and Jehane, and for Leigh who was there on the day when it
really mattered

The author

John Spiers is Health Policy Adviser to the Social Market Foundation in London. He has been Chairman of Brighton District Health Authority and of Brighton Health Care NHS Trust – responsible for five NHS hospitals and a budget of £100 million. He is co-author of *How To Be A Street-wise Patient: Getting the best from the NHS for you and yours.*

He has extensive Whitehall experience, as an adviser to the Prime Minister on the Citizen's and the Patient's Charter (in the Cabinet Office) and serving on ministerial and NHS Executive advisory groups on the Charter, on openness in the NHS, corporate governance and Board development, communications, hospital design and the patients' environment. He has served on the Executive and the Council of the National Association of Health Authorities and Trusts. He once turned up at one of his own hospitals in a wheelchair, to see what really happened to patients.

He established the first Clinical Performance Improvement Unit in the NHS, and appointed the first ever Patient's Advocate in an NHS hospital.

The author holds a First Class Honours degree in Modern History from the University of Sussex, which also awarded him an honorary doctorate in 1994. He is a member of the Institute of Health Services Management Policy Advisory Group, of the Board of the International Health Policy and Management Institute, and is a Visiting Fellow at the NHS Staff College, Wales.

A Fellow of the Royal Society of Arts, he is also Chairman of the Advisory Board of The Centre for Health Services Management at the University of Nottingham and of the educational charity the Trident Trust.

He has been Chairman and Managing Director of several publishing companies, and Chairman of the Southeast Thames Regional Health Authority management development centre. In 1986 his book publishing company won the Queen's Award for Export Achievement.

Contents

The NHS patient 147

The NHS staff 178

Foreword

On my first day as Director of the Social Market Foundation, I was accosted by a protester outside Westminster Town Hall. He shoved a protest leaflet into my hand and said, 'They are trying to run our public services like supermarkets'. 'Oh good,' I replied, and have since devoted my time at the Foundation to studying the ways in which public services can provide the same quality and variety as the best retail businesses.

In this task John Spiers has been an invaluable ally. He has brought to the NHS reforms his business experience as a remarkably successful entrepreneur. He has also brought a clear, jargon-free, literary style which allows him to communicate with experts and lay observers alike, as this book shows. Most important of all he has brought the reformers back time and time again to what really matters – consumer preference.

The National Health Service is a monopoly provider and a monopoly purchaser. It is highly centralized and tightly regulated. Its professional staff are well organized and its auxiliary staff are highly unionized. Those with a financial interest at stake have been allowed to become arbiters of what change is politically, even morally, acceptable.

John Spiers has not allowed any of this to stand in his way. He has developed his argument for patient power both in print and in practise with ideas like the patient advocate, which I am sure others will copy. He has not been content with the split between purchasing and providing remaining theoretical. He has pushed for more powerful purchasers and more responsive providers. Nor has he shown the traditional deference to consultants – insisting that they serve the patients not themselves. For this he has paid a high price but, I believe, he is right. Readers of this book will come to agree.

Daniel Finkelstein
Director, the Social
Market Foundation,
London
September 1995

Acknowledgements

Writing is the quickest route into debt. Mine is extensive. There are many friends and colleagues with whom I have had the privilege and the opportunity to discuss the dilemmas of public policy and service which I seek to address in this book. To them I owe much.

My partner Leigh Richardson, who has shared her extensive Health Service management experience with me, and Guy Howland, Policy and Publications Manager of the IHSM, persuaded me to bring this material together into a book. I owe to them a very special debt of gratitude for their friendship, their generosity of spirit, and for the privilege of many opportunities to discuss ideas together. These thanks are not easily encompassed in a conventional expression of gratitude.

The stylish, practical, and inimitably relevant leadership of Ray Rowden, Director of the IHSM, has been a source of inspiration and renewal. I am especially grateful, too, to Daniel Finkelstein, Director of the Social Market Foundation, and John Simmonds, of the University of Sussex, who, like Ray, have given me a great deal of personal encouragement and support, in the mutual attempt to understand cultural realities, political possibilities, and how to stimulate changes in practice.

I am indebted to The Rt. Hon. Mrs Virginia Bottomley MP, for appointing me to the Chairmanship of Brighton Health Authority in the first place, and for all the opportunities she has afforded me since 1991. My friends David Willetts MP, Sir Andrew Bowden MBE MP and the late Lord (Keith) Joseph CH, first encouraged me to take a part in the development of the NHS reforms. The Hon. Tom Sackville MP has generously shown me personal kindnesses, and enabled me to take part in his fundamental work on the improvement of the environment for care. My friend Keith Britto OBE has been an unfailing source of good sense since my days as an adviser on education reform in the late 1980s.

I have been fortunate to receive much personal and professional loyalty and friendship from Margaret Dann, of Brighton Health Care NHS Trust; Becky Williams, formerly of Brighton Health Care and now enlivening life at the BBC; and Pauline Sinkins, formerly of Brighton Health Care and now Communications Director for the South & West Regional Health Authority.

Many other friends and colleagues have shared with me conversations on the issues of policy and practice. Chris West, then Chief Executive of Portsmouth and South East Hampshire Health Authority, befriended me when I arrived in the NHS, and is much missed. Professor Alan Maynard, Director of the Centre for Health Economics at the University of York, has guided me to appreciate that rhetoric is not a substitute for evaluation, that cost and clinical effectiveness are interdependent, and that 'quality' is a very vague word.

Rick Nye, Deputy Director of The SMF, has always been generous with his time and guidance, as have Professor Eric Caines CB, Director of the Centre for Health Services Management, University of Nottingham; Stephen Prosser, Chief Executive of the NHS Staff College, Wales; Caroline Langridge, Head of the NHS Women's Unit; Dr Adam Darkins, Medical Director of Riverside Community Health NHS Trust; Steven Henning Sieverts, the independent management consultant; and Alys Harwood of the King's Fund Organisational Audit. I am grateful, too, to Marc Shaw of the Social Market Foundation, and Ben Marks of the IHSM.

My thanks are due to many other friends and colleagues during five momentous years. I would like to acknowledge here especially Dr Geoffrey Lockwood, George Kiloh, Sir Robert Balchin, Brian Rowson, Mark Fulbrook, William Norris, Professor Stephen Haseler, Alex Aiken, Barry Turner, John Bird, Phyllis Oliver, Alan Soutter, Sue Roe, Dr David G Green and Dr Gerald Donaghy.

Other friends in Whitehall, in the media, and in medical circles, not named here, know that I salute their spirit, too.

Camilla Behrens has been a most professional, supportive, and deft editor. I have, too, greatly valued the encouragement given to me by Andrew Bax and Gillian Nineham of Radcliffe Medical Press.

My uncle, Mr Alfred Root, is the real author of all my endeavours and he has supported me constantly with his love, judgement, and friendship. As he would say: 'It's a long way from Stanhope!'.

My greatest indebtedness is inadequately acknowledged in the dedication of this book to my children and to Leigh.

John Spiers
Salcombe, Devon

17 July 1995

Permissions

The quotations from TS Eliot *Little Gidding* (1942), Samuel Beckett *Waiting for Godot* (1955) and Tom Stoppard *Indian Ink* (1995) appear by kind permission of Faber & Faber Ltd. The quotation from Sir Peter Kemp *Beyond Next Steps* (1993) appears by kind permission of the Social Market Foundation.

I would like to thank the publishers of previously published pieces included in the book for permission to include them here.

The cover photograph is kindly supplied by Harry Gaston.

A note on the text

This book of essays is structured in sections, and to each chapter I have added a note on 'origins'.

There are a number of entirely new chapters. In addition, the book reprints a selection of my previously published articles and the text of some speeches. In preparing the material for publication here, I faced a choice between writing an entirely new book around these themes, or anchoring the book around my existing essays and speeches.

These were originally produced both as a contribution to and a commentary on change. It was suggested to me that these, in themselves, contribute to a history of the reforms, and that the original essays would be more useful if left as they were, in their original context. I have done my best to let the older material stand as it was.

I have added reference notes, reflections and annotations on subsequent developments. I have elucidated some points in the text itself and removed some repetition, both within and between the pieces. However, as a blacksmith strikes the same iron daily, I have allowed repetition to stand where it supports the development of the themes.

I have removed such inevitable salutations – 'I am grateful to have been invited here today...' – originally appropriate to a speech, but inappropriate in print.

Since June 1991 I have been speaking and writing on health issues regularly and widely – in each of the home countries, the USA and Australia. This is a selection of my work. Regretfully, my pieces on the importance of the 'healing estate' and the arts could not be accommodated. All the time I have struggled to contribute to developments, to understand, to think, to help to see the statue in the marble. I hope that the sound of the chisel chipping will not stop yet!

Chronology:
1942–1995

The place of publication is London, unless stated otherwise.

1942 (December) William Beveridge, *Social Insurance And Allied Services*, HMSO, Cmd. 6404.

1944 (February) Minister of Health, *A National Health Service*, White Paper, HMSO, Cmd. 6502.

1945 The King's Speech on 16 August announces NHS. New Ministry of Health to take over the functions of the old Local Government Board and the National Health Insurance Commissioner.

1946 National Health service established by *NHS Act*, supported by all parties. BMA opposed.

1948 NHS founding day, 5 July. Nationalizes 1000 hospitals previously run by charitable and voluntary bodies, and 550 hospitals run by local government. Minister of Health Aneurin Bevan Memorandum to Cabinet advising cost of running NHS to be substantially more than envisaged (13 December). Government actuary Sir George Epps had estimated total cost of NHS in its first year would be £170m. Actual cost was £242m, and by 1952/3 had already grown to £384m. By 1995 it was £112m a day.

1962 Enoch Powell's Hospital Plan published: Minister of Health, *A Hospital Plan For England And Wales*, HMSO, Cmd. 1604.

1971 DHSS, *National Health Service Reorganisation: Consultative Document*, HMSO.
DHSS, White Paper, *Better Services For The Mentally Handicapped*, HMSO.

1972 Secretary of State for Social Security, *National Health Service Reorganisation: England*, HMSO, Cmd. 5055.
AL Cochrane, *Effectiveness And Efficiency: Random Reflections On Health Services*, Nuffield Provincial Hospitals Trust – fundamental text.

1975 DHSS, White Paper, *Better Services For The Mentally Ill*, HMSO.

1979 Royal Commission on the NHS, *Report*, HMSO, Cmd. 7615.
DHSS, *Patients First*, HMSO.
(3 May) Mrs Thatcher wins General Election: majority 43.

1983 (9 June) Mrs Thatcher wins second General Election: majority 144, largest of any party since 1945.
(October) Griffiths Report, *NHS Management Enquiry Report*, DHSS. The first serious inquiry into the management of the NHS recommended radical changes in structure. NHS said to be suffering from 'institutionalized stagnation' in which it was 'extremely difficult to achieve change'.
Industrial action over pay(including strikes) by NHS Ancillary Workers, begins in May, ends mid-December.

1985 Alain Enthoven, *Reflections On The Management Of The NHS*, Nuffield Provincial Hospitals Trust; the scholar who originated the idea of the internal market.
(January) Norman Fowler, Secretary of State for DHSS, submits paper to Mrs Thatcher on future of NHS.

1987 (April) National Audit Office, *Competitive Tendering For Support Services In The National Health Service*, HMSO, HC 318.
(11 June) Mrs Thatcher wins third General Election.
(July) New Secretary of State John Moore and Mrs Thatcher discuss fundamental NHS review.
(November) Secretary of State for Social Security, *et al., Promoting Better Health*, HMSO.

1988 (January) Mrs Thatcher sets up Ministerial group for Health review, chaired by herself. Concentrates on reform of administrative structures. Emphasis on access, choice, effectiveness, devolved decision making. Includes Mrs Thatcher, John Moore, Tony Newton, Nigel Lawson, John Major and advisers.
(February) Efficiency Unit, *Management in Government, The Next Steps,* HMSO.
(March) Sir Roy Griffiths, *Community Care: An Agenda For Action*, HMSO.
(March) John Moore submits paper on long-term options, advising self-governing Trusts and purchaser/provider split. Mrs Thatcher notes 'there was at that time virtually no information about costs within the NHS'.
(March/April) PM holds two seminars at Chequers, for doctors and then for administrators.
(May) Nigel Lawson submits paper querying internal market. John Major proposes alternative financial arrangements. No.10 Policy Unit strongly in favour of money following patient, purchaser/provider split and independent hospital Trusts. Proposes GP fund holder device.
(July) PM splits DHSS, leaving John Moore as Secretary of State for Social Security and appointing Kenneth Clarke for more forceful

development. As Secretary of State for Health, Kenneth Clarke supports fund holding and develops concept.

(November) White Paper, proposing internal market and new contract for GPs.

1989 (January) Mrs Thatcher chairs twenty-fourth meeting of Ministerial group on NHS. Publishes White Paper; Department of Health, *Working For Patients,* HMSO, Cmd. 555. Strident BMA campaign begins. Audit Commission remit to be extended to NHS.

(February) Department of Health, *Indicative Prescribing Budgets For General Medical Practitioners*, Working Paper No. 4, HMSO.

(November) Department of Health, *Caring For People. Community Care In The Next Decade And Beyond*, HMSO – the government's response to the 1988 Griffiths Report.

1990 (1 April) First wave of NHS Trusts established: 57 open for business.

(1 April) New GP contract in force.

(June) NHS Trust Federation formed.

(1 August) NAHAT formed by the merger of National Association of Health Authorities and The Society of Family Practitioner Committees.

(1 October) New dentist contract in force.

(27 November) John Major wins leadership of Conservative Party after resignation of Mrs Thatcher; becomes Prime Minister the following day.

1991 (23 March) John Major first mentions idea of Citizen's Charter: speech to Conservative Central Council, Stockport.

(April) First comprehensive strategy for Research And Development in NHS launched, led by Professor (now Sir) Michael Peckham.

(October) Department of Health, *The Patient's Charter*, HMSO.

(July) White Paper, *The Citizen's Charter: Raising The Standard,* HMSO, Cmd. 1599.

1992 (January) NHS Management Executive, *Local Voices, The Views Of Local People In Purchasing For Health*. Department Of Health.

(February) NCEPOD, *The Report of the National Confidential Enquiry into Perioperative Deaths*, 1991/1992 (1 April 1991 to 31 March 1992),The National Confidential Enquiry into Perioperative Deaths, by EA Campling, HB Devlin, RW Hoile, JN Lunn. Scrutiny commences!

(9 April) John Major wins General Election on soap box; not widely forecast or expected in NHS; majority 21; promises 'classless society'.

(12 April) Virginia Bottomley moves up from Minister of Health to enter Cabinet as Secretary of State.

(18 July) John Smith replaces Neil Kinnock as leader of the Labour Party.

(July) White Paper, *The Health of the Nation*, HMSO, Cmd. 1986.

(October) First Charter Marks awarded.

(23 October) Sir Bernard Tomlinson's report published, recommending cuts and closures for London's hospitals.

(12 November) Norman Lamont, Chancellor of the Exchequer, launches Private Finance Initiative in Autumn Statement (*Hansard*, col. 996).

(November) *Citizen's Charter: First Report 1992*, HMSO, Cmd. 2101.

1993 (January) Bill Murray, *Environments For Quality Care*, NHS Estates, HMSO.

(1 April) Third wave of NHS Trusts, including Brighton Health Care.

(April) 'The Calman Report'. *Hospital Doctors: Training for the Future*. The Report of the Working Group on Specialist Medical Training, Department of Health, (Chairman, Dr Kenneth Calman).

(July) White Paper on *Open Government*, HMSO, Cmd. 2290.

(October) Department of Health, *Managing The New NHS: The Government's Proposals For The NHS Management Executive, Regional Health Authorities and Other Matters*.

(October) Department of Health, *Changing Childbirth*, Report of the Expert Maternity Group, HMSO.

1994 (March) *The Citizen's Charter – Second Report*, HMSO, Cmd. 2540.

(April) Department of Health, *Code of Conduct. Code of Accountability. Corporate Governance in the NHS*.

(19 May) John Smith dies unexpectedly.

(May) White Paper, *Competing For Quality – Buying Better Public Services*, HMSO, Cmd. 1730.

(May) 'The Wilson Report'. *Being Heard, The Report Of A Review Committee On NHS Complaints Procedures*, Department Of Health.

(June) NHS Executive, *The Patient's Charter: Hospital and Ambulance Services. Comparative Performance Guide 1993-1994*, Leeds. The second set of tables were published in July 1995.

(20 July) David Hunt succeeds William Waldegrave as Chancellor of the Duchy of Lancaster (and Head of the Office of Public Service and Science, responsible for the Citizen's Charter). Brian Hilton CB, then Head of the Citizen's Charter Unit in the Cabinet Office, with direct access to the PM, reported to the Chancellor.

(21 July) Tony Blair becomes leader of the Labour Party.

1995 (5 July) John Major defeats John Redwood and re-elected leader of Conservative Party. In Cabinet reshuffle Stephen Dorrell replaces Virginia Bottomley (who becomes Secretary of State for National Heritage); Roger Freeman succeeds David Hunt (on his resignation from the Cabinet).

Secretaries of State

1 Department of Health and Social Security

   Patrick Jenkin (May 1979 – September 1981)
   Norman Fowler (September 1981 – June 1987)
   John Moore (June 1987 – July 1988)

2 Department of Social Security

   John Moore (July 1988 – July 1989)
   Tony Newton (July 1989 – April 1992)
   Peter Lilley (April 1992 –)

3 Department of Health

   Kenneth Clarke (July 1988 – November 1990)
   William Waldegrave (November 1990 – April 1992)
   Virginia Bottomley (April 1992 – July 1995)
   Stephen Dorrell (July 1995 –)

Introduction

The patient's view, and a free society

My purpose is to try to see the world through the patient's eyes. And to help to change it. This book tells something of what one Chairman of a large NHS Hospitals Trust has seen and experienced in trying to do so.

My belief is that the system should start with the patient, and focus on what really happens to patients. We should assume that patients can act in their own best interests. And that it is they who can best define and give weight to these as they balance other choices.

Health care should be about people, not paper-chases; about individuals, not abstracted 'populations'; about serving the community by enabling local people to have power in the management of their own care and in running their own lives. Most vitally, it should deliver care that is effective for patients. There is, too, a proper anxiety about the poor, and an ethical commitment to their health care. There are deep practical, philosophic and political difficulties. In thinking about the dilemmas of health care and its evolution, we should, vitally, keep in focus the underlying question: why do we want a free society, and what kind of society is this to be?[1]

One answer to what kind of a society is one that ensures that everyone has good health care. And that this should improve lives. It is not obvious how to do it, but we have some good clues. As we try, we should keep in mind a key attitude: that is, that there are no 'patients' on the NHS waiting list, but people. It is only individuals, not 'experts', who can know how to satisfy their own wants, which may be different to the 'needs' specified for them by social scientists. Evidence shows, too, that much of what medicine does is based on diagnosis and treatment which is uncertain, ambiguous or perverse. Very large sums could be re-directed from wasteful, even harmful, treatments, to positive investments in disease prevention and health education. As technology, age, and wants press harder on budgets, we as a society cannot afford the huge waste of ineffective or even damaging care. Nor can the individual who receives it. On the validity of 'needs' analysis, one commentator has written of the 'results of prejudice,

preference, professional blindness, failure of moral nerve, and condition-
ing, which parade as the grand and obvious discoveries of objective
scientific method'.[2] In making many judgements, patients are as likely to
be rational as professionals.

This book – built round my concept of 'the invisible hospital' and
deployment of the literary idea of 'the secret garden' – is not about
architecture or gardening. It is about individual health care in a system
which generally confiscates power from individuals, often undermines
them psychologically, and does not know very much about what it
achieves for individuals. The 'invisible hospital' is what patients see and
experience, but which managers, doctors and nurses too often don't see.
The 'secret garden' is the private world of professionals, which is
unknown, untouched and unaccountable to ordinary people. In both
locations it is ordinary men, women and children like us, from what John
Ruskin called 'multitudinous, marred humanity' – who see and experience
'the invisible hospital'. This is the cluster of attitudes and environments,
ways of seeing, feeling, and being treated, which need to change if patient
influence, wants, and power are to be real. Especially so, if the ethical
vision of community service, which the nation holds in its imagination and
expects from the NHS, is to be realized.

The 'invisible hospital' is a state of mind, and a physical reality. It is a
striking mirror of minds. It is there in the built environment.[3] It is there in
the attitude that discounts the individual. It is there in the limits of
imagination. It is there in the language of 'needs assessment', in 'planning',
and in 'strategy'. This language and culture jars sensibilities, when
managers disregard the ambiguity that the NHS must plan, but that plans
must be mediated by what local people say they want.

This difficulty becomes worse if local communities misinterpret the
evolution of health care change, confusing it with commercialization
which has no social consent. The regular call to bring back Matron is an
appeal for the security of childhood, and an affirmation that community
values not be substituted by marketing. People do not believe that hospitals
are there to make 'sales', or to acquire 'market share'; although they
should be efficient. The political market, which reflects unease, is the
disciplinary forum for that concern. It remains, however, a general pattern
of punishment; the individual can hardly influence specific individual care
and service quality.

There are important changes, too, in the 'internal market', as hospitals
lose jurisdiction. Here, a new community focus implies greater local
collaboration between purchasers and 'preferred providers' of health care
to deliver a single system of more managed care. Competition between
hospitals is receiving much less emphasis, community networks much
more. The first study of five-year strategy plans, produced by 66 English
authorities, shows how the internal market is being used to 'coherently
plan' services. Purchasers are 'seeking to mould the market to fit their

vision of a desirable configuration of health care services for their populations. The new pattern is for contract stability between purchasers and Trusts, which will themselves operate a hub and spoke arrangement of hospital care.' Consumer influence is weak.[4]

The development of community systems may stabilize multi-hospital Trusts and other units. This may represent value. But at the same time, we must seek new ways to give power to the individual, as we continue to press for cost-savings and improved quality. What does the patient 'prefer'? The need is to maintain community values, to shift care into community settings, *and* to empower the user. Unless all three objectives can be achieved the potentials open to us will not be achieved. That is, the self-management of care, the reality of care in the home, the awareness of what the individual alone can do to prevent disease. All this will remain a vision. The costs of failure, financially and psychologically, would genuinely be enormous.

The future of care

It was Hayek who said 'It is knowing what we have not known before that makes us wiser men'. It was Kipling who offered sage advice to a friend, embarked on a railway book in 1924: 'Make the platform speak. It should have some tales to tell'.[5]

Patients should be able to learn these tales from one another – a mutual need which interactive computers will offer and fulfil. Patients should be able to check where the best care is to be found – by reference to their own values – and be enabled to take individual personal responsibility. Yet we live in a culture which does not like to hear the truth, and which fears emotion.

It is a culture in which patients have been given the apparent status of consumers whose wants should be met, but without any power of sanction. For example, we know that pain and its management is a major concern of all patients. Supposing we said that the problem was that we do not manage pain well, and that this issue had to control policy. If we put the patient in charge of their own discharge – and if no patient left hospital until pain management was satisfactory – we would then *have* to make pain management our priority. Instead, we discharge patients in pain, unable to manage it properly, without always making suitable arrangements for community nursing or contact with carers. This reflects other priorities – waiting list targets, and management convenience. It gives the game away.[6]

Consumers are invariably poorly informed. Individual management actions are not given definition in terms of the patient's values. And for the patient there is no visible link between care and costs. The fundamentals of patient power, personal responsibility, and the explicit link between care and cost remain submerged. So, too, in the lack of price signals and opportunity cost, is the wider debate needed about rationing. All this is what theory predicts, since producers dominate political markets and consumers are sovereign in economic markets.

However, instead of welcoming open discussion it is tempting and too easy for health care managers and doctors to be busy being busy, and to rely on respect for medical mystery to avoid accountability. With the best will in the world, it is too easy to live (and thrive) in the 'invisible hospital'. Too easy to forget that individual health care is primarily about caring for one another. Too convenient to overlook that this should mean openly welcoming the wants of patients, expressed in terms of their *own* values and preferences.

Our aspiration and purpose ought not to be simply statistical. It should be individual. It should be to ensure that every individual patient influences and receives the highest quality of *individual* care. *Care*, not merely treatment. Care, in harmony with their own values and preferences. Care, whose outcome they help to ensure by being part and party (rather than part and parcel) to individual care choices. Care, in the location of their choice, and in a health system managed on the basis of open knowledge which then influences the public opportunity to think in different ways.

The future of health care is the management of chronic illness in the community. Chiefly in the home – with only the very ill in hospital. For this system to succeed, the engaged and involved ('empowered') patient needs to be a cardinal objective of public policy. They and we need help in recognizing genetic risk, reporting symptoms, changing life-styles, and in shared-management of treatments which accord with individual values. For most of what the NHS does is not about life-threatening disease, but about life-style choices.

On this view, health care is a consumer good. Self-managed care, the prevention of disease, better life-style cannot be 'delivered'. They are the result of individual preference and responsibility, and of the commitment of the empowered patient to shared management of their own care. But, as Shirley Letwin notes, 'The NHS was designed to satisfy "needs" rather than "wants". "Needs" are given by nature, and only experts, doctors and social scientists can know how to satisfy them. Therefore the patient is not seen as a consumer, deciding what he wants, but as a passive recipient of whatever the all-knowing powers on high decide that he ought to have. Therefore consumer sovereignty would defeat the purpose of a national health service.'[7]

Is defeat acceptable, and inevitable, for a free people seeking to exercise personal responsibility, and to carry the moral values of society? Clearly not, and we need to think hard and carefully about the alternatives. This is not to call for isolated individualism – that is not the ideal. It is to call for individualism within a strengthened sense of solidarity in society. This kind of community cannot be delivered by direction (or even leadership) but only by people voluntarily living under the same shared moral obligations. Patient power and choice need to be embedded in free institutions, and to strengthen them. As David Willetts has shown in his *Civic Conservatism*: 'The crucial Tory insight is that a community has to be embodied in real institutions which are essential to sustain traditions, values, patterns of behaviour'.[8] This is the agenda for reluctant incrementalists.

The future of planning

Clearly, the NHS reforms have improved management and efficiency. But they have also shown the limits of what can and cannot be achieved by an 'internal market' which lacks direct consumer payment, and which disconnects the individual from the compelling power of money. The reforms have clarified how the political market functions, and revealed the limits to patient power implied by the absence of price-conscious choice.

Yet, although individuals are capable of making decisions for themselves, it is a difficulty that, even in the reformed NHS, this job is done for individuals by outside authority – 'agents', Health Authorities, GPs, nurses, managers. This marginalizes direct consumer inputs into the development of mandatory standards, which is essential.

The challenge is to maintain the new efficiencies of the NHS, and to equip the consumer to exercise choice. Yet professional and consumer standards are often at variance.[9] For example, many hospital complaints departments send up replies to patients' letters for the signature of the Chairman. But these replies often seek to justify to patients *why things must be as they are*. They frequently do not 'answer' the patient's concerns, spoken or unspoken, at all. Complaints about poor communications can usually be analysed back to attitudes. In fact, the individual is isolated by the expert, not by the market.[10]

The nature and design of the environment matters as well. Too many NHS hospitals still reflect in their physical body the mind that says that patients do not matter. These buildings – which are 'planned' for local communities, possibly out of existence – speculate the obvious: that patients have no power or sanction.

Yet the local hospital remains a source of local loyalties and affection. It represents an idea rather than an institution. It is a representative sign of the integrity of a community, and a vital element in public consciousness. Its recurrence of ritual is a comforting source of continuity, quietude and consolation in a world increasingly dedicated to change. Hence, in part, the lack of social consent for planned and 'needed' change which health authorities 'know' is necessary. Hence, in part, anxiety about 'commercialization', spending on 'image', and increases in management costs. The affection reserved for local community hospitals, and the commitment to universal cover which they represent in the imagination of the nation, is one source of the evident unpersuasiveness of statistics when produced to justify closures. This is the denial of the intuitively untrue.

The bewilderment that ordinary people feel with the language of 'needs-based strategy', and purchasing for 'populations' reflects a deep imaginative community insight, one with which the NHS has still to come to terms. It is said that patient power 'would make planning impossible'. The 'problem' of the public is a long-standing difficulty. How to accommodate opinion *and* planning is a challenge for much more open discussion if there is to be social consent for public policy.

The Chairman's role

The law is a denial, too. Patients have virtually no rights enforceable in law. The official medical system disempowers, although it is a power game.

Instead of individual power, patients have 'agents' – family doctors and nurses. But these do not inevitably involve them in deciding how they want to be treated. Nor are patients usually involved in deciding who to be sent to if they need to see a specialist. There is often a choice of treatments, and of who to see. The family doctor will know – reliably, if informally – about who is most sensitive to the values of the individual patient, who listens best, who is up-to-date, who is practised and who is preaching. This knowledge is un-commonly shared. The GP is not required to take the patient's views into account. Unless the individual patient has power around money; unless the individual patient has power around knowledge; unless the individual patient is valued as an individual – not as 'your case', not as a 'finished consultant episode', not as 'the hip in bed 9' – the NHS reforms may well succeed financially, but they will fail socially.

For government, reform of the NHS was not primarily about patient power, despite the rhetoric of 'choice'. It was a problem of costs and a response to a financial crisis. (Although the reform process in fact suppressed debate on funding alternatives, notably on compulsory health insurance, over which anxiety concerning the American experience of the uninsured remains a powerful political factor.) However, many supporters saw reform as an opportunity to introduce private consumer service *attitudes*; some urged private sector management and investment. For others, the personal testament was to help change the experience of how patients are treated, maintaining community commitments, and querying treatment options and outcomes themselves.[11]

The reform process itself has made it evident that health care is a social process, and a social construction. We need to try to find ways to improve the whole experience, and to sort out the relative importance of those factors which affect health outcomes. This includes clarifying with the patient – before they are entangled in the system – the point in a clinical relationship at which they want to make decisions about their own care. For how you are cared for is a health outcome in itself.[12]

Where does the NHS Trust Chairman fit into all this? My view is that the chief (only?) justification of that job is to get these issues into open debate. Each Chairman should ask of their own invisible hospital: 'What is it like to go through this place?'. It is their job to see that every detail speaks, and to see every detail that speaks. It is their job to discover power and knowledge and to give it back to patients. As I did so, history records, local doctors sought an opportunity to vote against this view.[13] But it is one that needs to prevail if the territory in which patient power should be legitimate is to be explored and mapped.

What *is* it like to go through this place?

How does the consumer judge?

'Outcomes' has become a very busy word. What works, what doesn't, and what does this doctor and hospital actually do? What are the alternative treatment strategies?

We are looking for the delivery of better outcomes in three dimensions: in clinical outcomes, in cost-effective outcomes, and in patient-determined outcomes (my answer to my question, 'whose evidence?'). These are interdependent, but they are different. We know it is difficult to assess clinical outcomes, in part because until recently we have hardly tried, in part because of many intrinsic and elusive dilemmas and impediments.[14]

Instead, the NHS has been paternalist, centralist, collectivist in 'knowing' what the individual patient 'needs', and so it has hardly been necessary to ask. We do not systematically track patients after treatment. It is little surprise that there is so little data on what works best, and what is actually done, although the true costs of poor quality are enormous, and research shows startling practice variations.[15] Our policy goal is improvement and emulation. This is succinctly stated by Steven Henning Sieverts 'Our goal, in fact, should be a system in which some are much better than others, and in which none are unacceptable'.[16]

How does the consumer judge?

Very difficult indeed. There are no individual sanctions to ensure that the question should be addressed. In the real world, people are being diagnosed with serious illnesses every day. Yet, five years after the NHS reform act, none of the published 'performance' information helps the consumer to identify which hospitals or doctors have unacceptably high rates of complication, or the poorest clinical outcomes. Patients do not yet have access to what other patients report – on such vital issues as how they were treated, and did it work for them. Nor is there guidance on the location of centres of expertise and best practice, and on which doctors are up to date and have recently been re-trained and re-accredited to practice. There is no reliable, systematic, up-to-date information on where to go to see a specialist – for example, on breast cancer, where services have been the cause of such widespread concern. Good information cannot be studied by the user. Consumers are uncertain about the incidence of illness and its cost, about which doctors to trust, about how to situate their own values at the core of their care.[17]

But these are very relevant questions. A leader writer in *The Guardian* put this memorably. Commenting on the refusal to tackle the real issues – mortality and morbidity tables: 'All opponents should be asked one question. If you were having to parachute from a plane tomorrow and you knew that one parachute packer never made a mistake but the other had a 20 per cent error rate, would you want to know who had packed your chute?'[18]

In a real market, providers listen to what users want. But in the 'internal market' the NHS insistently, unavoidably (and unpopularly) passes 'information' out. It pushes information at people. When they do not respond – or when they respond in their own terms (not turning up; 'inappropriate self-referral'; 'won't complete drug regime') – more information is pushed at them. This exhibits a paternalist, collectivist belief in the superiority of bureaucracy. It is a belief in approved responses. Yet when patients are given genuine knowledge, they use it beneficially – as research on self-administered drug treatments has proved.[19] A real market, too, is enriched by the unexpected. This is how society changes successfully. Which 'planner', for example, could have created Penguin Books, which have formed part of the reading experience of almost everyone?

The NHS is in perpetual motion. But almost nothing is shared with patients about the outcomes of its treatments.[20] Yet anecdote, personal experience, and research about what patients suggest is a good outcome for them says that what people want is a 'good', caring doctor, a 'good' relationship, and some simple respect. They want to be treated kindly. They want to be in a place of peace and comfort. They want, as we all do, to understand what is happening to them. They want to be told what is going on around them. They want to be openly and reassuringly offered choices. They want to be seen and heard as themselves, as individuals.

They want to get better.[21] Most of this turns on seeing the patient as an individual, and listening carefully to what is said and what is unsaid.

Yet the State answers on the aggregate, and on the average. And the first studies of health authority 'purchasing plans' – the essential driving-wheel of choice and quality care – which are just emerging in summer 1995 show that consumers are hardly influencing what happens at all.[22]

The ribbon has not been cut for individual patient power. And, despite the NHS reforms, this launch is continually postponed. Ordinary patients have no power around money. Nor around clear and useable information on effective and alternative treatments: who does what best, where, and with what results. They are not influencing 'purchasing'.

Sceptics will point to Theodore Dalrymple's regular column 'If symptoms persist...' in *The Spectator*. Certainly, we need open discussion of the extent to which 'patient power' is a romantic notion. There is an issue that, in a free society, some individuals refuse to accept that life-style has a health content, or that health consequences are an individual responsibility. Equally, patient power should not be a mantra with no meaning. That is, offered as 'policy' but intended as a substitute for a real market. All this can, of course, be avoided, subsumed and captured as just a matter of systems analysis and process improvement. This would be an error.

The NHS reforms: unexpected consequences

Clearly, the NHS reforms have 'worked'.[23] They have enabled us to get at the realities of NHS psychology, and to build a greater understanding of what we do now, and to think more about how this might be changed. An important result (and a consequence?) has been that waiting lists have fallen.[24] More is being done – hopefully for good outcomes. Even antagonists who argue that the NHS reforms have failed, say that they should not be underestimated.[25] Proponents propose that these gains are contingent on the reforms, not merely simultaneous.

But it is not easy to be conclusive. We are warned that 'Scepticism in the face of facts is an essential safeguard' given the pervasiveness of paradox[26] – and at least what goes on in the care environment is less taken for granted than it was five years ago.

There are, however, many unexpected consequences of the reforms. One is the continuing openness of apparently closed debates. First, on the fundamental structure of NHS financing, which the absence of patient power reiterates.[27] Second, if insurance is not on the political agenda, how to find other ways to place power with the people from whom it derives. In the reformed NHS patients cannot *individually* impact on the behaviour of budget-holders. Instead, decisions are made for them by health authorities and family doctors. Now, there is the possibility that patient influence will become a more distant prospect. This is a possible consequence of the new emphasis on 'collaborative' working, which could establish provider monopolies (secured around long-term A&E contracts). The NHS reforms were pivoted on the 'internal market'. If this is to be mediated by intensified 'collaboration', we must be sure that this focus will serve the community, and not be only a device to suit the system. A new balance must be struck between individual users and the provider – not only between the provider and the purchasing health authority. If collaboration is a device which changes the market, it remains essential to find new ways to empower the user.

This is a major difficulty for policy and practice.

Can we cut *that* ribbon, too?

The patient as fundholder

One commentator, Professor Calum Paton, has recently said that 'Neither services nor their locations are being chosen by patients or the public on any important scale. Many commentators naively add to this "yet", without seeing that the engine at the heart of the changes makes it less likely in the future. Regions (already acting as regional offices) have to "plan the market"...in this context communication with the public means public relations on behalf of the inevitable.'[28] Central controls, both political and managerial, are increasing. Winners and losers are being planned by regions, and the market is thus a transitional device which will see a hospital monopoly market settle down.

Paton observes, 'In the oxymoron of the managed market the limitations are now evident. The choice is either more privatization or more effective management of the system.' Paton would like greater co-ordination, with a close link between methods of resource allocation and planning models.

Yet different models of change are not without allies. One is growing understanding about the moral credentials of liberty and of markets, which are not merely a process of exchange but are uniquely associated with liberty. Another is rising expectations, which, as Arthur Seldon has argued, governments alone will not be able to meet.[29] A third is the evolution of more patient power from existing reforms. This could be patient fundholding.

The GP fundholder device has succeeded in making hospitals more responsive to what doctors have asked for on behalf of their patients. It now offers the potential to be an instrument of more power-sharing with patients. Patient fundholding, as I have proposed, would be an evolutionary step in practices where GPs are budget-holders. The internal market has strengthened the hand of GP fundholders as the agent of the patient, but they still assign patients, who do not necessarily have any choice. The user has no bargaining position over price, nor quality. For, even with the agent system, and for all the benefits of fundholding, the GP fundholder is a synthetic patient. And the Health authority is a synthetic GP fundholder.

Patient fundholding is not 'the voucher', nor is it direct consumer payment. But it would actively involve patients in decisions about the most appropriate provider, spending money already collected in taxes and allocated to the GP. The challenge of meeting unlimited demand with limited resources would be a shared one. It would shift mental expectations, from a service led by 'needs' to a service seeking to deliver wants and quality as defined by the patient.

Just as all change needs allies, the GP fundholder might be one in making this broader definition of budget-holding work. By this device – which would be realistic and able to be delivered in a political market – money would really follow the patient. Co-payment would also be possible (and would prompt a top-up insurance market). Patient fundholding, with the patient aware of costs and choices and invited to share the decision, would develop the existing system one more stage. It would also be more politically saleable than insurance, or of the transfer of assets to private ownership. GP fundholding has reversed the hospital/primary care power relationship. Patient fundholding would bring purchasing to the patient. It would, too, further develop the doctor/patient relationship. The limits of patient power in a state health system would become more explicit, too.

The status and influence of self-help groups would need to be augmented – their role is vital as advocate, counsellor, and support. A major investment in treatment-specific interactive videos is essential, too, and in advocacy.[30] We should at the same time, and in the absence of 'exit' opportunities, strengthen representative and consultative 'voice' organizations. There are 206 Community Health Councils in England and Wales, which could be converted into outcomes councils.[31]

The worth of the State

We need a health system which avoids public sector monopoly and the suppression of competition. One that avoids suppressing the citizen's ability to spend more than the political authorities wish to extract by taxation. David Green states the classical liberal view that 'It is not obvious in advance who will provide the best standard of care for patients or the most cost-effective care or the most clinically successful treatment. It remains to be discovered.'[32]

Competition allows us to discover information – who will serve consumers best, and which services are preferred by the users from amongst the alternatives, as well as what prices will emerge as those that cannot bettered by actual or potential rivals. It is competition which generates the information which people need to consume as they wish – including consuming health care. An alternative to state provision is a health care strategy based on personal responsibility. If this is not politically feasible, the state system itself must adapt to the fullest extent of its frontier. An alternative to tax-based provision would require individuals to make provision against ill health. The community would need to insist that the less fortunate be a responsibility for society. Community responsibility needs to be rebuilt, after 50 years of welfarism. Health care reform has the potential to create what Green has called a public domain which is not political.

David Green states a persistent anxiety, that 'The "right" to health care has turned out to be a command from the government instructing individuals to spend their money on a public sector monopoly which permits the providers to be the sole judges of their own merits.' The alternative, an insurance system, would increase funding and strengthen individual responsibility, but it has other difficulties. Costs are a concern, as are the problems of 'moral hazard', adverse selection, and pre-existing conditions. It would be necessary to ensure that the standard available to the poor under an insurance contract (in their case, from tax revenues, to ensure both cover and *their* power to have their preferences respected) would be high enough, and at least as good as is presently available. The social disadvantages of the poor could be counter-balanced to some extent by a weighted-voucher, as Julian Le Grand has suggested.[33]

The need to set limits on spending continues to be a problem in the 'political market'. An 'economic market' – in which the contributory negligence of the individual would inevitably be a factor – has merits as well as demerits. David Green again: 'The alternative is for consumers themselves to be conscious of cost by choosing an insurance policy which they consider to be right for them in the light of the price and services covered. But, too many consumers have succumbed to the allure of the claim that improved consumer choice and free health care can go hand in hand. The fact is that consumer *choice* is only possible with consumer *payment*. Perhaps the greatest irony of all is that the vast majority of people are paying in taxation the full cost of the services they receive. Yet, because they have surrendered up their buying power by handing over taxes to the government, they have also surrendered their ability to choose.'

Those who dismiss this view have the challenge of demonstrating how patients can be given power in other ways.

John Stuart Mill offers us this classical, synoptic, policy guidance: 'A government cannot have too much of the kind of activity which does not impede, but aids and stimulates, individual exertion and development. The mischief begins when, instead of calling forth the activity and powers of individuals and bodies, it substitutes its own activity for theirs; when, instead of informing, advising, and upon occasions, denouncing, it makes them work in fetters, or bids them stand aside and does their work instead of them. The worth of a State, in the long run, is the worth of the individuals composing it...'[34]

Prevention, the real problem

But this is not an economic market, but a political one. To do best for patients, the instruments at hand must be used, and evolved. The Patient's Charter and the NHS 'performance' tables need to extend their reach. What matters to consumers? Certainly, how long does the ambulance take to get here? Certainly, existing measures of 'activity' matter. But these are limited in their reach, in their imaginative power, in their ability to prompt active, informed choice about alternative treatments, hospitals, and doctors. We need to know not only is this hospital capable of giving good care, but does it actually do it? Patients want to know which doctor, which hospital, which treatment – where will I get better best?

We also need to focus on the real problem. This is not mainly about hospitals, although when patients need to go to one it should be to one that is emulating the best. The real problem, however, is not amenable to 'charter-action'. It is how successfully each of us can commit *ourselves* to disease prevention, to changes in life-style, to our recognition of inherited genetic-risk to which we are open, and to the challenge of individual responsibility and self-motivated care.

For the NHS has a walk-on part only, after environmental and class factors have pre-determined what is likely to happen to individuals ('health status'). Once again, the apostolic answers include a shared understanding of uncertainty in medicine and more patient power over one's own life. This requires the end of medical mystery, and the construction of individual patient power. Probably power around money and around interactive information sources – the multimedia computer, the interactive video, on-line information, and a market in which the health service learns instead of teaches. 'Quality' (to be imprecise) is the fundamental objective.

For best outcomes we need to ask the patient. We have decided to try to improve processes, as a way to improve outcomes. But we need to go directly to the outcomes, too. This requires us to believe in the unique knowledge of the patient, including valuing their knowledge of what to them is an acceptable outcome. It is not possible to achieve a satisfactory outcome without the patient's report – from where the patient, sits, stands, walks up stairs, breathes breathlessly, or carries a bag. This is a collegiate issue, to be handled with consumers and with the health organization together. A good start would be to ask both staff and users which six things really matter to them. These should be the basis for a new Patient's (and Mental Health) Charter. How much of a difference has the Patient's Charter made to quality, now that it has substantially improved management ? Consider what one writer, Nicholas Negroponte, has said in another context: 'If you have to test something carefully to see the difference it makes, then it is not making enough of a difference in the first place.' And: 'If you have to measure carefully to see any difference at all, maybe we are not working on things that matter enough.'[35]

The Imperial Guard

Meanwhile, the survival problems of governments are always a significant influence.

Keith Middlemas has masterfully demonstrated that a crisis in the state (itself paradoxically weak and strong, monolithic and plural) has prevailed throughout the life of the NHS.[36] As he shows, this has been brought about by the failure of government and of state agencies to achieve the aims they have set themselves – or would like to have set themselves. And, despite all the changes in political imagination, Mrs Thatcher herself found that in a political market-place governments did not prevail when confronted by the opposition or non-cooperation of strong, 'veto' institutions. In our context, these include the BMA – a trade union, which Kenneth Clarke has called 'a very powerful, Imperial Guard-type organization in politics' – as well as the Royal medical and nursing colleges, on whose ultimate compliance governments rely[37]. Yet it is not opposition, but alchemy, which we seek.

Middlemas offers an analysis which helps us think about recent difficulties in managing change. He clarifies an omnipresent difficulty for what he calls 'the actual state (the government of the day and the state machinery put, temporarily, at its particular disposal by the last election)' in seeking to live up to what is expected of 'the formal or conceptual state – whose duty is to declare and uphold the values and norms of behaviour in society'. As he says: 'In theory, of course, 'the public' accepts the conceptual state's declaratory and coercive roles as legitimate, but in practice the real public contests the actual state's claims on a significant and increasing number of occasions where these conflict with individuals' or collectives' self-interest.'[38]

Analysed in this framework, recent difficulties over scrutinizing professional practice, setting improvement targets, and encouraging greater patient influence (which arose in 1994–95 between doctors, managers and Trust Chairmen) were not created by individuals. These clashes were a symptom of long-term cultural and political struggles about power and veto over government and governance. This has an extensive history. These antipathies have to be seen in the changing context of the shifting political contract between an enlarged state and agreed social responsibilities.

The state continues to define a hypothetical national interest, and in the wider nation the argument continues as to what this is in health care and how to deliver it. The answers have not been left to a Hobbesian free-market; nor, indeed enabled to be expressed in a fully functioning 'internal market'. The political market seems likely to ensure that governments will continue to promise universal care and a coherent national system, as they confront the pressures of technology, demography and demand which will press on costs.

Equally, in the reformed NHS vested-interests seeking a permanent veto are finding their brokerage position changing in an increasingly open, accountable (and computer-based) society. Here, conflict arises as the attempt is made to run the system on the basis of knowledge, with information the currency of decision-making. Relative expectations and ideas are changing concerning those judgements, and over who is a legitimate participant in these discussions.

In managing the NHS, government still seeks to avoid unmodulated and politically expensive conflict. But understanding about unexpected variance and irrationality in clinical practice suggests that change in these relationships is necessary again. Tensions as to whose writ is to run, for whom, and for which results are a constant. Definitions of outputs are changing, and this needs to amend both formal and informal relationships. The 1940s are ceasing to be the only persuasive and fundamental reference point. New definitions of accountability, openness, and service expectations are shaping a new mainstream discourse. The voice and involvement of the patient is the premise for the best possible care.

It remains a key challenge for a democratic policy to sort out the new basis on which trade-offs between professional vested-interests and patient wants are to be decided. Mrs Thatcher, the great animator (practical, not ideological; instinctive, but not invariably insistent) realized that politicians have to deal with what exists, not with what ought not to exist. With her uncanny political instincts, Mrs Thatcher, who, as Ranelagh notes, had to think in several worlds simultaneously, excluded the NHS from her 'wars of movement'. Not for her Rupert Brooke's cry 'Come and die, it'll be great fun' when war broke out in 1914. Instead, a more limited tactical 'war of position' and coalition was fought. The NHS reforms were a new compromise settlement. Now half a decade old, it may require revisiting, as endemic problems unfold and unexpected consequences (and opportunities) unravel. The NHS 'internal market' is not shifting resources or services on the fulcrum of patient choice or power.

Indeed, it is increasingly obvious that no such fulcrum was set in place. The BMA and the Royal Colleges – which remain convenient for government as regulatory and training organizations, and who keep costs in check – understand this well.

It seems unlikely in the immediate future that any government will seek to reshape the way that these non-parliamentary, non-elected, peak organizations contest control vis-a-vis the state and its NHS Trust local branches. Yet dealings between government and doctor organizations remain an uneasy truce of hesitancy and evasion. To make a significant difference in this relationship it will be necessary to achieve change in common wisdoms. Major rule changes, deregulation, a large government majority, and at least a hint of a direct war of movement to shift opinion would be required. A carefully planned, cohesive, long-term effort would be necessary to change public perceptions and understanding of a profession which has remained supported by public opinion in a privileged category throughout the Thatcher changes. The materials on the irrationality, unexpected variability and outcomes of clinical practice (and of unacceptable patient events) are documented, persuasive and to hand. But it would be politically costly and a noisy business to deploy them.

As it is, patients have no individual power over providers. And the Treasury effectively endorses the elite BMA and Royal College position and status. Yet a positive response to more informed patients will require changes in contracts, and modernized working relationships in multi-disciplinary teams. Changes in the selection, socialization, and purposes of the professionals need review.

There remains, then, a mismatch between a modern, mass consumer-society energized by informed choice and which is democratic and market-oriented, and a society structured and powerfully managed by an elite in a political market. In this important sense, the NHS has been exempted from renewal. There is, too, a deeply intrusive and comprehensive problem here for the global competitiveness of the UK. There is a problem, too, for our hopes of greater social cohesion and community, and of personal responsibility. The NHS is the largest employer and the biggest 'business' in the country. The negative impact of these evasions on economic life, on national psychology, on attitudes to competitiveness is not to be underestimated. They may be a necessary compromise in a political market, but it is not an inexpensive deal. Nor is it obviously the bargain required to achieve the best patient outcomes.[39]

But fundamental persuasive power remains with the carriers of mystery – with Philip Larkin's priest and doctor running over the fields.[40] The public willingly subordinates itself to medical mystery. Government ability to achieve social consent and public allegiance remains the lesser. A professionally-derived definition of the public interest remains persuasive to press and public. This will remain an uneasy, and, in some estimates, an illegitimate truce, for it is based on arguable claims about where best judgements of patient's interests actually lie.

Deregulation, demystification, and patient empowerment cluster as a trinity in a corner of British life in which there is the wish noted by Emerson never 'to hear alteration more.' The grounds on which some gains may be made are reconciliation around clinical, cost and patient views of 'effectiveness'. The question of 'whose evidence?' is fundamental, and it may become a contest over values, rights, and expectations. Here, the exercise of legitimate political authority (as the consumers' party) and the claims of professional elites remain unresolved in the political market. And perhaps they must remain uncontested in an economic market since politics prevents access to that. The more reason for finding ways to evolve from the existing reforms to give knowledge, power, and choice to patients.

As Middlemas details (and Timmins, Ranelagh, Butler and the Prime Minister herself confirm), Mrs Thatcher worked with a model of the political world which allowed for a much greater level of conflict than her post-war settlement predecessors. Yet she adopted absolute flexibility if strategy required it. When it came to NHS reform, she decided against a strategy based on financial restructuring for which the direct political risks were too great. In present political conditions, we cannot realistically therefore expect a compulsory insurance health system to be proposed. Policy options instead need to look at evolutionary steps which can build personal responsibility, involve individual patients in personal care decisions, and make price and quality more explicit.

John Gray, meanwhile, has reminded us that 'For a conservative, political life is a perpetual choice among necessary evils.' It is 'the politics of imperfection.'[41]

Going digital

Even so, there are reasons to be cheerful. Change in a complex technological, modern society cannot be controlled by any one profession. And global technological change will generate social change. In multi-media, in fibre optics, in computers and networks, exponential change will pass the momentum to the ordinary consumer. This will impinge on doctors abundantly. It will dilute their diagnostic monopoly and re-assess their rationality.

Here lies the unfulfilled potential for patient power. For information will be universally accessible – and the demand for missing information will be ineluctable. Change will be driven by responses to hard data. Information will be withdrawn from data banks by users and potential users at little cost. And as these cost and access barriers are removed, 'professional' defences (after all, a historical adaptation, not God-given) will necessarily change. It will not be acceptable for public employees not to have the information to start with, nor to share it. It will not be possible for people to do their jobs without it – and this itself will generate the change.

This is the consumer-science of a new generation. The filtering and design of information will be a design issue for the *user*, not the projector. It is a nice irony that the end of computer mystery will be the end of medical mystery.

Medical information will necessarily and inevitably be more widely shared. The computer may well be the final invention, but its innovations are still preliminary. As 'my wants and knowledge' replace 'your mystery' the opportunity for best care will spread across the classes. This revolution in information for patients requires new attitudes to their need to have it. It requires new content, and new thinking about how to get it to patients. It requires, too, an active programme to help people benefit from it by advocacy and counselling. The recent experiences of similar patients will be called up from the home computer, shared with potential patients, and be a major influence on choice. This new knowledge, of patient's experiences of outcomes (and of who did what, where) will be an essential factor in the patient-GP fundholding relationship.

The decreasing costs, increasing power, and exploding presence of the user-friendly, interactive, omnipresent computer is the key. As the 20th century closes, we are flooded with information – except on the health outcomes information that matters most fundamentally to our lives. This situation is impermanent. As Nicholas Negroponte says: 'In fact, the notion of "tell me more" is very much part of multi-media.' 'Why not?' will be the patient's question. This will empower the unempowered in wider society. For the educative multi-media computer – which 'knows' its user – will ensure that basic levels of education will not be the barrier that they presently comprise. Provision will then have to be a nimble response. The need is for a change in the distribution of intelligence.

Computing, patient values, and informed health care will converge. For a multi-media computer is not merely an improved leaflet. Digital culture focuses on the individual; we will not be able to sustain a system which offers individual care on a statistical, 'population' basis. We will need to plan, but on the basis of what we learn from the people. Indeed, it is clear already that when we do not so – buying 'appropriate' numbers of prostate operations for 60-year-old men – we waste resources, and often do harm.[42] The huge resources presently spent on unnecessary interventions, and on things that do not work, will be released for what patients want. If there is a rise in demand for 'ineffective' care, this difficulty will need to be met by informed debate (and by price?).

In health facilities it will be necessary to document all action in care through the computer, so that outcomes can be analysed on the basis of what was done. The information that can be accessed – about outcomes, and standards, and other patient's *experiences* for example – will be analysed by the home computer, where alternative treatments will be assessed with reference to the values of the particular individual.

The impact on professional secretiveness and status will be dynamic. For, adopting and adapting Negroponte, the digital age has four very powerful qualities that will impact on public policy, and on patient power : it is decentralizing, globalizing, harmonizing, and empowering. This will localize in its impact on the ability of medicine to hide its responsibilities for its inefficiencies. It will, too, finally end the 1939–45 War. We are in the last moments of an NHS characterized by a '1939–45 war-just-ended' mentality of post-war welfarism, of a 'New Jerusalem'. In a new digital age – whether or not the NHS wishes to trust its patients – the patients will want information they can trust. For new technologies generate new behaviours. It is science itself which will change the basis of medical mystery and its veto over change.

None of this would have been a surprise to 19th century railway engineers and projectors. As a leading article in *The Engineer* noted almost exactly 100 years ago: 'We have been repeatedly told that the race [to Scotland] is dangerous; that the men in charge of the train are overworked; that the speed is so tremendous that the passengers' health must suffer; that there is no time to avoid collisions; that the risks of running off the line, breaking the rails, bursting the engine, breaking bridges, and so on are simply enormous. All this is an admirable and instructive example of the way in which history repeats itself...All the fine old arguments have been trotted out.'[43]

Yet there are new expectations. There is growing understanding. There are new social (and community) architectures being built all around us. These are focusing the invisible hospital, and unlocking the secret garden.

As they do so, patient power will not be a rebellion, but a reality.

Notes

1   See Willetts D (1994) *Civic Conservatism*, the Social Market Foundation, London, p.55. Also, Willetts D (1992) *Modern Conservatism*, Penguin Books, London; Gray J (1991) *A Conservative Disposition. Individualism, the free market, and the common life*, Centre for Policy Studies, London; Gray J (1994) *The Undoing of Conservatism*, The SMF, London; Gray J (1992) *The Moral Foundations of Society*, IEA Health & Welfare Unit, London; Green DG (1993) *Reinventing Civil Society: The Rediscovery of Welfare Without Politics*, IEA Health & Welfare Unit, London; Buchanan JM (1975) *The Limits of Liberty: Between Anarchy and Leviathan*, University of Chicago Press,

Chicago; Green DG (1995) The Morality of Welfare Reform: The Case for Unashamed Dismantling of the Welfare State, address to Mont Pelerin Society regional meeting, Cape Town, September.

2   Willard LD (1982) Needs and Medicine, *J. Med. Phil.*, **7,** 3, pp.259–73; also, see Letwin SR (1992) *The Anatomy of Thatcherism*, Fontana, London, p.204.

3   For examples of an alternative vision, see Murray W (1993) *Environments for Quality Care*, NHS Estates, HMSO, London, January, and (1994) *Better By Design: Pursuit of Excellence in Health Care Buildings,* London, NHS Estates, HMSO June. Some think none of this emphasis on design and art matters, and that Mozart is a German beer; one board member I met seemed to think that *Modern Painters* is a works dept. memo.

4   Redmayne S *et al.* (1995) *Reshaping the NHS: Strategies, Priorities and Resource Allocation*, NAHAT, Birmingham, June. Also, Brindle D (1995) Future shock in hospital, *The Guardian* (Society section), June 14, p.4, and Paton C (1995) Present dangers and future threats: some perverse incentives in the NHS reforms, *BMJ*, **310,** 6989, May 13, pp. 1245–48.

5   Hayek FA (1960) *The Constitution of Liberty*, Routledge & Kegan Paul, London, p. 41. Richards J, Mackenzie JM (1988) *The Railway Station, A Social History*, Oxford University Press, Oxford, p.13.

6   Suggested to me by Haydn Cook, Chief Executive, Northallerton Health NHS Trust; my 'spin'.

7   Letwin R (1992) op. cit., p.204.

8   Willetts D (1994) op. cit., p.55.

9   Williamson C (1992) *Whose Standards? Consumer and Professional Standards in Health Care*, Open University Press, Buckingham.

10 How are we to use the data on complaints that we have, and what do they mean? In July 1995 William Reid, Health Service Ombudsman, cited the case of one couple who wanted to know the qualifications of the staff who were caring for their baby. The Health Authority refused. Mr Reid : 'What's wrong with them asking? Why shouldn't they know?' *Health Service Commissioner's Annual Report for 1994–95*, HMSO, London. Also, Audit Commission report (1993) *What seems to be the matter: Communication Between Hospitals and Patients*, HMSO, London.

11 Sources for the high-politics of NHS reform/Thatcherism are already voluminous. In addition to obvious ministerial autobiographies/biographies see Banham J (1995) *The Anatomy of Change*, Orion edition, London; Butler J (1992) *Patients, Policies and Politics, Before and After 'Working for Patients'*, Open University Press, Buckingham; Letwin SR (1992) *The Anatomy of Thatcherism*, Fontana, London; Middlemas K (1991) *Power, Competition and The State, Vol. 3. The End of the Postwar Era: Britain since 1974*, Macmillan, London; Mohan J (1995) *A National Health Service? The Restructuring of Health Care in Britain since 1979*, Macmillan, London; Ranelagh J (1991) *Thatcher's People. An insider's account of the politics, the power and the personalities*, HarperCollins, London; Riddell P (1991) *The Thatcher Era, And Its Legacy*, Oxford, Blackwell; Skidelsky, R (ed.) (1989) *Thatcherism*, Blackwell, Oxford; Timmins N (1995) *The Five Giants, A Biography of the*

Welfare State, HarperCollins, London; Willetts D (June 1989) *Reforming the Health Service*, Conservative Political Centre, London.

12   See also Malby B (1995) (Fellow, King's Fund College) Measuring Outcomes: Are we making progress?, Speech to conference on Clinical effectiveness and outcomes, July 17, London on these sensitivities. Also, the inspirational career-work of Brian Edwards.

13   Hall C (1994) The Brighton Amputation, *The Independent*, 9 September; Limb M (1994) One for the record, *The Health Service Journal*, September 15.

14   See e.g. Delamothe T (ed.) (1994) *Outcomes into Clinical Practice*, BMJ Publishing, London, and Kelson M (1995) *Consumer Involvement Initiatives in Clinical Audit and Outcomes*, College of Health/Clinical Outcomes Consumer Sub-Group, London.

15   Audit commission report (1995) *The Doctor's Tale: the Work of Hospital Doctors in England and Wales*, HMSO, London; Yates, J (1995) *Private Eye, Heart and Hip*, Churchill Livingstone/IHSM, London; (1995) Audit Commission, *Setting the Record Straight*, London, HMSO, June.

16   Private communication, July 1995.

17   Here, over five years, there has been little change. See Enthoven A (1991) The Internal market revisited, in (1991) *Internalising the Market: Quality, information and choice*, IHSM, London, pp.33–4; Neuberger J (1994) What sort of information should be available to the public in an open society? in Marrinker M (ed.) (1994) *Controversies in Health Care Policies, Challenges to Practice*, BMJ Group, London; Harrison, S, Pollitt, C (1994) *Controlling Health Professionals, The Future of Work and Organisation in the NHS*, Open University Press, Buckingham. Also, Bradburn, J. *et al.* (1994) Eye Opener, Health Service Journal, August 4, pp.20–1.

18   Editorial, Matters of fact, life and death, *The Guardian*, June 11, 1994. Mrs Bottomley at Health Select Committee, May 11 1995, Lawrence H (1995) 'League Tables' for England? *Healthcare Parliamentary Monitor*, 154, May 22, p.5.

19   Lowe CJ *et al.* (1995) Effects of self medication programme on knowledge of drugs and compliance with treatment in elderly patients, *BMJ*, **312**, 6989, May 13, pp. 1229–31.

20   Compare American consumer data. For example, the guide to Washington, DC area hospitals, *Washington Consumers' Checkbook*; also Gambone JC, Reiter RC (1993) *Prepared for Health Care, A Consumer's Guide to Medical Decisions*, Great Performance Inc., Beavertton, Oregon.

21   Malby (1995), op. cit.

22   Redmayne S *et al.* (1995) op. cit. See also Bottomley V (1995) The New NHS: Continuity and Change, Lecture to the Royal Society of Medicine, London, June 20; Brindle D (1995) Peace in our Time? *The Guardian*, Society section, June 28; Hunt P (1995) Speech to Royal College of Nursing conference, Harrogate, reported by Brindle D (1995) Health chief seeks yearly contract end, *The Guardian*, May 16, and Hunt P (1995) NHS Reforms, Letter to *The Times*, July 11, p.17; Bottomley V (1995) *Lessons, Challenges, & Opportunities of Health Reform*, Lecture at Harvard Medical School, May 31, specially

published as a booklet by the NHS Executive; Green DG (ed.) (1990) *The NHS Reforms: Whatever Happened to Consumer Choice?* IEA Health & Welfare Unit, London. For warnings on likely political management given by Professor Alan Enthoven and Professor Alan Maynard, in January 1991, see *Internalising the Market: Quality, Information and Choice*, IHSM, London: We have had the language of a market, but not its reality. On similar USA market changes, see Sieverts SH (1995) When the going gets tough, does mission still matter? Presentation to the John C Bartlett Journal Club, at 43rd annual forum of the Forum for Health Care Planning, San Francisco, California, August 18. (Steven Henning Sieverts is an American health services manager who recently moved to Britain, where he is working from north London as an independent consultant, and helping to set up a new private sector 'managed care' scheme to be run by doctors.)

23 Marrinker M (ed.) (1994) op. cit., p. 11. Facts are 'values'. Data for evaluation are ambiguous. In addition, medical emergencies (or more than half of NHS work) is not subject to purchaser/provider contracting, except by the new 'total fundholders', who are few. See Robinson R, Le Grand J (eds) (1993) *Evaluating the NHS Reforms*, King's Fund Institute, London; Robinson R, Le Grand J Contracting and the purchaser-provider split, in Saltman RB, Van Otter, C (eds) (1995) *Implementing Planned Markets in Health Care*, Open University Press, Buckingham; Harrison S, Hunter DJ, Pollitt C, (1990) *The Dynamics of British Health Policy*, Routledge, London; Harris A (1994) How should changes in primary health care be evaluated?, in Marrinker M (ed.) *Controversies in Health Care Policies, Challenges to Practice*, BMJ Publishing; Murley R (1995) *Patients or Customers: Are the NHS Reforms Working?* IEA Health & Welfare Unit, London; McHugh J (1995) Can Reform Stem the Health Care Crisis?, *British Journal of Health Care Management*, **1**, (7) 16 June, pp. 343–5; Walsh D (1995) The internal market in health – sham or saviour? *British Journal of Health Care Management*, **1**, (7) June 16, pp. 352–5. Also, (1994) *OECD Economic Surveys: United Kingdom*, OECD, and (1994) Social and Community Planning Research, *British Social Attitudes Survey, 11th Report*, London, November. Klein R (1995) The New Politics of the NHS, Longman, London. Third edition is indispensable.

24 See *NHS Quarterly Review*, Summer 1995 (January – March), Leeds, Dept of Health, NHS Executive, pp. 5–8.

25 My reading is that the Labour Party has capitulated to the reforms, which it would however like to re-label. *Renewing the NHS, Labour's Agenda for a healthier Britain*, Labour Party, London, June 1995.

26 See chapter on Evidence, paradox and consensus, in Marrinker M (1994) op. cit.

27 Skidelsky R (1995) CPC Jubilee Lecture, February 21, in Cooke AB (ed.) *The Future of Conservatism*, Conservative Political Centre, London. See Butler (1992) and Timmins (1995) for suppression of financial debate during reform process. Also, for alternatives to tax-funding, Seldon A (1977) *Charge*, Temple Smith, London; London; Seldon A (1986) *The Riddle of the Voucher*, IEA, London; Green DG (1988) *Everyone a Private Patient, An Analysis of the Structural Flaws in the NHS and How They Could be Remedied*, IEA, London; and Seldon A (1990) *Capitalism*, Blackwell, Oxford. Timmins notes (1995): 'In all the furore about what the reforms would mean, it was barely

noticed that a review triggered by a financial crisis had in fact done nothing about refinancing the NHS. Rather, it has become almost a celebration of the service's success...' p.467. Seldon A (1995) sets out the policy alternatives, The Economic Fundamentals, in Murley (ed.) (1995) op. cit.

28   Paton C (1995) op.cit., p.1245.

29   Seldon A (1990) *Capitalism*, Blackwell, Oxford.

30   Darkins A (1994) Shared Decision Making in Health Care Systems, in *Proceedings from the Annual Research Conference 1994, Profession, business or trade*: Do the professions have a future? The Law Society Research and Policy Planning Unit, London, pp. 73–8. On maternity services, see Robinson, M, Sim F, Chappel J (1993) Which Maternity Unit? Who makes the choice? *Journal of Public Health Medicine*, **1**, (3) pp. 277–80. Also, Williamson C (1992) op. cit; (1994) Harrison S, Pollitt C op. cit. GP fundholders have been more willing to reflect demand by individuals, but are still able to undermine consumer choices, for example on an individual's preference not to have day-surgery.

31   An influential inner London CHC chairman, Annabelle May, pointed out that likely developments may further emasculate them. May A (1995) Teach new watchdogs new tricks, *The Health Service Journal*, July 20, p. 21; also (1995) *Report of the Working Group on the Implications of the Change in the Establishing Arrangements for Community Health Councils*, Leeds, NHS Executive, April; (1995) *CHCs at the Millennium: a strategic discussion paper*, London, The King's Fund, May; see also, for the discouragemnt of patient insights on the GMC, Robinson J (1988) *A Patient Voice at the GMC: A lay member's view of the General Medical Council*, London, Health Rights report, 1.

32   Private communication, July 1995. David Green has argued similarly in other publications. See list in note 24, p. 13, in this book.

33   Le Grand J (1989) Markets, welfare and equality, in Le Grand J, Estrin S (eds) (1989) *Market Socialism*, Oxford University Press, Oxford.

34   Mill JS (1859) *On Liberty*, in Gray J (ed.) *On Liberty and Other Essays*, Oxford University Press, Oxford, 1991, pp.127–8.

35   Negroponte N (1995) *Being Digital*, Hodder & Stoughton, London, pp. 99–100. Other quotations, pp. 69, 229. I have drawn in detail on the ideas and insights of this exceptional book on multimedia and digital culture ; the specific extrapolations about NHS culture and patient power are, however, my own. See also Wyke A (1994) Peering into 2010: A Survey of the Future of Medicine, *The Economist*, March 19.

36   Middlemas K (1991) *Power, Competition and The State. Volume 3, The End of the Postwar Era: Britain since 1974*, Macmillan, London. Also, Skidelsky R (1993) *Interests and Obsessions, Historical Essays*, Macmillan, London, pp.184–8, and Ranelagh (1991) op.cit., p.220.

37   Interview, in Timmins N (1995) op cit., p.466.

38   Middlemas, op. cit., p.xv., p. 280, pp. 414–9, p.280.

39   See Rosenthal MM, (1995) *The Incompetent Doctor. Behind Closed Doors.*

Buckingham, Open University Press, on the untouched norms characteristic of medicine, and my review (1995) Now help is at hand, *The Health Service Journal*, May 4, pp. 43–5. It is an international concern. See Gindrich N (1995) *To Renew America*, HarperCollins, New York, especially p.173. Also, on the redistribution of power from the individual to the state, and Gray's introduction, de Jouvenel B (1952) *The Ethics of Redistribution*, Gray J (ed.) (1990) Liberty Press, Indianapolis.

40   Larkin P (1953) not quite quoted from 'Days', in Thwaite, A. (ed.) *Collected Poems*, The Marvell Press/Faber & Faber, London, p.67.

41   Gray J (1991) op. cit., p.31.

42   Darkins A (1994) op.cit.

43   Leading article in *The Engineer*, 30 August 1895, quoted in Simmons J (1991) *Railways, An Anthology*, Collins, London.

The NHS reforms and patient power

We shall not cease from exploration
And the end of all our exploring
Will be to arrive where we started
And know the place for the first time.

TS Eliot, *Little Gidding* (1942)

It's your country, and we've got it.

Flora Crewe, in *Indian Ink*, by Tom Stoppard (1995)

The first shock of a great earthquake...

Charles Dickens, Dombey and Son (1846–7)

1

The wind in the NHS willows:

starting to reform the NHS, the first six months

I came entirely new to the Health Service in May 1991, becoming Chairman of Brighton District Health Authority responsible for five hospitals and a budget of £100m. I am in my first two hundred days in the job, and I *do* hesitate before such an audience of managers, doctors and Board members. So, as well as trying to absorb all I can about the NHS, and the context of public service reform, I have been relaxing from the tension by re-reading the books of my childhood including *The Wind in the Willows*. I was prompted to call this talk 'The wind in the NHS willows', or, 'Were the dangers of the wild wood overstated, and the opportunities of the big wide world understated?' The wild wood being the 'managed market', and now the 'steady state'.

You may remember your *Wind in the Willows* when Mole was talking to Rat on the riverbank about the Big Wide World. He said, as an enthusiast from the old NHS, and for keeping out of the wild wood, let alone the big wide world 'The Big Wide World is something that doesn't matter either to you or to me. I have never been there and I'm never going there, nor you either if you have any sense at all. Don't ever refer to it again please. Now then, here's our backwater, where we can have our lunch'!

I suspect that, if the NHS was like that, it is not like that now. For we are now there, in the big wide world. And, after six months of the government's health reforms (which came into force on 1 April, 1991), what are the issues as they seem from the point of view of a local District Chairman?

The 1980s were about limiting the power of the state and about the devolution of power to the localities.[1] The revolution has now reached the NHS. In devolving power and in expressing respect for the difference that management can make. This can be the end of many time-honoured centralized procedures with our activity driven by overly detailed instruction and direction from above. Markets are not a tool of government; the responsibility of government is, instead, to create the framework and the conditions for them to function in the knowledge of discovered and changing circumstance. It is the persuasiveness of experience that gives them legitimacy. The NHS reforms combine two conservative traditions: those of community and shared responsibility, and those of free markets compatible with community.[2]

Indeed, Alan Peacock, speaking of the work of the philosopher Michael Novak, has in my view rightly argued that Novak demonstrates that 'The economic benefits of capitalism need not be bought at the cost of adherence to spiritual values.'[3]

One useful way to frame a discussion may be to say that we are looking at some of the most difficult questions of how organizations do and do not change, and of how organizations learn, and we are doing it in the political spotlight, in an exposed service where politics and human emotion daily collide. For, as Michael Portillo has said 'The role of the reformer goes through bandit country.'[4] There are key commitments, and there are important questions already evident. The declared and explicit commitments form the framework: to establish health needs; to improve health promotion; to drive against tobacco use; to develop efficient management; to build new information systems; to establish new local alliances for better acute and community care. Each of the evolving questions are clear to those of us with private experience in private enterprise, but seem more surprising to some NHS managers. Each is focused on patients; each is about the exercise of power to achieve health gain and patient gain; each is about establishing genuine facts. All this is about managing targets, about delivering proven/better care, and about doing it in public light. In essence, the message of all these questions is that it is the customer that makes the difference. Thank goodness we now have a system that is to be purchaser driven.

Matthew Arnold said that history was 'a vast Mississippi of falsehood', and Voltaire that it was 'a cluster of fables that has been agreed upon'. Henry Ford's comment is too well known to quote, and we know that history is a trick played by the past upon historians. Yet, after a mere six months, we are asked to understand, analyse and write instant history.

What we can, I think, already see are six questions that the reforms pose.

First, how do we open up the system to fact, both for incentive and for control, to achieve quality and with outcome data? Audit is king, and Howard Davies is our patron saint![5]

Second, how do we make the system work, so that the NHS is genuinely owned by its users? – Not in the way that unprivatized British Rail is 'owned' by its users; not in the way that the Soviet Union was 'owned' by its people; not in the way that the NHS has been owned by producers. That is, how do we turn the system *outwards* towards the customer, both to the commissioner as agent and the patient as the individual recipient? Indeed, how do we put power into patients' hands? Clearly, the expansion of the GP fundholder initiative is one of the keys, as is the effective development of purchasing authorities which are locally responsive. As Sir Colin Walker said of each today 'They must be properly heard.'[6] I believe that the market will ensure that they are.

Third, how can we improve the patient's experience? In Brian Edwards' formulation, how *they* are treated as well as how their condition is treated. What does the customer want, and how do we change attitudes to patients so that they get it?

Fourth, what *is* quality? How can we improve cost-effective care? How is it delivered? By whom? How is it measured? And who does what when it is not delivered? Clearly, the development of good computer-based systems is vital; there is a great deal we can learn from the private health sector, too.

Fifth, how do we have honest, open, sensible discussions with the public about the complexities of these issues and our responsibilities, now that we have a delegated structure of local decision-making?

Sixth, and underpinning all these questions, whose writ is to run? Who is in control, of what, and at which level of the organization? For providers, this is about management roles in delivering a professionally managed, patient-friendly, responsive service as it is defined by the purchasers. For the latter, it is about ensuring that the service they identify to be needed is actually delivered.

These messages are reflected in what the Secretary of State for Health identified as 'The unprecedented level of discussion in the NHS'.[7] These questions will *not* go away. Not at *any* level of funding. Not with *any* structural adjustment of the system. Not with *any* added devices to increase choice. *Not* with any expansion or reduction of private, competitive health care. *Not* with any rejigging, and *not* with any changed political mandate. They are the fundamentals of the new frame of mind which is *the* major consequence of the reforms. The key battles, which are now localizing, are about these questions.

We are taking many initiatives already in Brighton. I am looking for immediate developments this year. I have put in place a communications audit, with John McKay Associates; we have taken other communication skills into the system with a company called Hallett Arendt; we have appointed Malcolm Miles of British Health Care Arts to look at the patients' environment from the patients' point of view. We are looking for catalysts which will encourage staff to understand and to contribute to the changes that we seek. For example, the refurbishment of our Regency but decayed out-patient building is being looked at in every detail to make sure that it is totally patient-friendly. We are in touch with a major airline for advice on staff training in these cultural changes. We are seeking to use clear language in clear communications. This means setting an open and an unbureaucratic style: for example, using innovative full-page advertisements in the local evening newspaper; and introducing new literature; for example, we do not want to say something intimidating like 'Acute Services Hospital Review – Consultation Document J79/B91', instead, we are now outlining our plans to the public in an attractive illustrated four-colour leaflet, which I have entitled 'We Want to Spend £100 million on *You*'. This is actively building communication skills.

There is an important general point here. We need two separate languages – first, a precise professional language in which we describe our intentions, strategy and expectations; and, second, a populist language in which we communicate to ordinary people. It is essential to think about the perception of language when we adopt terminology which can obstruct understanding. We have allowed our professional language to escape into the popular world where entirely different words are needed if we are to be vibrant, informative and persuasive. Terms like 'opt-out', 'human resources', 'fundholding', 'purchaser/provider split', 'extracontractual referral', and even 'contracts' are bewildering, alienating and thus futile as instruments of communication. They actively undermine social consent. They may serve the purposes of civil servants as descriptive professional language. They do no service to the politics of consent.

We are also setting targets for every part of the organization. Not only on the specifics of the Patient's Charter, but on those issues that are not much discussed, such as how effectively the internal mail system operates in our hospitals unit.[8]

We are looking to see quick changes in careers for women. I have 117 consultant medical staff of whom only 15 are women. I employ 6868 people of whom 5512 are women. There are no female executives on my Health Authority (although there are two excellent female Non-Executive Directors (NEDs)). The District Advisory Team is all male. The Unit Management Team in the hospitals unit has only one female representative. There are five excellent female senior managers in the Community and Mental Health Services Unit, led by Alan Bedford.[9] When I arrived I asked for two lists, which had to be produced by hand: first, the top 50 salaries, excluding consultants[10] – there were not many women; second, the top 25 most promotable and promising management candidates – mostly women. We have a new committee whose task is to review this. I think it is important. The vanguard must lead the rearguard.

Let us not underestimate what has been achieved in six months. A year ago people said 'We can't contract. We can't get the data.' We are gradually changing, piece by piece, the deeply embedded welfare culture that runs surprisingly deep and wide and in unexpected places.[11] The question is not whether the reforms are working, but has a genuine process of change begun, and clearly I think it has. Service delivery is, of course, an ongoing dynamic process. It is in the nature of health care that we can never get to a point where we can say 'We've done it!' However, a philosophy of practice, of adaptive change by concrete collaboration, is enabling us to work out in practical, local detail how to improve health, especially on making choices. We also need to ask the obvious questions that are asked in private business. What skills do we need at the top? Who are we going to promote? Who are the heroes of the service to be? In my view, people like the surgeon Lord McColl[12], like Tim Richardson (a GP fundholder) – people who really believe it is the customer that makes the difference. The NHS equivalent, if you like, of heroes of mine like Michael Novak, whose *The Spirit of Democratic Capitalism,* has just been republished by the IEA.[13] If we are really to believe that it is the customer who makes the difference, this means learning a great deal about the similarities between the public and the private enterprise, and about the differences: whether these are logical and meaningful; whether they are necessary or absurd; whether they are worth adopting or adapting. As Roy Forman of BUPA has said 'We must look at how we can successfully co-operate and not clash.' As a Trust, we will also compete!

Now, as Darwin puts it in *The Origin of Species,* we will discuss in a little more detail the struggle for existence: contracts, activity levels and delivery. I am not going to talk about how important it is to price properly, precisely, and in specialisms – we all know that has to be done. I want to talk instead, briefly, about what we have established as negotiable and what is not. In the first six months, we have been able to set out what it is worth arguing about and what is not. Inevitably, new issues arose: for example, loyalty to the organization and whether it is acceptable to campaign against the organization – delicate, difficult, provoking.

The effort is to achieve change by management and not only by adding more money to budgets. The issue of loyalty to the organization will become paramount.[14] In a successful enterprise it is critical that there should be free speech, but conflicts should be resolved in private. Consultants accuse managers of being an occupying force. I have great unease about these relationships. We have been told that the NHS is an organization where many mutiny but few jump overboard. Clearly, the role both of Chief Executive and Chairman is to seek common aims with the consultants, but there is an issue of loyalty and of power. The traditional medical role of personal advocacy for patients may be moving elsewhere, which is a major shift. Clinicians have a key contribution to make in the management of directorates (although not all directorate heads need be consultants).

The form that the NHS has been in since 1948 has powerfully directed its culture. Not least because clinicians are politically very acute, powerful and listened to by the public.[15] When governments force change, ranks close. I think we need to admit that to change and to run a new organization will need us to engage in some honest conflict and struggle. The struggles that have been important centrally are now localizing, but this remains a problem of governing and of leadership, not of management. Whose writ is to run?

There are those who think that it is not the writ of the Secretary of State, or the Regional General Manager, or the DHA Chairman, or the Director of Operations in the Trust hospital. People who think that have some difficult adjustments ahead, and they will only learn by events. A dramatic parallel was suggested to me by my Vice-Chairman, John Simmonds. He said to me that David Lloyd George had this problem with his generals. He asked 'Who runs the military?' A good question after enormous failure and disaster. When he succeeded Asquith as Prime Minister he said 'I run the military', and we won the war.

The real challenge is about how the organization really runs, at its core. The argument about this should be happening up and down the country, as able and good men and women with long service and expertise see the delicate fabric of their institution changing around them. Many have a different notion of what control is, and what the purpose of the service should be.

We have to find ways to help clinicians to strengthen the effective delivery of their management roles in ways which *coincide* with the needs of the organization, for the best use of resources, and to meet the priorities of the purchasers. There is, too, an issue about the lack of female consultants – this a genuine, national, social issue.[16] There is, too, a major issue about public information about the career details of all clinicians, their specialisms, their outcome records, what we know about secondary infection and second, unnecessary operations. Why shouldn't the public have this information?[17]

Providers are being asked to consider both what they do now and what they could do. They are subject to profound organizational change. However, it would be difficult to respond quickly and effectively to change required by commissioners if they do not have the right to hire and fire consultants. Job plans are a help, but if they are to monitor and review work with effective power of discipline they will need to negotiate fixed-term contracts so that they have the opportunity to respond to the changing needs of the market. Accreditation is an issue.[18] So, too, is the question of replacing, or not replacing, consultants on retirement, depending upon the level of demand that the provider can attract.[19]

Let us not underestimate what it is we are asking providers to do. Commissioners have emphasized strategic leadership to meet real-world need. Providers are changing from a public-service welfare culture to a genuine services-management system where they must attract and manage funds. This means they must now ask many difficult questions. Who are our target customer groups? Who are our current customers, and what do they expect of us? What characteristics do they value? What will they pay for? How are their needs/expectations changing, and how do we research these? How can we give them what they want? What is the core service and what the periphery? What extras can we offer at a low cost? How can we train our people to deliver individual personal service?

We *have* established that it is not negotiable that we are going to sort this service out once and for all. The organization has learned that the status quo is not an option. It is not an option to think 'producer', not patient. It is not an option to refuse to live within the available resources. It is not an option to retain cosy referral patterns that go back to medical school. It is not an option to over-deliver activity, or to deliver a year's activity in six months, disregarding contracts and demanding a lifeboat. Furthermore, it is not an option to ignore the GP fundholder. Of course, it is essential that consultant managers should help to negotiate new contracts, but it is not negotiable to refuse to sign up to that contract when it is finalized.

Consultants are generally taking a very positive attitude, and they are learning not only about management strains but also about some of the personal characteristics of some of their consultant colleagues! If Trusts are to function flexibly in a dynamic market, they will need to look hard at job plans, at accreditation, and at fixed-term contracts for all if they are to function flexibly in the market. We need to resolve these issues with all concerned and we should not underestimate what we are asking providers to do.[20] There are serious resource issues, and if consultants are going to sign up to deliver change, we must look very carefully at these. It will best be done by studying how local processes are really managed.

Three quick points about GP fundholders. First, they are identifying unmet needs (as, indeed, are extracontractual referrals). They are specifying service needs and helping to establish a new equilibrium. Second, they are showing that small changes locally can produce very large consequences. Third, they are raising a question about elective surgery: what is its priority to be? Should the GP fundholder influence this more than the consultant?

Cultural change is being implemented at the top of the organization. We are starting to try to get modern information technology in place. There is good progress in getting consultants engaged in managing the process of change. However, cultural change does not reach right down the organization, and this is very difficult to achieve – not only in public service, but in those private companies that some of you run. To ensure that everyone in contact with the public *actually* changes what they believe and how they behave requires meticulous training, retraining, revisiting, motivating, enthusing, making staff feel valued, and rewarding them. It means focusing our new attitude and tone in partnership with our staff; it means managers interpreting this vision and being committed to it themselves. It is not easy to ensure that changes have actually happened, continue to happen and are managed in detail.

Outcomes are important. If the public is to understand the rationale of our decisions, if we are to have an NHS in which people have confidence and know *why* they have confidence, we are going to have to tackle outcomes and publish the data. I believe this will rapidly become nationally non-negotiable. Despite its complexity, it must be faced. In Brighton we plan to run an open Health Authority seminar to ask how we can discuss such questions with the local community. This is not a stick with which to beat consultants. We must find a way of engaging them in that process. They do not have this data themselves, but would benefit from it. After all, the word 'prove' is buried in the word 'improvement'.

Six months on there are a number of unresolved dilemmas. Will the commercial stringency of the market be mediated by political change? The government is both banker and legislative policeman. Will the political will be there to maintain the changes? I believe it will, and it is vital to keep our nerve. Will the resources for preventive medicine be provided as well as those for hi-tech care? *The Health of the Nation* encourages the hope that it will be. How will we resolve professional struggles about power? To what extent will significant competition arise between providers? Will genuine choice be possible? Will purchasers gain the information to enable them to make fully informed choices? To what extent will purchasers make quality decisions, disregarding the local consequences for weaker providers – how much failure in the market place will central government allow? Will capital be available promptly, more flexibly, in a less cumbersome process?[21] Change should drive more capital, and capital drive more change.

There are many other issues, not least in discovering whether the new provider Trusts can learn how to maintain a business position, to invest in the costs associated with new technologies for futures difficult to forecast. Can they learn to exploit assets, shift from a labour to a capital base, sustain competitive advantage, identify and respond to new needs? Can they generate a marketing culture at every level within the organization? Can they increase quality, reduce costs, grow capacity, grow markets, maintain themselves in a dynamic marketplace? Can they succeed in establishing who the customers really are – the patients – in the minds of every member of the staff?[22]

Two last points – on truth and emotion. If we are to build confidence in the public service, we have to demonstrate the benefits to patients and to staff frankly and openly. We should be quite clear and quite unambiguous about how we as Districts make our decisions and how these affect the service. We should acknowledge the emotion that exists. We should recognize these emotional concerns and address them honestly. This is to recognize that our patients (our customers) generally do not think logically, and especially when the level of NHS debate has been dragged so low. They respond emotionally, irrespective of the fact that we are making major advances in provision. So, when we have to make tough choices, these must be seen to be carefully considered and costed, the result of carefully examining the alternatives in the interests of the patient.[23]

I believe the moral-moorings of the NHS are tightly anchored to new and firmer local riverbanks. The reforms were probably the only practical way we could have addressed the issues that David Green and the IEA have persistently raised. Dr Green has pointed out that by basing the NHS on universal, 'free' care, successful mutual communities were suppressed, and there was substituted an institution necessarily in permanent crisis since there is no satisfactory link between budgetary assignment and demand.[24]

Clearly, if all that we do is to build a new structure on an old culture we will change little. Equally, we need to concentrate on the implementation of change, distinguishing means and ends.

It must now become a service driven by the purchaser on behalf of the patient. The reforms were essential. They were our last chance. Two courageous Secretaries of State have delivered the opportunity.[25] If we keep our nerve, they will endure. The opportunities of the 'big wide world', of greater gains for patients are within our grasp. It is up to us to deliver them in a dynamic but evolutionary market.

Notes

1   By mid-1994 the public debate about the accountability of the new NHS purchasing authorities and of provider Trusts had become excitable, with those on the left convinced that those public services not yet privatized comprised an unelected state dominated by allegedly unaccountable quangos. Daniel Finkelstein contributed an important corrective to this debate, 'Hail the quangocracy, bane of interfering politicians', *The Times*, London, 30 January 1995, p.6. See also, Hunt P (1993) Still open to question. *Health Service Journal*, 16 December, p.21. For a contrary view to Finkelstein's, see Kaufman G (1994) 'The blank checks of government', *The Guardian*, London, 30 December, and Wright A (1995) *Beyond The Patronage State*. The Fabian Society, London. For the broad context see Willman J (1994) The Civil Service. In: *The Major Effect,* (eds) D Kavanagh and A Seldon, Macmillan, London. Also, *The Nolan Report, Standards in Public Life, First Report of the Committee on Standards in Public Life.* HMSO, London, 1995.

2   The important recent work on these points is Willetts D (1992) *Modern Conservatism.* Penguin Books, London, and his *Civic Conservatism,* The Social Market Foundation, London. See also Robin Letwin S (1992) *The Anatomy of Thatcherism.* Fontana, London; and Harris R (1989) *The Conservative Community, the Roots of Thatcherism – and its Future.* Centre For Policy Studies, London. When Mrs Thatcher left No. 10, Harris continued as her Assistant; he was previously, Director of Conservative Research Department (1985–9) and then a member of the PM's Policy Unit (1989–90). See also Gray J (1993) *Beyond the New Right: Markets, Government and the Common Environment.* Routledge, London and New York; and (1995) Hollowing out the Core. *The Guardian,* London, 8 March. Gray (1992) *The Moral Foundations of Market Institutions.* IEA Health and Welfare Unit, London, is now a classic statement.

3   Alan Peacock, Introduction in Novak M (1991) *The Spirit of Democratic Capitalism*, 2nd edn. Institute of Economic Affairs, London.

4   The Rt. Hon. Michael Portillo MP, Secretary of State for Employment, 1994–95; Secretary of State for Defence, 1995–.

5   Howard Davies, Director General, Confederation of British Industry, 1992–5; Deputy Governor of the Bank of England, 1995–; originally, a diplomat; Controller, Audit Commission, 1987–92, the period when this piece was originally prepared. See his important study (1992) *Fighting Leviathan: Building Social Markets That Work*. The Social Market Foundation, London.

6   Sir Colin Walker, Chairman, National Blood Authority, 1993–; landowner and farmer; Chairman, East Anglian RHA 1987–94.

7   The Rt. Hon. William Waldegrave MP, Secretary of State for Health, 1990–2; Chancellor of the Duchy of Lancaster, 1992–4 (responsible for the Citizen's Charter); Minister of Agriculture, Fisheries and Food, 1994–95; Chief Secretary to Treasury, 1995–.

8   During my first induction visits, a consultant told me that no distinction was made on any of our five campuses between junk-mail distributed internally and such vital information as path. lab. results. The telephone link between the principal operating theatre at the HQ Hospital and the path. lab. had been broken and left broken (whereas, in the USA, there would be an interactive video link). We studied creating an internal market for mail and other services, to rationalize intradepartmental dealings and to build an understanding of the costs these impose. We found that we did not have the data, the systems, or the technology to do it.

9   Alan Bedford, subsequently the founding Chief Executive of the South Downs Health NHS Trust, Brighton; a leading activist in the NHS Trust Federation; since 1995 Chief Executive of East Sussex Health Authority; one of the half dozen best managers I have worked with in 35 years.

10   Consultants salaries. I asked for a list. I obtained it for circulation to the Board. I was advised that the list would be collected up from Board members at the end of the meeting. I ensured that Board members retained the document. This information should be publicly available and the statutory instrument burying it in secrecy should be changed. Indeed, as H Brendan Devlin has suggested, this system of peer review should be more openly developed to help manage effectiveness. In my view, patients should influence merit awards.

11   Not least in 'wet' Tory circles, and surprisingly widely in the constituency associations. See Gilmour, Lord, *Dancing with Dogma, Britain Under Thatcherism*, Simon & Schuster (1992).

12   Lord McColl of Dulwich (life peer, 1989); Professor of Surgery, United Medical Schools of Guy's and St Thomas' Hospitals, 1971–; Director of Surgery, 1985–; Consultant Surgeon, Guy's, and King's, 1971–; Lewisham, 1983–; Parliamentary Private Secretary to the Prime Minister, House of Lords, and a Deputy Speaker, 1994–.

13   Michael Novak, op.cit.

14   Roy Lilley caused a major national stir when he addressed these issues in his

regular column. See (1994) 'Wrong Priorities', *Healthcare Today*, November/December; also, Macdonald V (1994) The Men who Killed Sir Lancelot Spratt. *The Sunday Telegraph*, 20 November.

15 I have subsequently sought to unravel the cultural problems of medical mystery and its influence. See especially 'From medical mystery to public rationality', in this book (p.46), and Spiers J, Lilley R(1995) *How to be a Street-wise Patient*, (in press), for the damaging influence of mystery.

16 See 'Games our mothers never taught us how to play' in this book (p.193).

17 While Chairman of Brighton Health Care NHS Trust I had a questionnaire designed and circulated to all consultants and senior managers, as the basis for a Who's Who, which we were to publish. Even though the response from consultants was good (despite warnings I was given that 'they will never wear it'), this was not published during my time in office. I have since proposed at the highest level that the Patient's Charter should require it to be done. The information included could accumulate to include outcome data.

18 See my (1995) *'The Prison of Awe': Democracy, Personal Responsibility, and Patient Power*, SMF.

19 What do we do with the consultants who are found to have been delivering ineffective care on a large scale? What has happened to all those ENT surgeons now that demand for grommets has dramatically reduced? Do we let them go, or allow them to adopt new procedures without R&D demonstrating clinical and cost effectiveness? Are they admitting into beds patients who would previously not have been admitted? Shouldn't we be told?

20 Nearly four years later the Audit Commission reported that these medical manpower and training issues were still hardly being addressed. See *The Doctor's Tale: The Work of Hospital Doctors in England and Wales,* HMSO, London, 1995; and John Yates *Serving Two Masters; Consultants, The National Health Service and Private Medicine,* London, Dispatches Report, Channel 4 Television/Birmingham, *Inter-Authority Comparisons and Consultancy,* Health Services Management Centre, University of Birmingham, 1995, and his subsequent book (1995) *Private Eye, Heart and Hip*, Churchill Livingstone, London, in association with the Institute of Health Services Management. See also Holland C (1995) John Yates: Serving the issues of equity (Profile*). British Journal of Health Care Management, 1,* (No.3), pp.128–30. When Brighton Health Care NHS Trust established its Clinical Performance Improvement Unit, a senior consultant told me that the next move should be five-year rolling contracts for consultants. I minuted the conversation.

21 It certainly looks like it now. The Hon. Tom Sackville MP, Parliamentary Under-Secretary of State, Department of Health, 1992–; previously a whip; has provided innovative leadership both on the private finance initiative and on the environment, architecture and design; one of the most consistently effective ministers in John Major's government, who has done a great deal for better patient care. I remain a member of his advisory group. See Willetts D (1993) *The Opportunities for Private Funding in the NHS.* The Social Market Foundation, London. For the strategic objectives fundamental to the reforms see *The Health of the Nation, a Consultative Document for Health in England.* HMSO (Cm.1523), London, May 1991.

22 When this speech was made I was Chairman of the unreconstructed Brighton DHA, both purchaser and provider. Brighton Health Care NHS Trust had been a first-wave applicant for Trust status, but withdrew. The recriminatory waves were still swamping confidence and flair when I arrived in April 1991. It was my decision to stabilize the situation, and to defer a further application until the third wave. Brighton went into shadow Trust form in November 1992 and went live on 1 April 1993.

23 When I arrived at Brighton management was tinkering with the attractions of a strapline. 'The primacy of patients' (shades of Desmond Morris?) was about to be adopted. I rewrote this as 'Putting patients interests first'. On my exit, Robert Kilroy-Silk, in his column in the *Daily Mail*, rewrote this as 'Putting doctors interests first'. I was never able to convince my Chief Executive of the attractions of a logo. An important opportunity has, too, been missed by the National Health Service Management Executive (NHSME) in not requiring its logo to be used by all NHS units alongside their own identifying livery. So local people have no easy way of knowing that the Easy Access Premier Oaktree Trust is an NHS outfit, and when they see the improvements they say 'Oh, you've gone private, have you?'

24 See Green DG (1992) Health: freedom and responsibility. In: D Anderson and G Frost (eds) *HUBRIS, The Tempting of Modern Conservatives.* Centre For Policy Studies, London. Also, by Green DG (1980) *Mutual Aid or Welfare State.* Allen & Unwin, London; and with Cromwell L (1985) *Working Class Patients and the Medical Establishment.* Temple Smith/Gower, London; and (1985) The changing attitudes to the state. In: A Seldon (ed.), *The 'New Right' Enlightenment: The Spectre that Haunts the Left.* Economic & Literary Books, Sevenoaks; and (1986) *Challenge To The NHS.* IEA, Hobart Paperback 23, London; and (1987) *The New Right: The Counter Revolution in Political, Economic and Social Thought.* Wheatsheaf Books, Brighton; and (1988) *Everyone a Private Patient, an Analysis of the Structural Flaws in the NHS and How They Could Be Remedied.* IEA, London; and *Reinventing Civil Society: The Rediscovery of Welfare Without Politics.* IEA, London.

25 The Rt. Hon. Kenneth Clarke MP, Chancellor of the Exchequer, 1993–; Secretary of State for Health, 1988–90; Education and Science, 1990–2; Home Department 1992–3; who inspired people as well as a BMA-inspired poster ('What do you call a man who does not listen to his doctors' advice?'); and the Rt. Hon. William Waldegrave MP, ibid.

This paper was given as an address at Queen Elizabeth II Hall, Westminster on 12 November 1991 to a conference on the first six months of the Health Service reforms, organized by The Institute Of Economic Affairs Health Unit, headed by Dr David G Green. It has not previously been published. I print here the full text, even though restricted time only allowed two- thirds of it to be delivered on the day.

On 'effectiveness' I have recently delivered a series of speeches which there has not been space to print in this book. These include 'To See the Statue in the Marble: How to get Better Outcomes', New South Wales Government Conference on Outcomes, Sydney, NSW, 12 August 1994; 'I Cannot Tell a Lie – I Did it With my Little Hatchet. Getting the Best Outcomes from the NHS Reforms', address to the International Health Policy and Management Institute Annual Conference, Washington, DC, September 1994.

See my articles: (1995) The outsider's view of risk management. *Clinical Risk,* **1,** (No.2), 89-93; and (1995) Life's long journey needs good partners. *Better Health Briefing,* Sydney, January, pp.16-17; these summarize key points made in this series of lectures.

New South Wales (whose Director is the former head of the NHS in Wales, GB, John Wyn Owen CBE) is offering international leadership on outcomes management. See *Getting It Right, Focusing on the Outcomes of Health Services and Programmes.* NSW Government, Sydney, April 1994; the discussion paper *A Healthy Future.* NSW Government, Sydney, June 1994; the *Program and Abstracts, Guide To The First NSW Health Outcomes Conference.* NSW Health Department, Sydney, August 1994, and the daily *Key Issues and Messages Report* issued during the conference; also, *NSW Health Outcomes Newsletter.* NSW Health Department, Sydney, **1,** July 1994 (continuing); see also the quarterly *Health Outcomes Bulletin.* Australian Institute of Health and Welfare, Canberra.

2

Provide, but not rule:

or, night thoughts of a Trust Chairman
on making purchasing work

To me – an 'insider-outsider' – what is happening to the NHS is both magical and fascinating – inspirational, difficult, challenging.[1] Purchasing and patient views are the pivot on which the new NHS turns. This places a special emphasis on practical action, on determined leadership, on proving effective clinical and other interventions, and on taking professional and public opinion with us. We are changing attitudes, pace, styles, processes, systems and methods, in many settings across a huge canvas. It is the sight and sound of a great ocean liner turning about. And is that not the GP, no longer kept in the soot below deck, waving confidently from the crow's nest?

Purchasing was launched down the ramp a while after the champagne bottles had cracked against the bows of Trusts. Though slower to sea initially, there is now real distinction, thoughtfulness, sensitivity, responsiveness and quality focus in many purchasing plans. The development of purchasing is bringing fundamental issues into focus. But purchasing leadership is uneven. It varies widely, as do provider responses. Purchasers vary from 'Atilla the Purchaser' ('as sweet as a razor'), whose providers think they have been 'nibbled down to the wishbone', from those purchasers managing with a light touch ('like a mouse with gloves') to providers, no doubt like 'Bessy Bighead' (the cowgirl in *Under Milk Wood*), who was kissed once in the pig sty when she was not looking, and never kissed again although she was looking all the time.[2]

What has to be done? What will it take?
What is in the way?

The wind and weather is still choppy. We have not yet cleared away the barnacle blight of an age. In these difficult waters let us ask, first, where have we got to; what has got to be done if purchasing is to be effective in buying health care and changing health provision? What will it take to do it? What is in the way? In posing these questions I recognize that my focus is to some extent limited by my background as Chairman of an acute Trust. However, the vital concerns of community, social, mental health, disability and other services, need to be addressed on common principles. There is in all aspects of what we do the necessity to drive change down the purchasing chain.

Where have we got to (in England)?

It is clear that providers have worked hard to get hospitals and other services into shape so that they can handle the market, while at the same time trying to abandon the old 'factory mentality'. Waiting lists are down, activity up. There are new clinics, new approaches to mental health. Costs are being attacked and core issues of power, incentive, outcome, contract and structure are being whispered (and, even sometimes, addressed). Intelligent providers are learning that they depend on customers and they are trying to lead by taking quality to the market.

Purchasers have set up in the difficult business of making up a new formula and implementing it. Critically, they must develop and implement a new vision of the shape and future of clinical and other health care. Yet already they are accused of being process-driven. Block contracts show a surprising ability to survive. Acute purchasing seems to be better developed than community purchasing. Even there, the rhetoric of effectiveness – by which we must mean both clinical effectiveness and cost effectiveness, which are interdependent – is not yet matched by adequate measurement, even though there is increasing emphasis on buying medical protocols and guidelines to improve the management of specific conditions.

What is it we want?

Purchasing may be more precarious than we realize. If we do not drive it and develop it, we may lose it. If we are to justify the transaction costs and deliver better care, then purchasing has not only to work, but has to be *seen* to work and to be patient-led. It must also be believed in by patients if national policy is to be delivered. It has to offer determined leadership to build public understanding, and to get into practical, tangible, performance management and outcome. This requires more precise measures of concepts like 'health gain' and 'effectiveness' than are as yet contained in most purchasing plans. Quality is not an 'insurance' issue. There is a disturbing attitude in some provider units, that it is acceptable to increase insurance without tackling the clinical practice that makes the insurance risk an issue.

We have, too, to get dynamic relationships into place, with purchasers and providers a righthand to each other in a system with room both for collaboration and for confrontation, where needed. If collaboration becomes collusion, we will not deliver the necessary changes. We need to ensure that we not only have research but development. Health promotion and prevention of sickness matter. We need more thought, too, so that we deliver policy objectives such as acute down-sizing, which requires sensitive local and political management. We must face the considerable challenge of getting the bulk of purchasing up to the pace of the leaders.

There are clearly some fundamentals for purchaser success. First, try to be a winner in weighted capitation. Second, be in a district where there are clear local choices – not in a rural area served by only one local hospital. Third, focus on contracts for health, not on contracts for specific services. Fourth, impose financial penalties and offer incentives for failing to deliver or for exceeding standards. Force your providers to be more actively managed, not administered. Put costs, productivity, systems and data on the critical list. Get into the measurement business. Think quantitatively, but do not merely define quality by crude numerical measures. Furthermore, to transform work, encourage a listening and not a confiscatory management style.

What will it take to do it all?

It requires leadership – clarity of thought and courage – to pursue the hard agenda. For the danger, if leadership is not there, is that the market will be run from the acute units and Trusts by the consultant body and compliant managers, as it has been for so long. This will restrict community shifts and outcome management. We do *have* to get hold of the momentum problem in purchasing, or we will slip back. This is, I think, especially true for an activity like purchasing, which is least likely to capture the interest of the public. Purchasers have no shrouds to wave. It is the *hospitals* who constantly get into trouble through change, and who use 'trouble' to restrict change. The public still thinks health care is 'hospitals' – and, more specifically, bed numbers. They do not know who the purchasers are. That has to change, but it will not do so unless we take communication skills seriously – giving them status at ·Board level, ·budgeting for them, developing them, staffing them.

Leadership

It is not sufficient to have a very able person as purchasing chairman. They have to be tough and demanding. They must be appointed as change-agents. The key imperative is for purchaser chairmen and boards to be tough, demanding and communicating. If purchasing is to go forward, we need to recognize that this is where the opportunities are for the brightest; this is where leadership needs to be; this is where the management of public understanding needs to be most creatively led. The bulk of the service has to shift into the fifth gear where Dorset, Southampton and South West Hampshire, Portsmouth and South East Hampshire, East Sussex (which is giving a strong lead on public communications) and others are already driving.[3] We do need providers who think with a purchasing mentality – that is a gain. But we need *purchasers* who think with a purchasing mentality, and especially those who say 'we only want to buy *if...*'. Let us move towards 'approved provider' status and accreditation. That ball was kicked into touch three or four years ago. Let us get that ball back.

There is an unremarked but common cultural interest between provider Trust chairmen and purchaser chairmen – they should share the commitment to drive cultural change, to help build learning, listening, responsive organizations focused on the patients interests. They are the people who must help to deliver the most change. In my experience, those who are the most insistent on change are new to the service. The old NHS boards could stop things happening; the new ones can make things happen. They do not feel that nothing can be done. They do not feel it is not their responsibility, and they are not going native.[4] Instead, they believe they can afford to drive change.

More than executives, they can afford to dare, afford to get it wrong, afford to say 'This isn't working', and can even sometimes afford to lose. Nor are they scared stiff of doctors. Coming from the private sector, they know what competitive life is like and are accustomed to leadership. They know, too, that we must not only transform work from below, but change behaviour above, too.

What constrains the market?

A recent Economic and Social Research Council briefing on Quasi Markets in Health, Social Care, Education and Housing[5] reflects a common anxiety that it is very difficult to achieve change in quasi-markets – despite changes in expectations and in attitudes about attitudes. If this is so, it is a disappointment to all those who were missionaries of the internal market. For the whole point of markets is that they produce solutions by their own dynamic, which are not predictable or generated by 'rational' planners. John Cooper, Chief Executive of The Royal Free, Hampstead NHS Trust, has pointed out in discussion with me that in the public sector in the UK, and particularly in the Health Service, there remains a huge ideological commitment to rationality and planning, despite its evident failure.[6] Yet the notion that the market *might* work has injected a crucial sense of jeopardy and rivalry. There are, nevertheless, evident constraints on the development of the present market, and on its potential for delivering efficiency, value, responsiveness, choice, quality and a reshaped service.

Despite all the structural changes, structure is still a problem. It is an unpriced service, with no concept of opportunity-cost identified to the public, whose expectations are rising constantly, irrespective of NHS investment levels. There are political restrictions on market dynamism. We still have a major capacity issue to resolve there. Fiscal incentives to top-up cash and to bring new providers into the market, seem to me to be essential.[7] For example, if we are to cut the 100+ week wait for a *first* appointment in orthopaedics in a number of south coast Trusts (a political time-bomb in itself), we need to expand the work done by the private sector, who now do 25% of hip operations. We need, too, more freedoms for access to capital markets, and flexibility for Trusts to control (and to shed) assets in response to purchasers wishes. We need a greater tolerance of risk, more of which needs to be taken by the Treasury.[8]

The practical constraints include:

- the availability of alternative suppliers, especially in rural areas

- the management of political noise, with anxiety enhanced the closer we come to a general election

- limited public understanding of change and its probable benefits – the communications deficit

- public belief in the rationality of medicine and medical mysteries – where hospital doctors produce miracles but managers do not, and where outcome understanding is negligible[9]

- the shadow of the waiting list queue on the corner – 'how can you close a hospital if my mother has been waiting 18 months?'

- the disability of a system based on cost equals average price, which offers no incentive to a provider to do better or to build necessary reserves. For why create a surplus which one cannot keep and use to motivate staff and improve quality? Without cost per case there will be no real competition between hospitals. Meanwhile, private providers are not inhibited by having no price freedoms, and surplus NHS capacity cannot be competitively traded

- the IT deficit – we are a long way behind in the measurement business and in evidence-based clinical decision-making, as Dr Brian Mawhinney constantly emphasizes.

These are overall constraints on the key objectives of efficiency and value, responsiveness, consumer choice and quality, and equity.

To deliver these objectives the market structure requires specific characteristics: genuine competition for providers to offer the lowest price compatible with a quality service; a structure discouraging poor suppliers and drawing in new ones; purchaser competitiveness and contestable purchasing so that no single purchaser can stabilize and control the market.

GP fundholders have intruded here; without them, single district purchasers would have created an even more serious distortion of the market. We need more intrusion. For example, we need: to develop quality IT as the basis for quality measurement to enable value added purchasing; reduced administrative and transaction costs; explicit provider motivation prompted by the certainty of potential market jeopardy; explicit purchaser motivation to serve the requirement of public support and legitimacy by building up local consent for what they propose to do.

Few of these conditions are yet in place. What the reforms have done is not to have *done it*, but to have created the tools with which it *could* be done. We now have to stimulate competition amongst providers. Reconfiguration may be essential – there are too many Trusts. We could increase efficiencies but this risks the establishment of new acute monopolies.[10] The reforms should encourage competitive bidding and tendering for services – not only on type of service offered but on price and quality. We do, too, need to ensure that as acute services change, community services are able to respond to this change by providing hospital-at-home services and outreach services in clinics. We will need managerial and business development for GPs, too. We cannot be happy with purchasing as process. Processing is for peas. *Purchasing should be about buying and delivering effective clinical intervention, for less cost, in appropriate settings, and with social consent.*

To deliver all this, there are basic issues and assumptions to test on staffing and medical education, where we need to 'design a new doctor' for both community settings and for acute clinical leadership. Computing, communication, business and managerial skills should be *de rigueur*.[11]

The precariousness of purchasing

Purchasing is at the top of the Ministerial agenda,[12] yet it may be more precarious than we realize. There are strong purchasing leaders, but the bulk of purchasers are not yet up to their pace. Purchasing may have suffered lots of quiet erosion and defeats, with purchasers giving up a lot of ground to difficult providers. We should, I think, be suspicious of the cosy idea that 'we are on our way, it's all going to be alright, trust us'. We still have to be clear and demanding if we are to demonstrate that purchasing is making a difference. We need to clarify that the reforms are tackling the *endemic* problems – they were not created by the reforms. The agenda is to be outcome- and evidence-based, not process-driven; to set objectivity, measurement, transparency, outcome and local focus on a pedestal, and to stand up and be counted for that.

We need to keep as much resource as possible close to the patient and away from administration, to demonstrate the value that the costs of purchasing activity deliver in patient care. As Claire Perry (Chief Executive, Bromley Health) has said,[13] we need to show that the changes made are worth more than the other ways we could have spent the money, so that we can build purchasing legitimacy, contestability of decisions, public support for priorities, and shift services from the acute to the primary sector. We need to demonstrate, too, that the shift to primary care gives added value in outcomes and changes in health status. All this is being shaken out of what Dickens in *Little Dorrit* calls 'destiny's dicebox'. Purchasers should ask three simple questions:

- does it work?

- does it improve the patient's health?

- does it do so from the patient's point of view?

Why not ask a patient 'Did what we deliver make you feel better? Has there been a real change from your perspective?' There are ways into this, for example, the USA model short form 36.[14] This is currently being used in over one hundred hospitals in the USA and Canada, by physicians, and for psychiatric care. The self-administered profile of physical, social and mental functioning before and after treatment is a data gain we can advocate. It does not cost a lot. It is not wildly hi-tec. It will not need 16 committees to pilot it. This is an opportunity for purchasing and patient leverage. We could ask the GPs to do this with us.

Where do GPs fit in?

A key issue is: who is to drive purchasing strategy and where do the GP fundholders fit in? To effect change it has been necessary to rely on awkwardly shaped, determined, pushy GP fundholders. It has suited the politics of the situation to let them successfully stir the water on cost, quality, setting, improved access, but there is a serious issue as to whether GPs should continue to drive services and reconfiguration unpoliced, unmonitored and unaccountable. They should *not* duplicate capital costs and staffing, either, but be gathered into cottage hospitals while we let GP fundholding-development run on.

On the debit side, GP fundholders are not accountable, as are other purchasers and providers. They do not hold public meetings with stakeholders. Partners do not meet in public. They have no annual public meeting. On the credit side, they *have* generated more change in three years than we have had in 40. They are not overly impressed by hospital consultants and they have exerted real leverage on the system. Equally, however, they are not trained managers, although we are pushing more and more power to them. I doubt if we will deliver national and local strategies, and avoid disintegration and chaos, unless the health commissions are in *overall* control – despite the distortion they represent in the market place. Integrated purchasing and resource allocation – guided by the ME but not managed in detail by it – is essential. The GP must be fully involved and there must be a common focus on local patch purchasing. If this is the right emphasis, we need to take account of the fact that purchasers must ensure that they have GPs' full support and commitment to their purchasing decisions. It has been said truly that contracts do not send patients anywhere, but GPs do. Strong purchasing leadership will not be sustained without GP co-operation.[15]

This does not undermine the critical point, which is that if the citadel of the medical professions is to be breached it does not seem sensible to pass *control* into the hands of another group of medics. Many ordinary GPs, too, are not necessarily coherent, strategic thinkers. Many still seem to be overemphasizing acute provision.

The role of the public

Purchasers have the key role of taking public attitudes seriously, and of promoting a wide basis of understanding and support. They have these factors to think about:

- the public still thinks health comes from hospitals
- the shadow of the waiting queue on the corner is a serious problem in managing acute down-sizing
- if we *really* believe we should be guided by the public and its wants, what do we do when the public is consulted and tells us things we do not want to hear? For example, on the closure of an uneconomic, well-loved children's hospital under royal patronage? Probably in a marginal seat. Probably occupied by a Government Minister.

The public and its role is a long-standing problem. How can purchasers prepare and lead opinions so that they can deliver support for acute down-sizing? This is one of the biggest current challenges. The other key aspect here is that public acceptance of the shift into the community is only likely if improved primary care is in place first.

How trusts will change

In response to purchasing pressures in the developing market, as well as innovations in clinical practice. Trusts will diversify. They will innovate, push back barriers, manage outreach services, reduce in numbers, make alliances with other Trusts, and with directly managed units, as well as with the private and voluntary sector and with other government agencies. These developments must be monitored to ask if they are establishing new monopolies. Are they genuinely delivering effective outcomes, enhancing choice, and increasing patient reference? For Trusts will clearly seek to impact on service configurations and we need these guarantees. Trusts will diversify, building on strength. They may also narrow their base, shedding services in which they are weak. Providers are pushing these initiatives. Purchasers should push for them, and look beyond their own boundaries, too.

Existing contracts with clinicians seem certain to need major change, if an optimal care model is to develop. We need more flexibility and local management scope to deliver national and local strategy. Better outcomes require better processes and mechanisms. This has inevitable and profound implications for doctors. Here, at Brighton, we are trying to look at everything we do in detail from the patient's point of view, and have just established the first-ever Clinical Performance Improvement Unit. Patient-focused care is the key strategic change agent at Brighton. Contracts, roles, rewards are fundamentals which we are opening up for real discussion, so that we can change the processes and the results of clinical care.[16]

We are very glad to have the help and support of Professor Eric Caines in this work. Eric is inspirational. He is rattling the dead wood. He is right. The strength of vested interest is evident, but what he is saying has needed saying for years. Job design, skill-mix review, the management of time, people and performance are huge issues. So, too, is professional performance. Shares in Caines have fluctuated; my advice is 'buy!'.[17]

The path to effective purchasing

Each step we take brings us closer to the fundamental reappraisal of the processes of care.

Effective purchasers are focusing on primary and secondary care in the home; bringing together health and social care provision from the users point of view; promoting access through primary care to a remodelled secondary and tertiary care sector as a back-up. They are commissioning across GP fundholding, locality purchasing, acute and community health services. This is to build resources in the community, especially at the interface between primary care and community health services. It requires a strategic review of acute care and the long-term direction of services in a five-year context, which informs annual contract negotiations.

This is to ensure that if there is less acute care, it is the most up-to-date, alongside effective accident and emergency services. Purchasers need to:

ensure day-case progress, and to get maximum outreach services, for example, mobile eye clinics in ophthalmology; to shift acute care out into the community, for example, with stroke care; to work effectively with other agencies, and to put them all together; to develop a purchasing strategy for particular local areas and for specific services, for example, maternity services based on community-based midwifery, looking at the resources available across all local sectors, including the voluntary sector and ensuring co-operation. The object is to provide for a future health care strategy with such fundamental characteristics as targets, and a plan for achieving them.[18]

Purchasers must face difficult decisions about priorities and objectives; set out the intended balance between acute, community and primary care; choose which health problems to tackle first; act as a link between health targets and detailed purchasing strategies. They must be backed up by realistic financial plans and an assessment of the resources required to deliver the strategy. Equally, they are reflecting on the fact that there are, as yet, few protocols for the evaluation of primary care developments, such as occupational therapy or ultrasound. Practice standards agreements need to be part of quality guarantees, and offer GPs opportunities to take an active part in purchasing health care and the services GPs will provide locally.

The purchaser who providers do not want to see

We have heard a good deal of emphasis on 'product sourcing' and on collaborative working. Yet providers will still have a view as to who they would prefer *not* to see on the other side of the table, holding the razor!

Such an individual would have a reputation for looking for door-openers, be suspicious of collusive possibilities in provider relations, and insist on knowing what is going on in a challenging, even a confrontational relationship.[19]

Here is a list of the characteristics of a purchaser that, believe me, provider executives prefer not to see.

- The purchasers would ask for the demonstration of measures of good integration.
- They will want a framework for real change, with targeted milestones which will require real and proper costings, with the purchaser saying 'On the 1st April 1995, that's it – cost per case or no business. And I want to audit the cost workings too, to be sure we avoid hidden cost-inflation.'
- They will emphasize clinically effective buying, not treatments bought

by numbers, and will want to contract, *via a provider*, with *individual* clinicians and their quality-tested services.

- Their strength will be in taking the public seriously, really understanding what they want, involving them rather than imposing on them, focusing on the whole person and making a reality of empowerment.

- They will prompt patients understanding that there is an issue called outcomes they should discuss with their GP.

- They will be hugely demanding of investment in screening, especially for patients who do not present themselves, so that patients are tested more and referred appropriately, with incentives to ensure that referrals go to the right place.

- They will cut contracts back to their core, clearly specifying change measures to get providers to specify what they do, and link these to clear incentives to deliver these change indicators (such as clinical protocols, and levels of day care), measuring the success of this change agenda against *Health of the Nation* and other targets.

- The monitoring and performance director will have power to use incentive for organizational development.

- The financial director will have power to remind providers that the opposite of cash flow is cash-ebb.

- The research director will be able to keep up to speed on clinical interventions which work, do not work, or which cause harm.

- The supplier development director will have power to seek new and alternative provider relationships.

- The Chief Executive will be able to take the Marks & Spencer view that you speak welcomingly to an entrepreneurial supplier by saying that if you can do better, I'll buy it.

Clearly, the purchaser must have access to provider clinical knowledge, and engage with it to reshape services, but remember the Russian proverb (which all doctors learn early in their careers) that the best way to defend your frontier is to be on both sides of it.

Purchasers need to keep pace with the huge changes in diagnostic techniques, change in treatments, and changes in such sophisticated areas as genetics. Purchasers should exert leverage on our environments – on buying quality through design awareness – to help transform the processes of health care. As processes change, so must our buildings, which must become more sensitively designed, lit, decorated, landscaped, from the patient's point of view (which includes looking up at the ceiling from a trolley). They must ensure, too, that provider medical directors represent medicine, and not medics, and help to drive the management agenda.[20] Homewood NHS Trust Chairman Roy Lilley would say that they also need a 'demolition contractor', to clear away the built acute detritus of centuries. Roy also urges competitive tendering for services by hospital doctors, to deliver what we are told cannot be done. Lastly, they should be realistic about the very real powers of providers to resist change, and be just a little sceptical of the new emphasis on collaboration that is emerging as the new wisdom. Remember what it says in *Alice in Wonderland* 'Once you have met the cake, you can't cut it'.

Day-to-day real life

In day-to-day local life, it is clear that contracts are the sum of relationships. To make them workable they must be built on the basis of good relations, co-operation, but some confrontation; and ultimately in this minuet it must be clear who is the dancing master to enable the market to develop *as a market*.

Our local experience so far produces the following guidance:

- be honest and open about objectives, on both sides
- sort out the timescales – it takes time to stripout capacity and shift services
- agree that quality costs time and money
- set out priorities to phase dislocation and shocks: success in achieving strategic change in a medium-term plan, relying on managing contracts in year. This involves profiling work sensibly, planning ahead for peaks in demand, ensuring that appropriate levels of emergency and urgent care are provided and monitoring that providers undertake no more work than they are contracted to do
- 'a no-surprises policy', with advance warning of dramatic changes
- get into collaborative working, with sticks and carrots; do not merely weigh, measure, ticket and price a provider
- build in floors and ceilings, and trigger mechanisms with pluses and minuses that 'bite' financially
- be aware that both sides want to improve performance and involve professionals without being captured by them
- set aside budgets for health promotion, preventive investment and targeting milestones for the *Health of the Nation* objectives in an action plan
- aside from shopping list exercises and bargains across the counter, build mutual understanding and develop incentives to encourage change in the

way we provide service (judged not only on price but on timings, locations and quality indices). Curtail rigmarole and open up direct-access to services, on a walk-in basis

- be explicit in the media, and invite the contestability of purchasing decisions

- ensure providers have the data and systems to do the job you pay them for – ask them 'Which services are not being used to full capacity? Your data and systems should tell you'

- look at why some disciplines are inefficient. What is happening on emergency cancellations, for example, which takes you into the real issues of power and control. Who does these operations? Who does the out-of-hours work, and with what results?

- ask 'When can you get to cost per case and, in the interim, to tariff-banding?'. Without cost per case, competition between hospitals will stumble along, not stride ahead. Spot-purchasing is the objective. Pragmatic initially, but programmatic soon

- focus on negotiating skills: mature, interpersonal skills, not game playing

- confirm an agreed approach to risk-sharing and information-sharing

- involve patients. It is no good if all extra costs (or new travel costs) are shifted onto patients by you buying a very inconvenient service. You are a proxy for patients, most of whom have no exit from poor services

- and why not ask for 'Gold Standards' – what measurable promises to patients does your provider *guarantee*? Will they pay for this to be delivered elsewhere if they fail to meet the guaranteed standard?[21]

Generally, purchasers must be strategically pushy, but 'in-year' we do need to bear and forebear with both sides of the banner equally seen.

All roads lead to outcomes

The governing idea must be quality. The key question is 'Is purchasing going to influence the practice of medicine?' Is there a rational basis for it to do so? Can purchasing really be based on hard knowledge? For a start, why are we not using the knowledge we already have to change practice and delivery? Purchaser interrogation of provider quality, costs, practice and results must go alongside purchasers demanding cost efficiencies.

We know well – for example from the NCEPOD studies[22] – that a number of lines of evident difficulty are revealed by research into medical practice. Medical decision-making produces major variations in practice patterns, inappropriate care, huge variations in physicians *own* perceptions of likely outcomes, and a wide range of uncertainty.[23] All this has worrying implications for informed consent, expert testimony and the use of consensus methods to develop practice guidelines. The issues are critical for purchasing decision-making, which turns on buying activity that improves the health status of the individual. We are dealing here with very problematic measurements and with key issues about power and power bases, but we have got to get to evidence-based decision-making.

Buying effective care

We may have to work at the simple things. The impact would still be significant. We need, too, to recognize that intermediate outcome measures such as 'Did the patient die in the car park?', are themselves insufficient. We need the long-term measures 'Did the patient have a fuller life? Did we produce the results we forecast?' We need to ask the patient and not only look in our own files.

Here are some simple things we might do. Remember, of what *we* decide people need, only 15% of interventions are known to be evaluated as effective. The other 70% we do not know about, and the rest are known to be ineffective or harmful but we are still doing them! More randomized control trials are vital. A profile of 132 minimally invasive surgical procedures, currently in use, shows that we have cost-effective information on only one. Nine are being evaluated in trials. The rest are in use outside the context of evaluation. If we are to see effective buying, purchasers must explicitly incorporate costs into decisions and practice guidelines. They must think quantitatively, create criteria of actual benefits, estimate the magnitudes of benefits, harms and costs with reasonable certainty and be sure that the benefits outweigh the harms and justify the cost.

First, the ME could put incentives into the corporate contracts of all purchasers to buy evidence-based care, and monitor it annually, to ensure they are buying proven care, not merely buying aggregate measures of organizational efficiency. We must not let the important – reducing waiting lists – drive out the urgent.

Let us deliver what we know works, buy clinical protocols, while realizing that they freeze consensus and need regular review, unlock the knowledge we already have. For example, we *know* that 90% of women who die of cervical cancer have never had a smear; buy smears and tackle the social issues as to why people do not present themselves. Do research and development into HPV (human papilloma virus) to which cervical cancer looks to be strongly linked. Immunize. Insist on an accredited course of action. Get the messages out. Do not rely on guidance outlines. They do not do it. Purchasers – action stations!

Really tackle smoking ban advertising and treble prices by taxation (politically explosive, I know!) Get into serious health promotion and sickness prevention. Get nine year olds to make videos about stopping from starting smoking, for nine year olds. Get into locality targeting, for example, Liverpool University's GIS (geographical information system) gets you down to postcodes so you can map out a disease (such as heart disease) on a postcode level. You could then do your clinics on that basis only.[24]

This is one way to think about how we should develop clinical performance and get our purchasing priorities right. This kind of specific thinking is basic to a reappraisal of the processes and delivery of care, to get quality, productivity, value for money, and the pay and reward incentives in place to incentivize and drive successful change.

Get rid of the idea that capital is the only solution and finesse decisions locally so that we do not let capital (or the requirements on doctor training) drive us into inappropriate developments we will not want or need.

Tackle the simple stuff: instead of complex operations on 89 year olds, help the elderly with asthma, backs, feet. Massage therapy and comfort may be a more effective alternative to triple toe and heel multiple corn by-passes, even though *they* can be written up in the medical journals.

Let us ask patients what they *want* (which we discover by enquiry), not decide what they *need* (which we decide on the basis of our prejudices and presumptions and which is driven by technology).

All this puts purchasing in the business of a conscious and explicit comparison of health outcomes and costs. On outcomes, most of all purchasers and providers have a very crisp relationship, billiard cue to ball. Outcomes push us *all* into managing for performance, managing for improved health status, analysing results patient-by-patient, procedure-by-procedure, purchase-by-purchase, clinician-by-clinician, which is how purchasers will soon want to buy. This is where we will hear the clink of metal on metal, where it matters.

This is the hard agenda where we must invest intellectual capital. It is not enough for purchasers to ask 'Where can we recycle money into patient care?', or, 'How high are provider overheads?', or, 'Do they manage their theatres properly?'.

Developing doctor-led IT at ward level

A critical issue is information technology (IT). We are very far behind in the measurement business, but if doctors are to know what works and purchasers are to buy it we will have to get to ward and GP level IT. To see and record who our patients are, what their conditions are, what we do, what happens, what it all costs and what the intermediate and long-term results actually are. To have all this analysed, mapped, with benefits, harms and costs tracked. With the difficulties of value judgements and surveillance procedures assessed, with the analysed data output available to all – usable for future clinical patient interfaces and consideration of alternative treatments.

We are a very long way away from this but we need to invest huge intellectual and managerial capital here, to equip purchasers to approach quality quantitatively and not by value judgement. This needs to be a doctor-led and a data-led investment. Most of all, doctor-led. For *they* need to know. *They* need the answers. *They* can create the advance in the intellectual infrastructure of medicine, to raise standards of performance for all professionals in all settings so that all players can be managed against expectations, the value expected to be added, and the result. We need to get started so that all professionals can use this data in their *own* consultations for patient benefit. Here, consultants can be invited to realize further *their* career commitments to the patient sitting on the other side of their desk.

A key step would be for every purchaser to follow Brighton's innovation and to ask *all* providers to establish a high-profile, top-of-the-office, Clinical Performance Unit. This would give us an audit on the local system as it develops, a whole series of case studies, with documentation of local clinical experience on how participating provider units, specialities and individual specialists perform, nurturing the good and disposing of the bad. This organizational innovation would bring clinical audit (which we might usefully rename 'Care Audit') into mainstream management, based on nationally set standards, taking us from productivity measures to outcome change. There are opportunities here, too, for providers to replicate such a performance unit, to contribute to measurement and the regulation and direction of the market.

All this gets us into the heartland of cost-effective clinical practice, into changing doctor training, into manpower supply and motivation, into contract incentive and reward. Into transparency, and into the team issues of multi-skilling, job plans, patient care paths and patient reference. If we are to get such things done, NEDs have to insist on them. This is why we need in purchasing authorities as well as providers not only people with industrial and business skills. We need change agents – not necessarily merely successful or merely safe people.

Using what we know: getting development from research

There is no harvest without seed. One test of how serious we are is to focus not only on the research knowledge, but on the development. The 'D' in 'R & D'. Using the knowledge we have now to achieve change. One lever would be new incentives in the annual performance monitoring of purchasers, to ensure they buy proven care, not merely aggregate measures of organizational efficiency. The important must not be driven out by the urgent. If we are to achieve this long-term strategy, purchasers will need to be rewarded for it.

We need, too, a more effective engagement of public health with finance, a mutual understanding of their agendas, so that fields of inquiry are turned into fields of action. A key test of our seriousness is to work with the various 'action stations' in place. There are many think-tanks: at Aberdeen, Bradford, Birmingham, Manchester, The King's Fund, Southampton, Nottingham, York, The Cochrane Centre at Oxford, and the Nuffield Institute at Leeds with its Outcomes Clearing House and the *Effectiveness Health Care Bulletins*. Look at Leeds – a success story. 10-15 calls a day. People are hungry for outcomes guidance on a basis of usage and discussion that cannot be challenged: scientific, credible, viable. The Nuffield Institute runs its two projects on £820 000, on short-term contracts. Yet we need stability and reassurance for places like Leeds so that good, senior, experienced people can interface with managers and professionals securely and on their own terms.

We need, too, to sort out the complementary strengths of the other centres and see how we can harness them. It is crucial that the regional R & D programmes are not lost either in the reshuffle of ME outposts – research *must* be kept at the top table, guiding strategy.[25]

Investment in purchasing development work means giving places like Leeds security, linking the centres, using their work for action, investing in the development agenda as well as in the research agenda, and in areas such as long-term chronic care where existing randomized control methodology is inappropriate, and for which we need to work up a new methodology. The R & D budget for England is 1.5% of total NHS funding; not a lot with such a research agenda.

The work that Professor Michael Peckham is doing on a national strategic framework for R & D is fundamental, as is that of Dr Graham Winyard (Deputy Chief Medical Officer), Yvonne Moores (Chief Nursing Officer) and others who are working on outcomes and at how we get professionals on board to develop specifications, quality standards, and to commit to them and implement them.[26]

Ultimately, the issue is who's writ is to run, for whom, and with what results. Key individuals, whose work impacts most on resources and quality, must now become accountable, for monopoly, power and leverage outside purchasing and Trust board control is hazardous for purchaser, Trust and patient. Getting to outcomes analysis openly is not merely an eccentricity on a par with campaigns for duo-decimal numbering or phonetic spelling – entertaining odysseys – it is at the core of all that we do. The emphasis on clinical audit as a private venture must shift as we move towards certification and re-certification of professionals, the accreditation and re-accreditation of facilities and services, and the likely competitive tendering by professionals for service contracts.

The big 'ifs'

'Payment on outcome', which some like Somerset Health Authority are leading, must come quickly. A system which only pays for a successful outcome, assessed according to agreed clinical measures *and a patient satisfaction survey*, will correct patient expectations and encourage consultants to consider, discuss and deliver outcomes.

- If capacity to benefit is to determine access to care.
- If decision making is to be based on cost data, effectiveness and outcome.
- If patients with identical health characteristics are to be given similar treatments, rather than widely varied treatments.
- If routine price and expenditure data in the NHS is to tell managers about the cost of treating patient episodes.
- If the volume and quality of evaluatory trials is to improve.
- If we are to insist on following procedures which work and to stop those which we know do not work.
- If the investment of £25m per annum in the NHS on data collection is to lead to it being used.
- If the Royal Colleges data on the confidential enquiry into peri-operative deaths is to be shared with non-clinical managers.
- If clinical interventions are to have a scientific base.
- If there are to be incentives for better practice.
- If confidentiality is to be questioned.
- If there is to be an open framework where the costs and benefits can be measured, quantified and valued.

If. If. If. And what **BIG IFs** they are. They will only be answered by purchaser insistence. So be it, if purchasing is to generate its dividends. All this sounds alarmingly daunting, but we *have* come a long way. Let me remind you how far. Let us not suffer from cultural amnesia of what the NHS was like as little as three years ago.

We all understand very clearly the 'why' of our changes. We are learning daily about the 'how' of actually delivering them. Purchasing leadership and intellectual clarity about the levers we need to pull, tough non-executive insistence, creative flair, communication skills and building public support are vital if we are to *prove* that we are delivering public benefits from the changes, and that we could not spend the money better in doing anything else.

To return to the initial question posed by the Admirals in Gold Braid 'Whose side are you on, anyway?'. Well, it is the patient's, isn't it? Which is why this all matters at all.

Notes

1   'Insider-outsider'. The phrase was coined by John Simmonds in his farewell speech as Chairman of Brighton DHA, April 1992.

2   The quoted phrases are, of course, from Dylan Thomas (1954) *Under Milk Wood.*

3   The NHS has been fortunate in its purchasing leadership, which has rescued it from the error of emphasizing provider Trusts in the early stages of the reforms. The health heroes here include Ian Carruthers (Dorset), Tony Shaw (Southampton & SW Hants), Chris West (Portsmouth & SE Hants), Claire Perry (Bromley). Alan Bedford (E Sussex) and Peter Catchpole (W Sussex) are newly appointed leaders, both 'ships of the line' who carry big guns. Dick Stockford, as Head of Purchasing at the NHS ME, was the architect of much of the strategic speed-up (and, one suspects, of much of what Dr Brian Mawhinney did to shift purchasing into top gear while Minister of Health). Stockford's influence as Head of Purchasing at Trent RHA now will be as national as ever.

4   I was misled by my natural optimism.

5   See 'Quasi Markets and Social Policy', Economic and Social Research Council, *Briefing,* **9**, (1993). Also, (1993) Le Grand J and Bartlett W, *Quasi Markets and Social Policy.* Macmillan Press, London.

6   John Cooper, now Chief Executive of Hammersmith Hospitals NHS Trust. Private communication, June 1994.

7   See Lord Robert Skidelsky, CPC Jubilee Lecture, 21 February 1995.

8   The Private Finance Initiative did, of course, pick this up.

9   I have developed my thinking on the 'rationality' of medicine, and the medical mystique, in a number of articles and speeches. See 'From medical mystery to public rationality' in this book (p.46).

10   The innovative work by Guy Howland, Policy Manager of the IHSM, is at the frontier here. We may come down to 25 hi-tech acute centres, and it will be essential, as with all markets, for the government to exercise regulation to

protect the public interest. See Howland G (1994) The Future of Healthcare. Keynote presentation to the *Annual Conference of AQH*, 28 September, in *Journal of the Association for Quality in Healthcare*, Winter 1995, **2**,(No.3), 98–105.

11 See the Audit Commission report, *The Doctor's Tale: The Work of Hospital Doctors in England and Wales.* HMSO, London, 1995.

12 See Dr Brian Mawhinney's series of speeches, collected and published as *Purchasing for health: a framework for action.* NHSME, Leeds, 1994; also, *Purchasing For Health, Involving Local People,* speech to National Purchasing Conference, Birmingham, 13 April 1994, NHSME, Leeds, 1994.

13 See Perry C (1994) *Purchasing For Change.* 'Speaking Up' series, No.2. NAHAT, Birmingham. (Based on a 1993 speech.)

14 USA Short Form 36. See Hays RD *et al.* (1991) Hospital quality trends: a short-form patient-based measure. *Medical Care, **29**,* No.7, 661–8.

15 Jackie Axelby, Private Communication February 1994.

16 See 'The view from Brighton Pier' in this book (p.120). The Central Health Outcomes Unit (CHOU), set up as an internal Department of Health Unit in July 1993, and the UK Clearing House for Health Outcomes (based at the Nuffield Institute for Health, University of Leeds), set up late in 1992, are two of the pivotal national initiatives.

17 Professor Eric Caines CB, Director of Personnel, NHS, 1990–93; Professor of Health Service Management, Nottingham University, 1993–; his wife, Karen Caines, was one of the people who, as a senior Civil Servant, helped create the Health Service Reforms.

18 See Shaw A (1993) *Models Of DHA/FHSA Co-operation.* Speech to NAHAT conference on 'Partners In Purchasing', London, 27 September, on which I have drawn here.

19 As I suggested was likely in November 1991, some of these conflicts are not only certain, they are essential. See 'The wind in the NHS willows', in this book (p.2).

20 Discussion of these issues is only beginning to be realistic as late as April 1995. See Turner S, Smidt L (1995) The role of the medical director. *British Journal of Health Care Management,* **1**, (No.3), 144–6. Also, Baker MR (1992) Role of the medical director. *British Journal of Hospital Medicine,* **47**, (No.2), 111–14.

21 See 'Performance the flag to fly' in this book (p.104) for an account of my introduction of 'Gold Standards' at Brighton.

22 See NCEPOD *The Report of the National Confidential Enquiry into Perioperative Deaths, 1991/1992* (1 April 1991 to 31 March 1992). London, The National Confidential Enquiry into Perioperative Deaths, EA Campling, HB Devlin, RW Hoile, JN Lunn. Also, Devlin HB (1995) Audit in Surgery: the National Confidential Enquiry into Perioperative Deaths. *Clinical Risk, London,* **1**, (No.3), May, 97–101.

23 The literature is, of course, huge. Amongst the work I have used is the landmark paper by David Eddy, on which I have drawn heavily and gratefully for what I say here about measurement, data collection, and the evident

difficulties of clinical practice. It is an extraordinary paper, and few medical directors draw it to the attention of their Chairmen (mine did not). See Eddy DM (1993) Medicine, money and mathematics. *Medical Audit News,* **3**, (No. 8); see also, *Compliance with Practice Guidelines: Clinical Autonomy Revisited,* presented by Nick Klazinga to the European Health Policy Forum, Brussels, 30 September, 1993; Maynard A (1993) Rational Decision Making in Health Care. *Annual Conference of the Operational Research Society,* York, 15 September; *Appropriateness in Clinical Care, A Handbook* (SETRHA, 1994) surveys issues and cites the major literature, while leaving room for development on what Trusts and purchasers need actually to do to encourage change in clinical practice. On the 'norms' characteristic of medicine (non-criticism, the exclusivity of professional judgement, the unwillingness to confront incompetence, the conspiracy of tolerance, the collegiate world bonded by a shared sense of vulnerability) see Rosenthal M (1995) *The Incompetent Doctor, Behind Closed Doors.* Open University Press, Buckingham.

24 Liverpool. See Reeve D (1991) Scale Models. *Health Service Journal,* 31 October, London, pp.39–40.

25 I am grateful to David Hunter, Professor of Health Policy and Management and Director of the Nuffield Institute for Health, University of Leeds for our conversations.

26 See May A (1994) Famous for 15 minutes? Interview with Professor Michael Peckham. *The Health Service Journal,* 17 February; and in *R & D Towards Knowledge-Based Care.* South West Thames Public Health Report, 1994.

This paper is the previously unpublished address I prepared for 'The Chairman's Conference' on Purchaser Development and Provider Relationships (of the Northern Health and Social Services Board in Belfast) on 2 December 1993. I am most grateful to Robert J Hanna CBE, the Chairman in question, for inviting me and prompting these 'night thoughts of a Trust Chairman'. On delivery, time ran out and I am glad to have the opportunity to publish in full what I had prepared. I have now added Notes on sources and some additional current comments are located there. Purchasing has moved forward, but the issues set out seem to me to be surprisingly current.

3

'Jellyfish slippery':

or, can the Patient's Charter deliver better health outcomes?

If patients really had power would there be *any* mixed wards? Wouldn't there be 300 cancer centres? Wouldn't everyone see a specialist? Wouldn't there be one-stop diagnosis? Wouldn't there be 24-hour out-patient access to consultants for cancer patients?[1]

The truth is that we have still hardly begun to give patients any real power or any informed choice. We struggle to get the system to respond to patients' wishes. It does not want to do it; it does not have the motivation to do it; and most people have no exit to a genuinely high quality and cost-effective alternative.

Where is the gun that will fire the shot that will hit the target to give patients real power?

There are severe limits on the effectiveness of the levers so far in place, and there seems little political will to work with new levers which would make the difference. I am sceptical about the value of the phalanx of present initiatives. The Patient's Charter (so far, innocent of measures tackling clinical quality), the CHCs (more variable than the weather), uneven (and politically hampered) purchasing initiatives, patient advocacy, and even the best patient workshops like the Wiltshire Users Network[2] do not amount to a 'choice revolution' in which the government openly trusts the patient.

There may be only one way to make patient power and informed choice a reality – to recognize that only money really talks. The GP fundholder, as a proxy for patients, shows that this is so. Patient fundholding, with patients holding the purchasing power on advice from the GP, is logically the next step, but this is forbidden territory. It means that wicked word 'the voucher'. It is taboo, just as was 'reunification', in Eric Honecker's East German workers' paradise. In my view, patient fundholding will eventually win the day, supplemented with tax incentives to encourage high quality, cost-efficient competition in a genuine health market where patients are informed, prudent customers who demand, choose and pay with their tax pounds.

For the present there is a 'Berlin wall' around this dynamic solution. The search for other levers for patient empowerment goes on, hampered as it is by the limits on publication of real knowledge about clinical performance and practice. In this context there is another expression that is making progress 'shared decision-making'. Will this prove to be useful, or another cul-de-sac into which the nuisance of non-executive energy and patient demand can be happily shunted by over-powerful doctors? Does it offer a genuine opportunity to think about and tackle some of the deep cultural problems in which all attempts at health reform are geologically embedded?

'Shared decision-making' makes some illuminating assumptions, not least about the apparently surprising idea that individual patients have special knowledge about themselves which they and only they can have. That they know how they want to live, if they can. That they know how they want to be treated, if they can get it. That their values matter to them. That they know what results have primacy for them. That they know what counts for them as a 'good result'.

The concept carries with it, too, the idea that we overestimate the rationality of medicine. A practical requirement is that doctors should become better at listening and at sympathetic communications. The notion suggests, too, that we can get better treatment and better outcomes than we now achieve. A bonus may, incidentally, include an answer to the problem of 'under-funding' – that demands on and for services can fall when patients are empowered; for example, when the very high probability of impotence and continuing incontinence is explained to candidates for a routine prostate operation, significant resources are released for other treatments.

In my experience at Brighton hospital clinicians are tempted to argue that *all* such notions are about disciplining doctors. Yet shared decision-making is not that. Indeed, it is the very opposite. It is about asking for a change in the leadership of the organization, not least in engaging doctors *with* patients in shared decision-making about their own care, the options open to them and the balance of risk and benefit.

Since so much of what the NHS does is not about life-threatening conditions, but about lifestyle choices, this will have big health benefits and free resources from ineffective to effective care.

It may also be the key to how we can carry professionals with us, to move from medical mystery and a system by which doctors limit changes in their own interests, to a culture of open information and choice. Inevitably, much of this is to query the 1948 NHS settlement about boundaries, structure, contract, incentive, reward, and who is a legitimate player in these debates. Critically, shared decision-making may help us to think about the psychology of doctors and their reluctance to take part in the critical analysis of practice.

Clearly, here, there are big international and historical differences of culture. The American doctor, for example, is far more open to performance measurement then his or her counterpart elsewhere.

We need to ask if this is only about power and money. Is this only about sticks, carrots and contracts, or is there something deeper going on? What about the role of fear in all this? Are doctors afraid to open up because de-mystifying practice *is* actually a very disempowering thing to be asking them to do? After all, if only 20% of what doctors do has been shown by systematic evaluation to be worth doing, what we are asking for in getting them to open up is very 'challenging'.

We need to find ways to show doctors that it is a positive step for them to accept de-mystification, if it is combined with mentoring, retraining and a sharing of their fear and uncertainty with patients. Indeed, this is likely to be very important for patients. For they, too, collude with doctors in not admitting the inadmissible. For doctors pretend that they can fix everything. We want them to pretend, because reality can be too awful. Perhaps in shared decision-making we can all face this fear together. This is surely all a bit like *The Wizard of Oz,* who needed to stay locked up in mystery because the contemplation of the reality of what he actually was, was too awful. The people of Oz conspired to keep it like that. They needed the fantasy too. It was not until Dorothy came along and dismantled the mystery and helped him face reality with confidence that everyone faced the fear together. In fact, it was dealt with better that way, and the wizard was able to come out of his citadel.

The NHS analogy seems clear: to make progress with shared decision-making we need lateral-thinking, clarity and understanding and we all need to want the same things. There needs to be an acceptance in good will that we are trying to create worthwhile new things, not to destroy good things to make way for bad. Doctors' anxiety is, of course, part of this cultural discussion.

In a sense, it is part of their conventional repertoire. In its place, we need the mutuality of all of us believing that doctors and patients can do their best *together.* Critically, we need to build a commitment from all the players to a coherent vision where patients are seen as legitimate players holding power. For doctors – notably for Brighton doctors – this is a new and to some a devastating notion. Here, of course, an outcomes focus is vital, for it is not *who* is in charge but *what* is in charge, that matters.

Patient empowerment on this model requires doctors to admit uncertainties about diagnosis, prognosis and treatment. Whether or not they should treat, if so, when and how? In shared decision-making these uncertainties would be *embraced* and used as a vehicle for patients to express their preferences about treatment. They would enable doctors to be more effective. We know this from those video disc programmes on breast cancer and prostate that are successfully being used now.

In shifting patient opinion and experience into the equation properly, and in engaging their values as a key to decision-making, we need to abandon the 'secret garden' notion of mystery in medicine. We need to embrace the idea that for doctors, management and patients the choice is between rationality and mystery. We need, too, to be aware of the potency and the fundamental power of persuasive control that mystery still represents, for if we are to replace mystery with rationality and to achieve an evidence-based service, we face the chastening difficulty that rationality is not yet comfortably and widely welcomed and understood by patients. This is why doctors still confidently address the public over the heads of health reformers. It is one of their methods of benefiting from the power relationship in which patients not only subordinate themselves to mystery, but *expect* to be subordinated. This culture of medical mystery is a control on how much we can achieve. It still sets the terms of many of our difficulties. It limits the freedom that management has to engage the public, since ordinary people are prone to being touched and fingered by the mystery.

Thus, it is very hard to get public support to change District General Hospitals, or to amend the power of the hospital clinician, or to shift resources into the community. The informed debate with the public, driven by outcomes understanding, that we need as we debate the future of health care, is greatly hindered by it.

Shared decision-making, however, looks like a key to finding an answer. We can find out from patients how they feel about the possible risks and benefits of treatments. We can set out clearly doctors perceptions about treatment and the choices they believe are available. We can summarise these choices, the associated risks, and assist the empowered patient to express a preference.

This is to move towards a market driven by patient preferences. If it were *combined* with a voucher, in patient fundholding, it would be very powerful indeed. We still, too, require to find ways of making doctors more committed stakeholders in the long-term tracking of patients and in working with their experiences and opinions.

The device of shared decision-making being built around the interactive disc and much better communication is a key element. It offers the opportunity for doctors and patients to interact in a new way. Interactive video programmes, for which we now need a very significant ministerial commitment and a big budget to make British programmes, can aid expert decision-making between doctors and patients. The essence is that they explore *together* the uncertainties that inevitably surround treatment decisions.

Not all doctors are against it. The good doctors see this new order and face it with confidence. It is a new enlightenment to which they can and will accommodate. We need to move forward with mutual confidence. We need to move away from some clinical certainties that were fossil-neat but unfounded in fact. We need, too, to measure what we do against international standards, for the world is not Brighton. We need to recognize, as the Scottish novelist Candia McWilliam has said, that 'provincial fame cuts the world into parishes'.[3]

If we are to empower patients, we need practical changes that work and that can be delivered in the present political world. If the voucher is not practical politics at present, shared decision-making surely is. It was Dylan Thomas in *Under Milk Wood*, who offered the notion of existence as 'Jellyfish slippery'. These practical changes could offer us a positive focus to empower patients and to validate and legitimize all we do based on proven outcomes and patient preferences. Both have been elusive. Now they must come into the NHS net, and with a fine mesh. For, as Max Weber wrote, efficiency is about doing the job right, effectiveness is about doing the right job.

Notes

1 See also my article (1995) Cancer care: putting patients interests first. *The Health Summary*, London, March, pp.2–3.

2 See Wiltshire Community Care User Involvement Network, *Second Annual Report*, April 1993–March 1994, WCCUIN, Devizes, 1994.

3 McWilliam C (1994) *Debateable Land.* Bloomsbury, London.

This article is reprinted from *The Health Summary*, London, February 1995, pp.7–9. Patient fundholding is further discussed in my article (1995) Next step is patient fundholding. *Hospital Doctor*, 4 May, pp.28–29, and in my *The 'Prison Of Awe'*, op.cit.

4

From 'voice' to sanction:

Community Health Councils, and model outcomes

Public services exist to satisfy individual needs. They must become accountable to the user, in parallel with private sector enterprises. But how?

Few NHS users can walk away to an alternative health service. Indeed, many are dependent long-term. For patients, 'empowerment' is the word constantly buzzing. Must it remain background noise in the least responsive of public services, a populist but unspecific mantra? Or can patients be given effective power?

This is a challenge that is perennially puzzling. 'Social marketeers' argue that there can be no user power without the prospect of user exit, and the specific encouragement of new market entrants which is not happening. The alternative is the 'voice' model of patient representation posed by Community Health Councils (CHCs). It remains a major difficulty that *neither* idea has been properly tried in the NHS.

The CHCs, set up as the patients' watchdog in 1973, remain a frail voice. The NHS market is politically restricted. Core (and especially clinical) services are not being market tested. The voucher, which would connect 'own cash' (or tax refund) to 'own health care' is 'verboten'. The NHS persistently avoids the challenge and discipline of patient power and the influence of consumer choice and expectation. As Daniel Finkelstein, Director of the Social Market Foundation, has written, the NHS uses expenditure 'as an index of compassion' but offers no index of outcomes, nor any effective patient sanctions.[1]

Now, the future of CHCs has been put into play by the Secretary of State for Health's proposals in *Managing The New NHS*, offering the abolition of Regional Health Authorities (responsible for CHCs) in April 1996. What can we make of this opportunity?[2]

Why not give CHCs a new, developmental, frontier role as Community *Outcomes* Councils? They could exercise sanctions over both provider and purchaser performance and themselves be made more clearly accountable. They could be part of a new framework of independent audit, and a culture of targeted local improvement. They could be reshaped, properly funded, as a real test of how realistic consumer representation can be as a method of empowering patients. They could be given the lead role in patient advocacy, patient audit, long-term patient tracking for outcomes analysis, and even work on patient fundholding with GPs on a trial basis. This innovation would show us how far patient power can go without the voucher.

The existing network of 206 locally-focused CHCs in England and Wales is the strongest machinery we have that speaks for patients' views. However, it is built on participation, not challenge. There is at present no sense in which the consumer speaks powerfully to the professional, in tones of insurgency or sanction.

CHCs have been viewed with suspicion by government as participants in trench warfare resistance to health care change, under Jacobin leadership. They have remained frugally funded, slightly staffed, hard-working and committed voluntary organizations of little account – the laity leading the lame – but have not withered away.

Instead, for 20 years they have been a symbolic, presentational expedient; a political necessity and a controllable nuisance. Their budgets tell the story of how little real influence and authority patients have. In 1992/3 the average level of CHC funding varied from £50 700 in North West Region to £88 600 in North West Thames. Most have staffs of two or three. CHCs are frictional, but with no hope of counterbalancing the phalanx of the BMA, the Royal Colleges and managerial networks. The problem is reinforced by the public's willing subordination to the medical mystique and ignorance about standards and comparative costs.[3]

What would a Community Outcomes Council (COC) do and how would it work? It would be open about effectiveness and efficiency. It would encourage an open, learning environment engaging purchasers, professionals, providers and patients in setting explicit standards incorporating the unique knowledge that only patients have.

The COC would be independent of the Health Authority, but would be given access to all the information that it holds. It would be consulted by it on its plans, publish a commentary on its strategy, and, through patient audit of the results, exercise sanctions through publicity.

This new body would work closely with GPs as the direct line from purchaser to patient. They would be given direct access to GPs as a right and would be part of the process of GP accountability – for example, reviewing referrals, and building on patient feedback – so that the patient voice is heard and acted upon.

The COC would need to be given the right of access to medical professionals, to focus on analysing clinical practice and counterbalance professional influence on the contracting process. Long-term patient tracking is critical to ensure that clinical guidelines and clinical pathways improve patient outcome, safety, and satisfaction especially if purchasers are to tell clinicians to do something different.

Fundamentally, the COC would be given power to require purchasers to publish improvement targets in every clinical discipline, taking full account of local patients' experiences and views. COCs too, would need explicit criteria for the public to judge their performance.

The COC would have an educative role, influencing public under-standing of clinical uncertainty, effective and ineffective treatment, and the medical mystique. It would help to build shared decision-making, the informed patient and a greater role for the individual in the management of their own care.

Perhaps the COC, with the GP, would effectively make the Health Authority obsolete. Clearly, the potential for turf fights is considerable, but the COCs could create an explicit framework which starts with the priority of patient values. It would push for the development of standardized consumer outcome measures, which could be incorporated into routine service delivery and standard reporting on results. For, even without the potential of consumer exit, we need to manage the service by science, by fact and by patient experience in a culture of outcomes-based thinking at a local level. Purchasers are not waltzing yet.

Will it work? It does nothing to link individual payments to individual preference or measured benefit, but it changes the job to be done by CHCs. The new model would be loyal to the outcome, not to local politics nor to the NHS structure. It would represent a broader definition of consumer interest and not be merely grievance-based.

COCs would need to come on board as the first bastion of change, not the last bastion of intransigence. The necessary conditions for their success would be a positive attitude, almost certainly under newly appointed local leadership. The trade-off would be substantial funding, the addition of new public health and new communication skills, and a national commitment to ensure that positive provider performance be rewarded by local pay linked to local improvement.

This initiative could be the basis, too, of a new National Patients Council, validated by its roots in the local patch. A key role would be to make sure that patients' experience and outcome counts in the make-up of local and national purchasing strategy.

There would be one further gain. Doctors presently claim all the knowledge of what patients want. COCs would draw on a new source of patient information which would help manage professionals. It would open up the basic issues of how decisions are taken, by whom, and on what basis, especially concerning clinical practice.

Notes

1 Finkelstein D (1992) Foreword to Howard Davies, *Fighting Leviathan, Building Social Markets That Work*. The Social Market Foundation, London, p.8.

2 *Managing the New NHS: The Government's Proposals for the NHS Management Executive, Regional Health Authorities and Other Matters.* Department of Health, London, October 1993.

3 See, Association of Community Health Councils for England and Wales (ACHEW), London, *Annual Report 1993/4*. Also, ACHEW's *Managing The New NHS: Ensuring Effective CHCs in the New Structure*. London, February 1994; NHS Management Executive, Leeds, Executive Letter EL(94)4, *The Operation of Community Health Councils;* Toby Harris (Director, ACHEW), The role of the Community Health Councils in relation to contracting, in *Papers On Quality and Contracts*. National Association of Quality Assurance in Health Care, Hereford 1990; Klein R (1989) *The Politics of the NHS,* 2nd edn. Longman, London and New York; Klein R, Lewis J (1976) *The Politics of Consumer Representation*. Centre For Studies in Social Policy, London. Also, for an example of a forcefully led and imaginative CHC, see The Tower Hamlets CHC, *Annual Report 1993–4,* and *Tower Hamlets Health Strategy Group, Annual report 1994*. An outstanding contribution to policy is Joule N (1995) *Sacrificing Dignity For Efficiency: A Report of a Survey of Policies, Practices and Preferences on Mixed Sex Hospital Wards*. Greater London Association of CHCs, London. One recent summary of empowerment initiatives demonstrates their limitations, see Fontes J, Howland G (1995) *Putting Power Into Patients' Hands, A Guide For Managers*. IHSM, London; and my critique (1995)'*The Prison Of Awe': Democracy, Public Policy, and Power for the Patient*. The Social Market Foundation, London.

This article appeared in *The Guardian* (Society section), London, 8 February 1995, curiously titled 'Model Mantras' by sub-editor.

The NHS and medical mystery

A wonderful fact to reflect upon, that every human creature is constituted
to be that profound secret and mystery to every other.

Charles Dickens, *A Tale Of Two Cities* (1859)

If Arthur Scargill had called his Trade Union The Royal College of Miners,
he'd have won.

John Spiers, speech on NHS reforms to the International Health Policy and
Management Institute Conference, Washington DC, September 1994

When the axe came into the forest, the trees said the handle is one of us.

Turkish proverb

There is nothing more difficult to take in hand, more perilous to conduct,
or more uncertain of success than to take a lead in the introduction of a
new order of things, because the innovation has for enemies all those who
have done well under the old conditions and lukewarm defenders in those
who may do well under new.

Niccolo Machiavelli, *The Prince* (1513)

5

From medical mystery to public rationality:

scrutiny, individual responsibility and the secret garden

Here are three questions to start.

1 Is trying to measure the performance of doctors like knitting with water?

2 Is this to seek to measure the unmeasurable, or can the publication of the first six NHS Performance League Table indicators[1] of some important aspects of NHS managerial performance assist them, us and patients, to move towards measurements of effectiveness of clinical practice?

3 Can we make progress on outcomes measurement, and to what extent can we make gains by much better management of process and structure?

These questions are at the heart of the NHS reforms. To ask them clearly is to set hard tests of the relatively soft initial measures, and to see where this might take us in building quality standards for the delivery of effective care. These are delicate issues, but they are fundamental. We need to build on peer review, too, where doctors respect one another, to extend this informal scrutiny and without mutually damaging and wasteful disputes. We have to improve and change clinical practice incrementally, and enhance outcomes management – with appropriate humility on all sides.

Inevitably, there will be some chess games, but we need to set out new rules as we move into a new era of informed choice in health services, focusing in all we do on where we want to get to.

If we are, too, truly serious about transforming the NHS into a genuinely customer-oriented enterprise, we need to make a reality of patient power by developing effective patient audit of services, arm-in-arm with purchasers. This needs to go well beyond the ordinary patient satisfaction survey, to ask the question that bites: did your treatment work for you? This is about listening best, not knowing best, if we are to improve clinical quality *and* customer service delivery in a patient-focused environment.

The context of all public service change is the new emphasis on running services for the people who pay for them, setting explicit standards and asking to be judged by them. This is to require management change for service improvement – by publicity, comparison and emulation – so we can all follow the best who get out ahead.

The *specific* context for the NHS is to move from a culture of mystery to one of rationality, to use information for choice and change. The key word is effectiveness – quality is too loose a word[2] – and to what extent it can be measured, proved and compared against explicit public standards which we set out and audit. The essence of quality is the performance of *individual* doctors and clinical teams – the performance of the whole and of its constituent parts.

It is clear that we do have a system of integrity and commitment. Most doctors and clinical teams work hard. Yet open information is a method which will enable us to see if we can further strengthen our organization, help teams to improve their work, and enable us all to function in an open economy. Open information should also assist us in delivering the public sector objective of getting the most and the best (whatever that is) from what we have to spend. It will help, too, to motivate our staff to do better, for morale (not least that of doctors and other professionals) matters. Our most essential imperative is *truly to believe* that our patients are the owners of the service, and that truly to satisfy our customers is *a requirement*, not a purpose alone. It is not resources we need to stress, but *resourcefulness* – to build on the best, to face deficiencies, and to remedy them.

For patients and for management, the choice is between rationality and mystery. If we believe in explicit improvement as a guiding reality, we must abandon the secret garden notion of mystery in medicine. This has a long history. It is older than Pepys. It was and is about how to ensure one is able to defend ones Guild boundaries, where people were 'inducted into the mystery and the art'. This was a process designed in an embryonic economy. It is no longer appropriate, which is not to say that it is not enormously powerful. Clearly, it is, but the mystery should be viewed now like the Easter Island Statues, or The Flag: powerful, but about things people no longer necessarily need rely on.

It is very striking that there are only four core, serious professions. They focus on the four things that frighten us all most. 'Death' – which gives the Churches their power. 'The military threat' from which the forces keep us safe. 'Crime and disorder' – from which the law keeps us secure inside our fences. And 'Disease' – from which doctors defend us. These four professions are the core structure that allow us to live in a civilized and orderly way. It is big stuff. It warns us to notice the potency, the fundamental power, the persuasive control of what goes on culturally inside a hospital, and of the power of mystery as we ask for change. The agenda for change asks us to replace mystery with rationality, to achieve an evidence-based service, and to carry forward a genuinely managed enterprise. Yet mystery still has an enormous influence. The secret garden is what children want. It is time to pass to adulthood. To achieve this, it is very important to involve the *recipients* of services – and here lies a chastening difficulty. The *flag of rationality* is not happily welcomed by practitioners or by users, either at the bewigged bar, by priests in their parishes, by soldiers in their barracks, or by doctors in their hospitals.

Indeed, if we ask why is it that doctors confidently address the public over the heads of Trust boards, one finds the power relationship in which patients not only subordinate themselves to the mystery, but *expect* to be subordinated. If one could video a doctor/patient consultation, this is what you would see. It was very striking to me when I spent half a day last year with a surgeon in his clinic, sitting at his elbow while patients came in for consultation. Most GPs, too – fundholders or not – would, I suspect, find it very difficult to address questions from patients as if they were not holders of mystery but of information. It is information that they need, however, to purchase effectively and for patients to make informed choices. It is information, objective and managed, which will intrude into the relationships of mystery which have built up over generations. Information, too, to enable choice and not only for reassurance, important though that is. We should notice, too, that the culture of medical mystery is a control on how much we can achieve. It sets the terms of our difficulties. It limits the freedom we have to engage the public, since ordinary people are prone to being touched and fingered by the mystery. It is very hard to induce public support to change the mystery to rationality, to reduce the scale of the District General Hospital (DGH) and the power of the hospital clinician. It is difficult enough for us, as insider-outsiders, who live alongside it and with the tribe of people who are its initiates. This analysis may be thought to be anthropology and ethnography, not management. Yet we are not dealing with the Pacific or Easter Islanders. It is not a Pacific puzzle, it is ours, and that mystique controls a huge chunk of our modern society. The informed debate we need on the future of health care is greatly hindered by it.

The key to change is to understand and to manage the potency of mystery, in the drive to rationality. We need to understand this as we argue that we have got to settle for less public ignorance. We must make a start, not wait until we have a cast-iron case for everything. We must use the knowledge that we have, to get it into action. That is why we must go hard for open management. All successful industry, all effective commerce meeting the needs of its customers, sets this as a fundamental of success and modernity.

The NHS is a federation of cultures. How we deal with the relationships of a federation of cultures which are in their essence about feelings is a major management dilemma, and it is politically sensitive. As we press for scrutiny and management action, it is noticeable that these have been collusive relationships. They have been about private bargaining, which is why they are so hard to manage. This is, too, why the culture bites so deep, and it may, indeed, be that the only way to conduct a federation of cultures is to tackle feelings. The functioning of this private culture can be seen in many details. Look at the old-style, conventional relationships between Chief Executives and clinicians, or between clinicians and nurses. They relate as if in a complicated dance. The doctor's power lies in part in the ability to manipulate this dance, and when doctors are asked to substitute a culture of rationality and to be managed on the basis of known evidence, they find this a very difficult change to make, even if they declare this change to be their objective. The very long lead-times in responding to new research signal this. However, the new players in the situation, outsiders, asked to lead change are giving us an opportunity to make big changes happen. The key is for people who know the system, but are not of it, to link with executive managers to build a new vision as a way forward and to deal with the troubles that arrive in the slipstream of change.

We are, here, indeed, only saying a few simple things about open government: on the micro-level – that it would be better for patients because we will be able to engage them in choices about their own care and its management; on the macro-level – that it would help an evolving NHS survive in an informed debate which would build social consent for change. For we are saying what successful organizations say has helped them to survive. We are noticing, too, that many great enterprises (Clyde Shipbuilders, Dunlop, IBM, Pan-American) do not necessarily persist. It takes thought to last. Enterprises that survive over time contrive constantly to improve as evidence-based systems, and as open, collaborative organizations that fundamentally believe in delivering guarantees to their users. The establishment of a culture of openness is a key element. All this is being driven by a fundamental factor, too, which is the search for improved health status and improved health care delivery.

Secret gardens, of course, offer in literature and in the imagination beguiling and special pleasures. They are the most magical of places – personal, private, protected, and as Francis Hodgson Burnett's novel *The Secret Garden* tells us 'It's the garden no-one can go into. It's the garden without a door. How I wish I could see what it's like.'[3]

Come into the largest secret garden of them all – our own NHS backyard. Come through the ivied, wicker gate, first pushed ajar by the Patient's Charter and now eased further open by the Performance League Tables. Come specifically into the secret garden of the hospital, where little is quite as it seems, and where, despite momentous changes, the fundamentals of management, competition and quality need to be taken further – probably, most critically, in ensuring that what we know is best practice is actually and *always* practised. If purchasing is to obtain effective care based on best known processes by using buyer muscle, we require the further development of real and useful measurements of effectiveness.

We need measures of clinical performance as well as of service performance. To achieve this betterment and improvement, we are, of course, talking about relationships. Quality is about getting better *through* people, and it is about management focusing people on quality, which means effectiveness and targets for doing better.

We do not yet know what performance in terms of effectiveness we are getting from each NHS Trust. Look at the secret garden, as it is now:

- where quality is asserted, not measured
- where we agree policies, but they do not easily become real
- where audit is private and not inevitably the prelude to action
- where data does not necessarily flower as information for change
- where, in public service value-terms, *merely to exist* is to be worthy, without the need to show measured returns or results
- where anonymity is the rule
- where competitiveness is minimal, and purchasing only just on the move
- where our NHS federation of cultures – including the dominant coalition between managers and hospital clinicians – offer their own definitions of appropriate measures of the value added
- where a variety of stakeholders (whom we must consult) seek to advance their own ends
- where Trust and Purchaser Boards do not commonly know if best practice is in hand, and
- what real – that is, clinical and patient reported – results actually are.

There is much informal, peer review and anecdotal comment, and it seems likely that most doctors do well in their work. Yet we now need to see if we can credibly move from informality to measurement, from approximate truths to precision, from precision to decision, from decision to action and reaction, and from there to competitive change driven by quality measurement of best practice and outcome debate, where clinicians demonstrate that they meet the standards they set and provide indicators of progress and where patients make choices. We can use this quality information, too, to enable the adjustment of activity, provision and location to go forward openly to finesse public decision. It will help us tackle fundamental medical workforce issues on clinical effectiveness and changes in medical/management relationships – we need help here.

Very few NHS Trusts fire 21-gun salutes to this flag. Clinical resistance to management, where it exists, argues that 'outcomes' is an exceedingly difficult and complex area. It is. There are fundamental problems, but it is *not* an area where no progress can be made. We need to set out the problems clearly and fairly (not least because the morale of doctors is important to us). We need to admit that we are a very long way behind on relevant IT investment to build uniform clinical records and uniform data sets which will enable us both to measure quality, and to interrogate past experience and practice guidelines.

The problems and the opportunities are clearly mostly focused on ensuring conformity to agreed standards of process and structure, making sure clinical teams are doing what they are supposed to be doing.

The challenges raise, too, concerns about training and the kinds of doctors we will want, especially in primary settings, where 'designing a new doctor' by changes in training could help us in the delivery of new service needs.

The secret garden is now a construction site. The mere act of *assembling* data on a range of indicators gives greater prominence and meaning to the data than does the mere reporting of any individual datum or studies. If ignorance is not bliss, the *comparison* of performance should prompt enquiry by Trust and health authority boards who need to ensure that best processes are followed and audited. The new League Tables should thus sharpen competitive edge, enhance entrepreneurship, drive and innovation. They should enable us to monitor trends, reflect changes in practice, and prompt continuous improvement. This is about going beyond the change in the NHS culture, with the purchaser/provider split, to changing the old command and control system of planning. New signals are being given at the top to the professionals that we know we are seeing the inevitable clash between two cultures, and that managers must get into discussion on these local issues. It must not be left to the byzantine formulations that emerge from discussion between the Department of Health, The Royal Colleges and the medical professionals.

Trust Managers now need to take the opportunities to check whether services achieve good results. In 1993 the Department of Health published an initial, but very limited group of clinical outcome indicators to check the work of purchasers on specific diseases, to begin to sort out what actually is going wrong. The challenge is to develop purchasing organizations to *think* in this way and *manage* in this way, and *instinctively* ask of an issue: what does the evidence tell me? How do I measure results? Are they as good as they should be? We need managers and all health care professionals to help clinicians to work in this way. We must reshape medical/clinical thinking and professional relationships. The recommendations of the Calman Report[4] must be delivered, and also supplemented so that we recruit different people to medical schools and socialize them differently.

In the magnificent film *Shadowlands*[5], Debra Winger (as Joy Gresham) says that when we hurt is when we learn. Fundamentally, it is the quality issues on best practice and on outcomes which we must tackle if we are to learn and to improve. Patient feedback, patient report and audit may be a key to this, too. In the NHS, patient feedback on our success is fuzzy and empowerment is conceptually in its infancy.

We need to ask, too, whether the professional performance levels of NHS clinicians are a mystery because they *deliberately* keep us out of the secret garden? Or, aside from their obviously anecdotal knowledge about their peers' clinical quality – on which their sense of status and self-esteem is based – do they really know hardly more than we do in many clinical areas?

This is not a quibble. Steven Henning Sieverts (an experienced and shrewd American Health Service manager who has recently come to work in England on change management) has pointed out to me that the reality seems to be that doctors actually are not very knowledgeable, in a disciplined and rigorous sense, about how the quality of their own clinical performance (diagnostic acumen, technical skill, therapeutic judgement, responsiveness to patients' needs and wishes, and sensitivity to the need to expend scarce resources wisely) or that of the doctors they work with, measures up. Measures up to what? Either to an objective set of standards or to a relative scale which compares similar clinicians to each other. We need to decide what we mean by measurement.

In part, the difficulty (and thus the mystery) is a product of the absence of hard data, but it goes deeper than that. We are only at the beginning of knowing what information needs to be collected and how it should be arrayed (in computer-ready formats) in order for anybody to be able to say with valid confidence 'Dr Smith is a better gastroenterologist than Dr Jones.' And, without that validity, where are the NHS reforms going?

It is very daunting to people like me, for whom ignorance is not bliss and who seek to link management to patient wants, to see how basic our problems actually are, and to set out what the challenge *really is* for both managers and doctors together.

We will not make progress until we confess the rudimentary nature of our tools. This is being exposed now by the developing market. We see more clearly that clinical record-keeping in British hospitals is far less developed than in the USA.

The challenge, in other words, is not just a matter of getting the doctors and managers to get to work on measuring the quality of clinical performance. Before they or anybody can do much with that task, we need first to invest substantial resources and intelligence in building the uniform clinical records and uniform data sets that must underlie any serious effort to measure clinical quality. We cannot compare doctors to each other, or to objective standards, if we do not know what they did to their patients and how the patients then fared. This requires the ward-level data inputs urged by the leading American Urologist Dr David Eddy[6], and it requires long-term patient tracking.

Steven Hennings Sieverts has pointed out to me that we still have to sort out just what we mean by 'outcomes'.[7] As we talk of pinning-down individual doctors and their performance, we see that for most medical services this is far from clear. As Sieverts says, even when we are looking at clearly definable disease episodes of patients without any significant co-morbidities (such as streptococcal pneumonia and simple undisplaced tibula fractures), where there are well-understood routes of recovery, how do we know the role that a particular doctor's performance played in the course of events? Did the choice of drug hinder or help? What effect did the patient's idiosyncratic behaviour have? Are we even certain that the recorded diagnosis was correct? Additionally, most modern medical care for most major diseases such as cancer, stroke, heart disease, AIDS, major trauma, major infections, and the like, does not involve just one doctor whose clinical behaviour determines the outcome. Not only do clinicians frequently practice in single-speciality teams, but there is always a multiplicity of other clinicians and other health professionals involved.

If something goes wrong, it may or may not be attributable to what any one of them did, and even if that could be pinpointed, how does that knowledge feed into the system to evaluate a particular surgeon's performance, when it was the radiologist misreading that led to the unfortunate result? We know that, frequently, different doctors involved with the same patient reach quite different diagnoses. Dr Eddy has shown the huge variations in outcome expectation that doctors advise for similar patients with similar conditions proposed for similar interventions.

Steven Henning Sieverts points out that it is even worse than this 'Even after we agree on a generalised definition – "outcome is how the patient did as a direct result of the treatment rendered during an episode of illness" – what do we in fact mean? Most patients who present in doctor's surgeries, after all, have real or imagined medical problems that will get better irrespective of what the doctor does, unless the doctor does harm. For conditions that do require clinical treatment, most don't lead to clear and total return to good health in the immediate term, even with the best of care.'

If we take seriously that we must take account of post-operative infection and anaesthetic complication rates, and of deaths during or following major procedures, there is a *powerful problem with data*.

For most medical care, of course, a desirable outcome is both *subjective* on the patient's part, and unknown in the kind of short-term where data can be readily collected. Moreover, the outcome is likely to be highly affected by the patient's behaviour patterns, lifestyle, environment and other factors beyond the reach of the medical care system. How are we going to make progress here?

Doctors, managers, and political leaders of all shapes and shades need to admit that we are in serious difficulties, especially if we want to make progress in generating an informed debate which allows us to finesse the politics of rationing, merger, service denial, shifted location and new patterns of investment.

Hiding in the shadows of the secret garden is helping no-one. Perhaps we need to re-focus the huge expenditure on clinical audit, to get us the IT and data we really need (and to get patient audit and tracking into play in a way that tells us meaningful things).

What can we learn from general American experience and current approaches to these difficulties? Will this help us make outcomes management a reality?

At present, huge amounts of money and effort are being spent in the USA on outcomes research. Necessarily, most of the focus is on very specific disease and treatment entities which offer relatively clean sequelae. To date, there is not a great deal to show from that research, and even less that is in a form that can be readily applied to a sound process for evaluating clinicians or hospital quality. Clearly, it is very important for that research to continue and expand – not only there, but here too. We must recognize, however, that even with the relatively much more advanced clinical databases available in the USA we are not yet ready to do much quality assessment based on outcomes. It will take time to bear fruit. But they *are* planting to reap.

If we cannot yet apply appropriate outcomes material, does this mean we can do nothing? Clearly, not. The current major debate on cancer treatments, and hugely variable results, opens the gates. This debate shows that we can make real progress, if we have the will and the courage to seek it.

As Dr Ian Fentiman said 'There's a tremendous amount of published data on what we should be doing but many (clinicians) have chosen to ignore it.'[8] The point, of course, is that we are quite able to measure quality in meaningful ways without looking at outcomes, by assuring conformity to standards of process and structure through accreditation programmes which include patients as assessors. This is the immediate key to progress and *purchasers* must grip it hard. It is the answer we can use now.

This is not to soften our commitment to outcomes, nor is it to weaken the need to get a patient database of the kind Dr David Eddy proposes, but it does bring into focus the need to base judgements about clinicians and hospitals on evaluating teams of professionals and their hospital in terms of adherence to standards and criteria. If we can use league tables, too, to show the community we serve that we are the best, they will have valid and objective reasons to feel ownership and to challenge GPs and Health Authority purchasing decisions, too.

A key area of daily disaster is breast cancer care in the UK. It affects one woman in 12. It kills some 15 000 women a year. Yet only now, in May

1994 (the original date of this paper being presented), have we got to the publication of ten minimum standards of care for women with breast cancer by the Cancer Relief Macmillan Fund (and its associated charity, Breast Cancer Care).[9] It tackles major regional variations in diagnosis, treatment and results. It shows unacceptable variations in approaches to cancer between districts, hospitals, and even doctors in the same hospital. We could save up to 3000 more lives a year if all women with breast cancer were given the best treatment available in the light of present knowledge.[10] Specialist, rigorously monitored care, best process and structure standards, and an open culture of information, advice and support in a reorganized system of care are all highlighted.

I do not believe there is any respectable argument against disclosure of what is known, and honesty about what is not known. But there is of course the 'fruiterer's gambit', the claim that we do not compare apples and pears, like with like. But when we do compare like with like the results are alarming. Death rates vary up to twofold among British districts, even between adjacent districts. Standards of care vary widely, especially between specialist and local district hospitals. Guidelines for the management of breast cancer, published in 1986[11], were still being widely ignored five years later, according to a *British Medical Journal* report earlier this year.[12]

15 000 women die of breast cancer in Britain each year. Only one in four patients studied by the Thames Cancer Registry[13] were shown to have had their cancer properly assessed; four out of ten women who should have been getting chemotherapy were not getting it. Britain is at the bottom of the league table that really counts on cancer. We are doing less well than any comparable country in Europe. Specialization matters. Professor John Yates (University of Birmingham) has reported that deaths from breast cancer surgery are six times higher for some surgeons than others, but that the reasons are not being investigated. In addition, surgeons who operate on at least 50 breast cancer patients a year have better skills and lower complication rates than those who operate on only a few. Five surgical teams from different hospitals who had performed 449 breast cancer operations had a death rate of 3.3% compared with five teams who had performed only 24 operations and had a death rate of 21%. Professor Yates' study of 128 surgical teams − or one in ten of those in England − found death rates following all types of surgery varying from 1% to more than 6%.[14] The information to allow the performance of hospitals and surgeons to be compared has been available for 30 years, but never been used. Why? Will purchasers use it now, and by weighting this to take account of the fact that many DGHs provide ongoing care and commonly admit the gravely ill and dying under their original surgeons, will they compare like with like? [15]

If we were a really serious service industry, we would buy best practice on breast cancer by buying the whole integrated service. Instead of letting screening, palliative care, radiotherapy separately, we would buy a seamless service. We are still buying bits of the old provider world; we need to challenge Chief Executives of purchaser and provider to become much more imaginative, genuinely to think 'seamless service' and actually deliver it, to stitch the whole experience together.

However, more than half of the district hospitals in England are providing substandard treatment for cancer patients because they do not have consultants with special training in cancer care. If this is so in this one area, what is the position in other disciplines? Do we know? What would be the impact of the approach of systematically buying only best possible standards? To make major gains, the recommendations of the Calman proposals in May 1994[16] must be appropriately funded to concentrate care in specialist units in England and Wales.

A critical issue is IT. We are very far behind in necessary investment, but if doctors are to know what works and purchasers are to buy it we will have to get to ward and GP level IT. Dr Eddy is right. We need to see and record who our patients are, what their conditions are, what we do, what happens, what it all costs, and what the intermediate and long-term results actually are. It needs to be analysed and mapped, with benefits, harms and costs tracked; with the difficulties of value judgements and surveillance procedures assessed, with the analysed data output available to all – usable for future clinical patient interfaces and consideration of alternative treatments.[17] We are a very long way away from this but we need to invest huge intellectual and managerial capital here, to equip purchasers to approach quality quantitatively and not by value judgement. This needs to be a doctor-led and a data-led investment. Most of all, doctor-led, for *they* need to know, *they* need the answers, *they* can create the advance in the intellectual infrastructure of medicine, to raise standards of performance for all professionals in all settings so that all players can be managed against expectations, the value expected to be added, and the result.

We need to get started so that all professionals can use this data in their *own* consultations for patient benefit. Here, consultants can be invited further to realize *their* career commitments to the patient sitting on the other side of the desk.

A key step would be for every purchaser to establish a high-profile, top-of-the-office, Clinical Performance Unit. This would give us an audit on the local system as it develops, a whole series of case studies, with documentation of local clinical experience on how participating provider units, specialities and individual specialists perform, nurturing the good and disposing of the bad. This organizational innovation would bring clinical audit (which we might usefully rename 'Care Audit') into mainstream management, based on nationally set standards, taking us from productivity measures to outcome change.

There are opportunities here, too, for providers to replicate such a

Performance Unit, to contribute to measurement and the regulation and direction of the market.

All this gets us into the heartland of changing clinical practice: into changing doctor training; into manpower supply and motivation; into contract incentive and reward; into transparency; and into the team issues of multi-skilling, job plans, patient care paths and patient reference. If we are to get such things done, NEDs have to insist on them. This is why we need, in purchasing authorities as well as providers, not only people with industrial and business skills; we need change agents – not necessarily merely successful or merely safe people.

Ultimately, the issue is who's writ is to run, for whom, and with what results. Key individuals, whose work impacts most on resources and quality must now become accountable. For monopoly, power and leverage outside purchasing and Trust Board control is hazardous for purchaser, trust and patient. The emphasis on clinical audit as a private venture must shift as we move towards certification and re-certification of professionals, the accreditation and re-accreditation of facilities and services, and competitive tendering both by professionals for service contracts and by management teams to deliver them.

A system which only pays for a successful outcome, assessed according to agreed clinical measures *and a patient satisfaction survey*, will correct patient expectations and encourage consultants to consider how to deliver targeted improved outcomes.

Yet, so far, our signals indicating good or unacceptable performance are weak and ineffective. One of the challenges of a non-profitmaking organization is to find ways to compensate for the weak influence that the recipients of services have when compared with the customers of profitmaking organizations, who can hit back and go away. To that extent the Patient's Charter and the League Tables are conceptual landmarks, but they need now to lead to measures of purchasing and quality that really bite, to deliver managed change. Clearly, neither is a comprehensive scheme. However, they do ask us to compete not only against others but against ourselves. They prompt further development in moving us from an organizational framework to a managed service, and they help us query the views and justifications of both managers and professionals who have their own perspective of what the organization should be doing, and what should be kept to itself by a public service.

Non-privatized services must be made more competitive, by having their performance critically analysed, while keeping paperwork under control. This ought to give a greater measure of choice, if people choose to exercise it. It should enable us to involve more people in the management of their own care. This must be what we mean by empowerment. It could help hospitals celebrate their strength, locate and improve their weaknesses. It is a learning process, in which we must pin down not only Trusts but *individuals*, for whom we need measures of individual comparative competence, as we move from relatively raw to more complex analysis of performance and the relative effectiveness of what we do. We need to think, too, about how staff, managers and patients can know if we are doing well or poorly against the standards we set, and who could do better. At present, effective measurement is made more difficult by the varying standards and demands of patients, purchasers, clinicians and management.

These different constituencies choose different measures because of their different interests. Our NHS organizations, in these terms, should not be seen as impersonal instruments guided by managers, but as shifting alliances of separate and effective relationships, where different groups advance their own interests. Proper outcome measures will enable us more easily to manage the clash of this federation of cultures, to amend the rigidities of the service, and to test the alternatives. The League Tables start us on the road to more effective measures, as does the market-testing programme. It may be, too, that to manage change we will have to develop multiple measures that accommodate the conflicting wishes of multiple constituencies. But measures are the new currency. They will, too, help us manage the dilemmas between the calls of our *values*, of our service challenges, and of political decision-making. The significant questions about performance measurements are thus not technical but conceptual. It is not only *how* to measure effectiveness but *what* to measure, and *why*. How these definitions are chosen and how used is clearly linked to key aspects of the organization's structure, shape, functioning, power relations and purposes.

The Management Executive has started the League Tables with six valuable, though hospital-centred, measures. It is probably important to start with issues that the public can understand easily and get a handle on. It is obviously desirable to assemble public understanding of how the service works and these new indicators enable us to see how a particular hospital, as a social organization, typically or untypically delivers some basics.

Let us stop ducking the issue: we are talking about life and death. The key facts at the heart of the secret garden are concealed from us: which doctor, which clinical team, which procedure, which competence, which significant variation, which lottery, which outcome, which purchaser, which provider. Indeed, it looks as if doctors themselves do not know.

This is not to demonize doctors. This is not a challenge to whether doctors work hard or devotedly. It is an issue of outcomes, not a measure of effort, nor of calm grandeur, and stoic (even heroic) energy. These issues *are* 'jellyfish slippery', but we have to get them into the net – not least by supporting Professor Michael Peckham's R&D programme.[19]

Professor Peckham, the Cochrane Centre and the *Effectiveness Bulletins*, show that we know a lot already, and we have to make sure we use the knowledge we have. As we go forward, we need to find more explicit, fair and reasonable measures of outcomes, common enough to mean something. They must be useful, in a necessary argument in which doctors need to believe and feel that they can use them. We cannot measure everything. Why not deal with the five most common conditions and our forecast of outcomes and the measures we can use in those situations. We could look at our diagnostic services (even assuming it is correct to say that early diagnosis improves outcome). We will probably find that success is a lot more common than failure. The simple measures commonly mentioned, peri-operative deaths, revision rates for arthroplasty, and perinatal mortality, are relatively rare events. The more common and less simple are necessarily more difficult, but we could look at the individual performance of clinicians, for example, on postoperative infection of wounds, postoperative length of stay, at unexpected recall. If we accumulate good data that is well recorded, we can observe the performance of individual doctors. Our interest is in best practice, in changing clinical practice, and in properly funded, good quality audit which is shared with management – not least to make the best use of what clinicians and the BMA constantly tell us is limited capacity. Purchasers will need to get public health medicine really into play.

To make sense of quality measures, we need to know a lot more about the structure of the population and the conditions we should be dealing with. We need, too, to reorganize the provision of care to get away from subjecting patients to 'the meddler' and to ensure access to a multi-disciplinary team of specialists whose performance is of much higher quality. Acute rationalization and changed work-flows can only sensibly happen on a quality basis, too.

The new accountability, greater patient influence, purchasing development, and the wider social decline of deference, all draw attention to medical myth, mystery and NHS reverence for holy relic. The public are entitled to know the name, qualifications, retraining experience, accreditation and results of any doctor and clinical team to whom they are sent. This is a major issue of public information.

How could we possibly tolerate the repetition of damaging behaviour and activities? Trusts pay the wages. Trusts must make the change. Unless, that is, we are to accept that Boards may not determine the most significant issues for their patients and their futures. Purchaser clocks, too, must now chime 'time'! In so far as best practice is concerned, the medical hierarchy cannot be sustained as it is. Purchasers must bite *on behalf* of patients. They must, too, greatly enhance the incidence and effectiveness of screening work and tackle non-attendance and re-attendance. Even so, our difficulty remains that individual consumer action is still not yet part of the system. Patients remain an indivisible collective group so far as consumer action is concerned. They pay their taxes, but they do not have the status and choices of an individual standing with his or her cash at the door. The State cuts the link between the provider and the users, substituting taxation for a direct transaction. We still have nothing like the voucher, or another enabling device to link 'own money' to 'own outcomes' while ensuring that the entire nation continues to receive health care coverage. Patient Audit involving purchasers in provider and purchaser audit may be one powerful new idea which we should explore. Whatever possible developments there are in this area, the governing idea must be quality. The key question is: Is purchasing going to influence the practice of medicine and is there a rational basis for it to do so? Can purchasing really be based on hard knowledge? Why are we not using the knowledge we already have to change practice and delivery? Purchaser interrogation of provider quality, costs, practice and results must go alongside purchasers demanding cost efficiencies.

Medical practice does vary hugely. We know well, for example from the NCEPOD studies, that a number of lines of evident difficulty are revealed by research into medical practice. Medical decision-making produces major variations in practice patterns, inappropriate care, huge variations in clinical perceptions of likely outcomes and a wide range of uncertainty.[20] All this has worrying implications for informed consent, expert testimony, and the use of consensus methods to develop practice guidelines.

If the objective is managerial excellence as well as clinical performance, we need sanctions for failure: publicity, clearly; public contumely, yes; a loss of purchaser faith in your service, too; patient concern and preferences coming into play, with a real impact on the main sources of the income of a Trust. The bottom line that matters is the health of the patient, not primarily the financial health of the Trust or Purchaser. Indeed, poor quality *should* have a negative impact on the Trust's finances. It should be a key NED concern.

The proper function of management is to ensure that *quality* is at least not behind what is being obtained elsewhere, and if possible, is giving an innovative lead.

On all this, Trust chairmen have a dilemma. They are here to be cultural change-makers but also to ensure that business plans are achieved. Their legitimacy comes from their place in the local community, and as a proxy for the patients' interests. We want open and full publication of as much data as possible – required or not by the League Tables. We can adjudicate conflicts between measures when the data is clear. It falls to the Chairman to lead the Board to insist on this point of view and to ask the Chief Executive to manage the consequences – including the impact on bottom line. Most fundamentally, all the data we collect and publish will be meaningless, too, unless purchasers act on it.

The NHS has to become a performance organization and a truly democratic and accessible body. We must break down the mystique of an untouchable culture where only initiates speak to initiates. We must create an open system, debatable and open to question by anybody, by people in the street, in their terms. We must challenge openly the pattern and quality of provision, and make purchasing decisions contestable.

The ME should look hard at purchasing contracts for quality, and at Trust business plans, and use leverage on Trusts to set out clinical processes and standards, prove their achievement, and feel the heat if they are not fulfilled. The difficulty of assessing performance should not deter managers and Boards from setting objectives and assessing results, to demonstrate if they are indeed doing well while also doing good. That is what Chief Executives are well paid to do.

We need to meet the need for perspective to assess the relationship between the purchaser, the State provider and the mixed economy of health, to deliver the ethical imperatives of the Health Service, and to conduct the necessary review of the welfare state which turns on knowing what quality is and what we are delivering. We need to develop a vision, to think through the consequences and the opportunities of the first six League Table indicators, how they fit in with research and development, with proven clinical methods, and with the improvement of the Health of the Nation.[21]

Frances Hodgson Burnett, CS Lewis, Lewis Carroll, AA Milne, Kenneth Grahame, all showed the magic of the secret garden. In our garden we need to plant assessment of every process, outcome scrutiny, comparison and competition, and we need to label everything – with no-one anonymous. The League Tables are a beacon whose light will illuminate the path by which we can now go further.

We have got to value the good performers who get out in front, who set the pace, and show what can be done; that is inspirational to all. They raise morale and get us to quality with a different tone, standard and commitment. We should not all be in line. Some of us should try to race ahead. As Eric Caines has said, it is about people being inspired into what they are capable of being and doing. The growth potential *is* huge. It is time to move on again.

Notes

1   *The Patient's Charter: Hospital and Ambulance Services. Comparative Performance Guide 1993–1994.* NHS Executive, Leeds, 1994. (The second set of tables were published in July 1995.) See 'Improving Clinical Effectiveness.' *NHS Management Executive Letter* (93) 115, 21 December 1993. Also, McColl AJ, Gulliford MC (1994) *Population Health Outcome Indicators of the NHS, A Feasibility Study.* Faculty of Health Medicine of The

Royal Colleges of Physicians of the United Kingdom, London, 1994. For a key to the door of Quality Adjusted Life Years see, for example, Williams A (1991) *Economics, QALYs and Medical Ethics: A Health Economist's Perspective.* Centre For Health Economics, Discussion Paper 121, York. Also, Drummond M, Torrance G, Mason J (1993) Cost-Effectiveness League Tables: More Harm Than Good? *Soc. Sci. Med.,* **37,** (No. 1), 33–40.

2   No-one has made this fundamental point more clearly and consistently than Professor Alan Maynard. Amongst his many contributions see (1993) *Wrong Targets? Wrong Policies?: Reflections on Health Care Reform in the Last Twenty Years'.* Speech to conference on 'Marketing and the Health Service', 28 January, London; (1994) *The Shaping of Health Care Systems.* Speech to the Ditchley Foundation, 20 May; (1993) *Rational Decision Making in Health Care.* Paper presented to the annual conference of the Operational Research Society, 15 September, York; with Bloor K (1995) Primary Care and Health Reform: the Need to Reflect Before Reforming. *Health Policy,* **31** 171–81. The article by Kind P (1990) Outcome Measurement Using Hospital Activity Data: Deaths After Surgical Procedures. *British Journal of Surgery, 77,* 1399–402 is a fundamental landmark. See also his *Hospital Deaths – The Missing Link.* Discussion Paper No. 44, Centre for Health Economics, University of York, 1988, and also the important collection of speeches in *But Will It Work, Doctor?* Report of a conference about involving users of health services in outcomes research, held at the King's Fund Centre, 9 November 1993, edited by Michael Dunning and Gill Needham, The Consumer Health Information Consortium etc., London, 1994. One way into the American literature is the text and extensive footnotes in Brook RH (1991) Quality of care: do we care? *Annals of Internal Medicine,* **115,** (No. 6), 486–90.

3   Francis Hodgson Burnett (1911) *The Secret Garden.* (Puffin edition, Penguin Books, 1993, London.) This speech was, of course given in April 1994. In the ensuing year we have gradually seen more of what the garden really contains, for example, the new Eurocare survey, which is following 800 000 cancer patients from 11 European countries has again emphasized how poorly managed cancer services are in the UK. See, Mihill C (1995) Euro Cancer List Shows Failings. *The Guardian*, 17 May, p.7, and Milton C (1995) Survival Rate Below Norm in British Cancer Cases. *The Times,* 17 May, p.7.

4   *The Calman Report. Hospital Doctors: Training for the Future.* The Report of the Working Group on Specialist Medical Training. Department of Health, London, April 1993. (Chairman, Dr Kenneth Calman.)

5   The love story of CS Lewis (played by Anthony Hopkins) and New York poet Joy Gresham (played by Debra Winger), directed by Sir Richard Attenborough, 1994.

6   See Eddy DM (1993) Medicine, Money and Mathematics. *Medical Audit News,* **3,** (No 8), (Report of address to American Urological Association, presented on October 21 1991, Chicago.)

7   Private discussion and communication, March 1994.

8   *Daily Telegraph*, London, 17 May 1994.

9   *Breast Cancer: How To Help Yourself.* Cancer Relief Macmillan Fund, London, 1994.

10 As cited in an internal, unpublished, Department of Health report, 1994; private information.

11 Consensus Development Conference: Treatment of Primary Breast Cancer. *British Medical Journal, 293,* 946–7. 11 October 1993.

12 Chouillet AM, Bell CMJ, Hiscox JG (1994) Management of Breast Cancer in South East England. *British Medical Journal,* **308,** *168–71.*

13 *Cancer in South East England, 1990. Cancer Incidence, Prevalence and Survival in Residents of the District Health Authorities in the Four Thames Regions.* Thames Cancer Registry, London, October 1993. See also: *Review of the Pattern of Cancer Services in England and Wales.* The Association of Cancer Physicians, London, April 1994 (Chairman, Professor JMA Whitehouse); and Swerdlow A (1994) *Atlas of Cancer Incidence in England and Wales.* Oxford University Press, Oxford.

14 John Yates *Variety is the Price of Death,* address to The Royal Society of Medicine, London, 11 April 1994. See also, Shaw CD, Costain DW (1994) *League Tables for Health Care.* Report for a Joint Meeting of the Forum on Quality in Health Care and the section on Measurement in Medicine, at the Royal Society of Medicine, 11 April, London.

15 See Professor Sir Reginald Murley (President, The Royal College of Surgeons, England 1977–80), letter to *The Times,* 20 April 1994.

16 New policy developments were prefaced by the Chief Medical Officer's report on the future of cancer services: Calman K (1994) *A Policy Framework For Commissioning Cancer Services.* Consultative Document, London. See also, the assessment of the report by Butler P (1994) A double-edged *sword. Health Service Journal,* 26 May 1994, London, pp.10–11, and the editorial *Cancer: a race against time,* in the same issue, p.17. The consultative document was re-published by the Department of Health with firm decisions under its original title on 24 April 1995. See also Mihill C (1995) Health Shake-Up to End Cancer 'Lottery'. *The Guardian,* 25 April, p.5; and Laurance J (1995) Specialist Centres to End Lottery of Cancer Treatment. *The Times,* 25 April, p.3. In February 1995 the Cancer Relief Macmillan Fund made information available to GPs on services available for breast cancer, one area where Britain does least well of all European countries. Its directory was not, however, available to patients. See Hawkes N (1995) Breast Cancer Directory Seeks to End 'Care Lottery'. *The Times,* 21 February, p.6. An important forward view was given in *Vision For Cancer: The Next 25 Years,* London, Imperial Cancer Research Fund, second draft, January 1995.

17 David M Eddy, op.cit.

18 NCEPOD, op.cit.

19 See comment also in 'Famous for 15 minutes?', Annabelle May interview with Professor Michael Peckham, *The Health Service Journal,* 17 February 1994, and in *R & D Towards Knowledge-Based Care.* South West Thames Public Health Report, 1994.

20 David M Eddy, op.cit.

21 *Compliance with Practice Guidelines: Clinical Autonomy Revisited,* presented by Nick Klazinga to the European Health Policy Forum, Brussels, 30

September 1993. See also: *Rational Decision Making in Health Care,* Professor Alan Maynard's address to Annual Conference of the Operational Research Society, York, 15 September 1993, and *Appropriateness in Clinical Care, A Handbook.* South East Thames Regional Health Authority, 1994. Also, *Clinical Effectiveness and Clinical Audit,* address by The Rt Hon Mrs Virginia Bottomley MP, Secretary of State for Health, Birmingham, 17 February 1994.

This chapter is built around the scaffolding of a speech given at the Royal Society of Medicine in London on 11 April 1994 to a joint meeting of the Forum on Quality in Health Care and the Society's Section on Measurement in Medicine. A brief summary of speeches that day entitled *League Tables For Health Care* was prepared by Charles D Shaw and David W Costain. I owe particular thanks to John Simmonds for our several conversations on the issues and ideas discussed in this chapter, and to David Costain for the original invitation to deliver the address. Steven Henning Sieverts deepened and broadened my understanding in our discussions which were prompted by his comments after reading the original address, to the very great benefit of the final version.

6

The invisible hospital:

or, what patients experience but managers often do not see

There is an 'invisible hospital', which patients see and experience, but managers often do not. There is a vital necessity for NEDs to be much more active and influential than conventional wisdom has thought they ought to be. It is they – and, perhaps, only they – who can identify the 'invisible hospital' for managers and fulfil the potential of the reforms to change it. Their responsibility is to ask themselves, as they visit their hospital, 'What is it like to go through this place?'

When in November 1992 I was invited to become Chairman of the proposed Brighton Health Care NHS Trust – the acute hospital provider in Brighton – I asked my non-executive colleagues to support two initiatives focused on accountability, quality and choice. First, that executive directors accustomed to rolling contracts should be offered fixed-term two-year contracts, with the emphasis on performance and accountability, and, second, the new Board should target an agenda insisting on quality (effectiveness) and choice. This would really take seriously our service to patients, and focus the organization on really carrying service through in the way that patients tell us they want it.[1] Clearly, it is not possible to achieve change without persuading the people in the organization that they want it, but it is a difficulty that the NHS does not seem to change unless there is no alternative. There are issues on which the Board has to insist. The Board is the only part of the organization that can enforce audit, improvement, better practice – and the fact that these do not exist are their fault as much as the employees' fault.

In NHS terms, this is revolutionary stuff. It implies and requires the development of the roles of Chairman and NED in new ways to ensure that we genuinely put patients' interests first. There is, too, the overriding responsibility of the Board for probity in the management of public money and assets owned by the public service, as the Cadbury Report establishes.[2] The lessons of the London Ambulance Service[3] and of Wessex Regional Health Authority[4] – as well as private sector problems, too – emphasize that NEDs must not only be better informed but must go further and take power for change.

It is clear from personal conversations with colleagues in the service that my wheelchair trip has become the subject both of myth and misconception. The event was not intended as a gimmick. It was not done to seek the limelight. Its purpose was to encourage management to see the service from the patient's point of view.

It was encouraging to see the independent report by the 'Access Action Group', set up in April 1993 in response to concerns expressed by patients and staff about the difficulties faced by disabled patients, visitors and staff within Brighton Health Care. We enabled disabled people to audit our sites, and our forward plans.

The Group, which was funded with £40 000 from the Trust for two successive years, said of the event 'We were involved in plans for this event, and two members of the Access Action Group, Bill and Kathy Goddon, escorted the Chairman throughout his session to ensure he was given an idea about what it is like to have a disability. As well as highlighting the problems experienced by disabled people in the Royal Sussex County Hospital, the trip also raised the profile of the Access Action Group and its work. The trip also meant that a number of problems were dealt with more quickly than they may otherwise have been.'[5]

My proposal to visit in a wheelchair was prompted by discussions with patients, who had said to me 'If you had to go through it you would soon change it.' It was, too, a way to get management to see the details of the patients experience and the problems of the environment – when conventional ways of doing this did not seem to me to be sufficient. The visit was on Friday 28 May 1993. The article in *The Sunday Times* which attracted national attention did not appear until 24 April 1994, almost a full year later. My article The 'Pravda' Mentality' for *The Health Summary,* January 1994, was prepared for a professional audience.

How could I visit like this and be unknown after two years in the job? I could not and I did not. I did not make the visit without any advance warning. The surprise was that even though it was known in advance so much was still un-fixed. Nor was I unrecognized by the staff – except for the unfortunate porter. The visit was not intended as a patronizing token. It was arranged by the Patients' Advocate and the Access Action Group set up by the Trust in April 1993. Two members played a major role: wheelchair user Mrs Kathy Goddon and her husband Bill Goddon, who has a serious visual disability. For part of the tour I was equipped with special glasses designed greatly to limit my vision, to help me experience what Bill Goddon had to deal with in the hospital. Many staff welcomed the tour. I was quoted afterwards as saying 'Staff are full of energy and ideas. We've got to find a way of tapping into these.'[6]

The visit provided material for the first episode of the new, eight-part 1995 series of the hospital drama *Cardiac Arrest* (BBC 1, 19 April 1995) when a new, and as yet unknown, manager borrowed a wheelchair and tested facilities to see if they were appropriate for the disabled. They were not. Another example of what Dickens called 'the triumphant imperfection of inconvenience.'

Nurse leader Mary Donn was right to tell a nursing conference in June 1992 'Well, the way to find out whether (everyone, including people with special needs can use our services) is to put the Chairman of the Health Authority or the Chief Executive in a wheelchair or else blindfold them and ask them to make their way around some of our premises. That may be the assertive way we need to behave if we are actually going to get improvements for people with special needs'.[7]

The presumption must be that the Chairman has the time to do the job, to become an insider without becoming captured by the system.[8] The NED comes at it as an outsider and has limited time, so they must be able to rely on the Chairman for information, advice, guidance and support to become truly effective. There is, surely, a great deal of room for thought about the development of the Chairman's office. This seems to me to require clear agenda management by the Chairman, and some organizational experimentation at the margins. If Chairmen are really to make a difference, they need their own full-time secretary/assistant ('eyes and ears'), not a shared or part-time secretary. They need a very strong vice-chairman – an important supporter to help drive change.[9] I believe, too, that we should experiment with a strengthening of the Chairman's office with a research assistant, that there should be short-term task forces chaired by NEDs: for example, to look at what performance indicators we need. To be at all useful NEDs need to ensure that they get the information they need, in a form they can use.[10] An obvious example is the financial information. There is, surely, too, a role for local special advisers to the Chairman and NEDs; in Brighton we are appointing a practising GP (who was formerly an NED on Brighton Health Authority), a local headmistress and a member of the management faculty of the University of Sussex. We need to look for catalysts for change, heroes and heroines within the system too.

In Brighton we are making many discoveries by pressing at the boundaries, and getting many surprises as we seek to develop these critical roles to improve service, for example, in January 1993 we launched two new campaigns, 'The Search For Quality' and 'The Search For choice', each seeking to produce *immediate* changes, with relatively low investment costs, with an emphasis on *pace*, to emphasize this new point of view. The 'Search For Quality' seeks to find 24 initiatives we can *deliver* by Easter this year.[11]

Inevitably, as NEDs seek to inspire and enthuse our colleagues, and as we exert pressure on the organization for change, wheels squeak, and squeaking wheels speak to us about what we need to do. Brighton Health Care launched its searches for quality and choice believing that a Trust should not wait to be prompted by purchaser guidelines. It should take quality and choice to the market, which it seeks to lead. If Trusts' freedoms, local discretion and accountability, are not to be mere rhetoric, we need to be seen to develop and deliver quality services, and in ways that patients can judge. 'Target quality in every detail' – that is easy to say, but it is not easy to deliver. The process of trying and the difficulties identified then tell us a great deal about the persistence of the old NHS culture and our difficulties in unveiling the new.

To achieve these changes takes strong leadership, and it is too much to expect a Chairman to do it alone. Unfortunately, too many of the best NEDs were forcibly retired on the grounds of age. This was a great loss, particularly at Brighton, and just when their detailed knowledge credibility, and their management experience in carrying people with them counted most.

We set the ball rolling by new training so that all telephone calls would be answered promptly and in a warm and helpful fashion. We are launching a returners newsletter and a returners day. We are examining the idea of a courtesy bus service to key sites to help patients, since we have very little parking. We established a new 'no questions asked' amnesty for the return of NHS equipment, and I said 'Forget about feeling guilty. Just bring the stuff back. It would help us to help other patients.'

We are attacking the 'sellotape' culture, eliminating crude sellotaped, tacky, fly-posted notices on walls and boards and providing decent noticeboards. We are training departments to reissue current, accurate and friendly notices in attractive and readable formats. We are encouraging executives to notice the large number of public notices which begin with the words 'Do Not...'. This is, of course, not unique to Brighton; it is endemic (as are some bewilderingly mole-like views, or lack of them) throughout the public service.

We are taking our out-patients seriously as living people by removing ten-year old copies of *Punch* and offering them todays newspapers and current magazines – the cost in a full year was £3000.

As Chairman, I have asked for large public information noticeboards outside each of our sites which will tell people how we are doing on the Patient's Charter, and which will be readable from the street. And we are going to return the personal effects of deceased patients to relatives in a good quality bag, not in an old box or a bin-liner.

We are also – fundamentally, and most centrally – setting in place a major project to ask patients on a continuing basis what it is that matters to *them*? What do *they* want, besides what we think they want?[12] The distressing thing, the really startling thing, is that all these initiatives are obvious, inexpensive to do, achievable and manageable, are a signal that the patients matter, but have been given no priority. I lost count of the number of managers whose first response to me was to say 'What? Why? You mean... we'll never get that done here.'

Much of this is about ceasing to be complacent about detail. It is about appreciating that every detail 'speaks' and needs to be managed and monitored. It takes time. It takes insistence from the top. It requires ownership at all levels. It requires the Chief Executive to be seen to believe in it, and not only when the Chairman is looking.

When we think in this way it leads us to focus on reward systems, on saying 'Thank you', and on being supportive of behaviour, not merely of performance. All this is about helping people see the 'invisible hospital' – the whole picture – and their own role in it. This self-knowledge is essential if people are to see how their work connects with everyone elses and with the patient's experience. It dramatizes the most fundamental point about every service industry, that every single transaction with a customer is a quality issue. Everything, from an incoming phone call to how people are written to, is a customer transaction. This is to focus us on a new image of the patient, whose interests and concerns are always put first. This is to welcome the patient who is more energetic and informed and, hopefully, more self-confident in using and influencing our services. It places a premium on creativity, flair, personality, style, energy, and originality, which have not been qualities previously much valued in the NHS. So, the searches for quality and choice set us to ask what do we do, why do we do it, how do we do it, who does it, what is the result, and what do patients think of it.

This has been a non-executive initiative, to which executive management signed up. For an outsider like me the negotiation produced many surprises, which point to difficulties that the NHS locally needs to address.

First, management sets deadlines, but they are not taken seriously in the way that they are in business. A priority in an aeroplane is instant, but when a Japanese competitor opens up next door to your business it is a shock. In the NHS 'urgent' actions tend to go onto a long list. Many people do not take priorities seriously since they have become accustomed to managers not meaning what they say (and not saying what they mean two days running). Or, if urgent priorities are taken seriously, the necessary actions still do not always get taken as people do not seem always to really understand what is being asked of them: for example, the initiative to improve noticeboards, to give them proper headings, to locate them in places where they could be useful, has not yet been delivered. Instead, the bureaucratic executive response was to stamp notices on the back as 'approved' (apparently irrespective of content or design) and put them on the old noticeboards. This was thought to be a sufficient change, even for noticeboards located in corridors with virtually no light. The attempt to see the noticeboard from the patients' point of view did *not* come into focus, despite the policy. Many executives do seem to find it extraordinarily difficult to see the service from the patients' view, and to recognize that old rubbish bags, broken signs, filthy loos, handwritten notices, sellotape and Blu-tac everywhere, are a serious organizational failing. Executives, too, often seem genuinely bewildered by how to achieve what the new culture asks them to do. They do not recognize that there are relevant skills and knowledge which they do not have, which NEDs do have (or should), and which they should take seriously.

There is, too, an extraordinary lack of visual imagination, although the project led by Bill Murray (himself a Trust Chief Executive) and published as the estates development report, *Environments For Quality Care*[13], demonstrates how some Trusts can and are making major changes, but to get a simple thing like a noticeboard redesigned, relocated and managed is a *huge* struggle. Equally, old-speak boundary and ownership conflicts hinder us, too. We do need to focus on common goals and to sort out the relationships between departments: for example, between Works, Estates and Hotel Services. Too much is left stranded on the boundaries between them: for example, a true one (from Brighton), Estates fixes a sign, but leaves a wrecked trolley lying on the floor beneath it – 'That's for Hotel Services'. No system for Works to tell them seems to exist. Hotel Services, too, have to be opened up by market testing to those who know how to deliver the best to which we are all accustomed *outside* the NHS.

It is not easy, either, to get people really to think about what quality means in our daily work, in how we behave. It is true that specifying service protocols, narrowing tolerances, and setting operational proce- dures does help, but executive mind-sets have to change, not because they are hit by a bucket by the Chairman[11], but because, unless they do change and show they believe in the change no-one down below will believe in the policies and deliver them. For people *know* who is committed and who is not. Chance remarks, glances, give the game away. It has to matter to the people at the top, and evidently to matter if it is to matter to those down below. Much of this is about what I call the 'invisible hospital', that is, the hospital that patients experience but managers do not. This blindness, this short-sightedness, is now severely dysfunctional, and it is here that non- executive influence on ways of looking, seeing and feeling can be vital if we are to go beyond 'new structures' to a genuinely new service approach.

Just look at what has been invisible to management. Look at the route through the Royal Sussex County Hospital at Brighton. Look at what our patients access audit has already showed us. (How typical are we?) Our maps do not say 'You are here'. They are colour coded, but we do not say how or why. They direct people to a customer care centre, but we do not have one. We have toilets which have no sign on the door. No-one knows how many toilets we have. We have lifts, but with no mini-directory in them to say what is on each floor. We do not say which floor gives which access to other buildings. We do not tell people which floor they are on when they are outside the lifts. We do not give directions as to what is on that floor. Our Social Work office (not signposted) has a door, hidden behind a cupboard. We do not tell people if they have an option to use the lift or stairs. We call the ENT department two different things within three feet of each other outside the department. We do not tell the public they can use our restaurant, although they can. We have no directory in A&E. We upgraded a building housing physiotherapy (and the management team) and put a handle on it which physiotherapy patients could not open.[15]

The initiative entitled 'The Search For Quality' has started to help us understand more about how the organization works, or does not work, and about what has previously been invisible and unattended. This is about shifting our priorities. I think it is clear that this would not have happened without the Chairman's insistence and intervention in setting an agenda for the executives. Indeed, the success or failure of the search both for quality and for choice is a test of whether or not NEDs can really achieve change, actually to put patients at the centre and turn the pyramid on its head. With these objectives in view NED roles need to continue to develop. This will take active effort. NEDs need to *insist* on forming a new regime. This is not about carpets alone. It is about shifting attitudes. We all of us, all the time, get distressing letters about the patient's experience 'Why has *this* happened to my husband?'. Managers have got to see, to give way to, and passionately to care about patients' concerns: the ugliness of the buildings, the tattiness, the cold food, the rudeness. It is newcomers, outsiders, who are helping them see it for the first time.

We need to find ways to manage so that we pick up all these 'details', each of us shocked when we find them. It is clear that being an NED will continue to be hard work. It will take staying power, energy, drive, determination and insistence on investing to get these details right, and right first time. It is important for NEDs to insist, in part because the market is not getting it done, and because it has not mattered to Chief Operating Officers. Purchasers are still managing budgets, buying volume, and it is still an uncomplaining market. So far there have been relatively few really significant shifts, despite what GP fundholders have done. The internal market is, in fact, still like the markets of the old Soviet Union where you could not get a car or a washing machine at any price. You did not expect to live to see one, so you were only too glad to get one of any kind, even a Trabant! Or, in the case of the NHS patient on a long waiting-list, when they do get in they do not really yell at the awfulness of much of the experience. Indeed, they report 'satisfaction'.

Instead, NEDs must get it done. To do so they must remain unsocialized by the NHS. So, do not let your energies be dissipated. Do not be inducted into the system. Remember whose heads rolls if you fail to deliver change. Indeed, I believe that it will steadily be demonstrated that the true, the real potential in the format of the NHS reforms, is that the NEDs and Chairmen are the ones who are learning to speak for the people, to insist on quality and on choice, while the executives run the shop. The executives are not wicked, they are doing their best, but they have always done things in other ways.[16] They are 'company people' who have grown up with the old culture. They do not yet control the system in a way recognizable to

NEDs. Generally, they honourably administer a federation of cultures, and calling administrators Managers does not make them so. Someone has to lead the change and to stop the old culture. I am told that in a previous effort to bring in outsiders, executives recruited from industry and the forces did not make it. The old culture did not allow it. It is vital that NEDs do make it, are powerful and insist on change. This is the most vital potential in the new reform format.

Indeed, it begins to look as if the only way in which the organization can haul itself around is by the distinctive contribution that NEDs can make. Their base must be to claim the right to speak for the people, for the local population whose service this is. This, much more than their qualifications in business, is their justification and the source of their authority. They have to make the agenda clear; help manage conflict; hold to the notion of the 'public voice'; support the good managers; ensure the delivery of quality and choice. The emergence of the controlling influence of NEDs may be the most important of all the unintended consequences of the reforms, and the most profound.

Critically, the key to the full asset utilization of Trusts is that clinicians should change the historic ways they have always worked. NEDs will need to give the fullest support to Chief Executives in encouraging this change. Inevitably, there is tension, for we are leading the service away from endorsing the highly developed NHS culture of consensus and compromise, which strongly militates against achieving some of the most difficult and conflict-producing aspects of the reforms.[17] We need, of course, to improve everyone's perception of the patient's physical environment. We need to recover or develop our empathy and perception of the patient's experience, to appreciate their position and what they feel. Tackling these issues will lead us directly into the core of the medical and nursing cultures which still dictate the main features of the overall NHS culture. Many people clearly find it disturbing to see and feel what the patient sees and feels, and the culture we are trying to change has, of course, been serving purposes which we now want to alter. The challenge to managers in changing cultures is about trying to create a new organizational environment where the opportunities for different purposes and for a more adventurous and creative management style can be enhanced. Thus, the need to ensure the emphasis on accountability must be right, but it is insufficient. Accountability should be clearly linked with dynamic management – valuing leadership, innovation, being less risk-adverse, trying new things, valuing where people are now and what they do now as the basis from which we can lead and encourage them to do new things.

I am not at all sure that in exerting pressure for improvement that purchasers should accept the provider view that every obvious improvement shall be itemized for costing purposes. I think John Simmonds (Chairman, Brighton Health Authority) was right when he said to me in conversation 'Providers should only be providers because they maintain certain standards, and it is the existence of these standards which justifies them entering the list of *potential* providers.' The ultimate key to establishing new standards and delivering them, is that we must be genuinely concerned with our employees as individuals. We are not. Yet we ask them to make the change, and genuinely to address the questions patients raise.

The NEDs have to roll out the map and to take control. The executives have to deliver the cultural and behavioural change, and we need to ask how we can bring the executives along with us? Is this more training? Is it creative ideas like sabbatical opportunities in the private sector? How do we build *the team* in this new world? We need to open out these issues and discuss them frankly. There is too much that is invisible, too many unstated assumptions, too much informal knowledge, too much secrecy. It is to the NED, who was not intended to say so, to speak the unspoken truths.

Notes

1 At this time I prepared a booklet intended for staff and patients entitled *Taking Strides Down Quality Street: Grasping the Quality Opportunities Of Trust Status in Brighton – The First 100 Days,* but in the event the Trust did not publish it. I devoted my New Year Message to it in December 1992. The idea was to carry people with us by making it clear what the Trust was all about. A short version of the unpublished booklet was presented to the Board in December 1992. Each initiative was given a target date for completion, with responsibility given to a lead Director; for example, a photographic 'Who's Who' of consultants was to be completed by 31 March 1993 (lead Director, Dr Nicholas Bishop, Medical Director).

2 *A Report Of The Committee On The Financial Aspects Of Corporate Governance. Gee, London, 1992.* See also 'The Cadbury Report on Corporate Governance'. *NAHAT Briefing,* No. **42**, Birmingham, March 1993. The then NHS Chief Executive, Sir Duncan Nichol CBE, had highlighted the implications of Cadbury for the NHS at a NAHAT conference in London in February 1993. See Sir Adrian Cadbury (1993) Effective Boards. *The Health Summary,* September, pp.7–8, edited version of speech to NAHAT conference, 16 September 1993. Also, EL(94)40, *Codes of Conduct and Accountability: Guidance.* NHS Executive, Leeds, 28 April 1994; the Leeds firm of solicitors Simpson Curtis issued a ten page commentary; the Department of Health finally issued a *Code of Conduct and Accountability,* London, 28 April 1994. I addressed these issues in a speech entitled *All Above Board; Or, How to Openly Ask the Public to Judge Us. Accountability in the NHS,* to a workshop at the NAHAT Annual Conference, Bournemouth, 17 June 1993.

3 On the London Ambulance Service, see Butler P (1993) '666' (News Focus), *The Health Service Journal,* 4 March, and *Report of the Enquiry into London*

Ambulance Service. Communications Directorate, SW Thames RHA, London, 1995.

4 On the Wessex RHA, see District Auditor, Wessex RHA, Public Interest Report, *The Statutory Report of the District Auditor of WRHA*, Winchester, 15 July 1992.

5 Brighton Health Care NHS Trust *Access Action Group: Review of Our First Year and Forward Plan for 1994/95*, (March 1994).

6 See 'Chairman Survives His "Lethal" Journey', *Brighton Health Care Bulletin*, No. **282**, p.2, July 1993.

7 See *The Patient's Charter: Achieving Objectives Through the Framework.* English National Board Study Day, 8 June 1992.

8 I was interested and encouraged when in June 1994 a senior manager just below Board level suggested to me in writing that the Trust needed a Chairman's Think/Action Tank, but time ran out. The Chairman's office in the reformed system is an undeveloped structure. If Chairmen are to be more interventionist, to be more concerned with implementation, to maintain momentum (as I think they must) they need to gain space and capacity to ensure that policy objects are achieved. For further discussion of some of these issues see the chapters 'Performance, The Flag To Fly' and 'Where Do Chairmen Get Their Information'.

Useful work on NEDs includes: Lilley R (1992) Welcome on Board, NAHAT, Birmingham; Langley M (1993) *The Role of the Chairman and the Non-Executive Director in the NHS in Wales.* Welsh Association Of Health Authorities and Trusts, Cowbridge, Wales; Andrew Wall (1993) *Healthy NHS Boards, Guidelines For Board Members.* NAHAT, Birmingham; Ferlie E, Ashburner L, Fitzgerald L (1993) Movers and Shakers. *Health Service Journal*, 18 November, pp. 25-26; Ferlie E, Ashburner L, Fitzgerald L (1993) *Board Teams – Roles and Relationships.* Research For Action Paper 10, Bristol, NHS Training Directorate; Ashburner L(1994) The Composition of NHS Trust Boards. *Health Services Management Research, 7*, (No.3), 154–64; and several articles by an effective NED (Vice-Chairman York Health Services Trust), Charlotte Williamson (1989) Less than the Sum of their Parts: A Lesson for DHAs. *Health Services Management,* June, *pp.114–17;* (1994) The Eyes Have It. *Health Service Journal,* 13 January, pp.22–4; (1994) You Are in my Power. *Health Service Journal,* 17 March, pp.25–6; (1994) Out of Time. *Health Service Journal,* 8 September, pp.28–9; (1995) Spice of Life. *Health Service Journal,* 23 March, pp.28–9; (1995) Gender Gap. *Health Service Journal*, 30 March, pp.27–9. See also Long R, Salter B (1994) Confusion and Control. *Health Service Journal,* 5 May, pp.18–20; Turrell A (1995) To be on the Board or not to be on the Board, is that the Question?. *The Cutting Edge Newsletter,* Centre For Health Services Management, University Of Nottingham, Issue 3, January, pp.4–6; my article (1995) Time For Fat Cats To Diet. *The Guardian,* (Society section), 1 March, and Caines E (1995) A Voice on the Board. *The Times,* 11 May, p.14. (Transparently about Brighton.) For a view of what NEDs are supposed to contribute in leadership, albeit at an angle, see Heffer S (1993) This is the time of year when wars break out. *The Spectator,* 17 July; and Davies P (1993) Your Disobedient Servant. *Health Service Journal,* London, 23 September. For what managers think of NEDs, see Limb M (1994)

The seats of power. *Health Service Journal,* 8 December, p.15. See also, *Who Runs Our Health* Service? The Occupational and Political Background of NHS Trust Chairs and Non-Executive Directors. Labour Research Department, London, 1994.

9 A very strong Vice-Chairman who shares a commitment to the agenda is essential. I was enormously fortunate to inherit John Simmonds as Vice-Chairman of Brighton Health Authority when I was appointed by Virginia Bottomley as Chairman at Brighton in April 1991. When I moved to head the Trust, John succeeded me. He shared my prejudice in favour of imagination, and was as shocked as I was at the prevalence of what Dickens had noted 130 years earlier 'Never imagine anything. Have no imagination at all.'

10 For more recent thoughts see 'Where do NHS Chairmen get their information' in this book (p.86).

11 Looking back on these initiatives I see that they represented one of my greatest struggles with inertia. It often seemed that a policy was signed, sealed, but was it delivered? In the attack on the sellotape culture, Marion Ryland (seconded from SE Thames RHA) did a wonderful job.

12 When I left Brighton in September 1994, calls to the main switchboard were being answered properly (and I regularly went there to say 'Thank you'), but we had no programme to ensure that extensions were answered once calls were switched through. The equipment amnesty in April 1993 worked, and it was essential for there to be unsupervized deposit points at each main door. As a member of the Patient's Charter Advisory Group I suggested to the Secretary of State for Health that the national campaign be entitled 'Help us to help you', and I was glad that this was adopted. My hope that every map we sent to a patient would carry a current message of good news had not been actioned, nor had my proposal for a courtesy bus service to carry patients between our five sites. We still lacked a photographic 'Who's Who' of staff in each ward, and of senior medical staff. The new Brighton Health Care Arts Trust (which had already attracted six figure funding from The Contemporary Arts Society) was stood down, after several trustees withdrew. We did successfully involve patients and visitors in the design of the new hospital.

I know that I was thought to have set a large agenda, but this should not have been necessary. The best private companies have been managed and focused on these priorities for some years. I believed it was essential to be an activist Chairman and to give a lead on giving power to patients. Some things worked. Bec Hanley and then Penny Dunman were inspired choices as successive Patient Advocates. In 1993/94 Penny saw 700 patients, a large number of whom were picked up when in difficulty in the system, given time as well as 'a slot', helped to know what they could get access to and how to get access to it, especially through help to get continuity of care and advice. The extension of the work of the Advocate to network with local advocates in Age Concern, mental health and disability groups was the Advocate's own initiative.

We renamed a ward after George Miles, the first baby born the day we became a Trust; we invited Doug Flowers, our longest serving member of staff, with 46 years service, to declare the Trust open. In August 1993 I began a regular open day for staff to see me on a confidential basis. In July 1994, to improve how we handled complaints from patients, I telephoned the complainer personally on the day I received any complaint letter. I had hoped to rename the breast cancer unit for a woman (and not, as at present, after a retired male doctor); the unit, however, initiated a programme of tape recording consultations for patients to take home and replay, and the Sussex Oncology Centre won a Charter Mark in 1994. We agreed to appoint a patient as an Associate Director of the Board, especially to advocate the interests of the elderly (agreed as policy, but not yet concluded?), and I had hoped to appoint a disabled patient to the same role, to reinforce the messages of the Patient Advocate and the Patient Access Group.

We also needed good signposting to the Patient Advocate's office; advertising boards as big as houses at each of our five sites campaigning against smoking; individual slogans on all our stationery against smoking, specific to the speciality (e.g. 'Smoking harms your baby', for Obs. & Gynae.); open days to schools; a regular quarterly report to the community, and genuine Annual Reporting to the patient. We had achieved wide circulation of the Board agenda and six public Board meetings annually. The first Annual Report was, in my view, an outstandingly effective piece of communication, but I do not know if an audit has been done to assess whether it reached patients. Would it have been different if our actual patients were the customers rather than the recipients of care purchased for them? In September 1994 seven 'Gold Standards' were introduced, in a developmental programme which made explicit promises to patients.

13 Murray B (1993) *Environments for Quality Care.* HMSO/NHS Estates, London.

14 One of my treasured mementoes of my time at Brighton is a small flower-bucket, painted gold, given to me by a friend at the time to remind me that I did regularly remark that it seemed impossible to get executive action unless people were hit with a bucket. On one or two occasions I was naughty and placed the bucket in front of me on the boardroom table.

15 My experience touring the site in a wheelchair, when advance notice had been given, produced many other examples. One result was the suggestion by Patients' Advocate Penny Dunman for a 'fresh eyes' debriefing programme for new staff from whom we could learn. The restaurant, open to patients, charged them more than staff. What is the message there?

16 They did, of course, come in under the old rules. See 'Do not wait for the cavalry: or, what is a Chief Executive for?' in this book (p.179).

17 We need to do a lot of thinking, even now in 1995, about how to encourage doctors to become committed stakeholders in their Trusts; we need a new model of ownership and accountability, and local engagement, to help raise standards. A stimulating idea which may have some parallels for NHS Trusts (and which was considered at the inception of the reforms – see Thatcher M (1993) *The Downing Street Years.* Chapter xx, Harper Collins, London) has again been put forward by Anthony Meredith (1995) *Teachers' Right To Buy: A New Model For State Schools.* The Social Market Foundation, London. He proposes that teachers be given a long-term stake, tangible rewards for success, and the scope to innovate by creating 'school businesses', taking over

all or part of existing state schools. This may offer more positive action than clinicians withdrawing into 'chambers'.

This material, where I first developed the concept of the 'invisible hospital', was prepared at the beginning of 1993, and has not previously been published in full. A short article appeared in *Health Direct,* the NAHAT journal for NEDs (now renamed *Health Director*), April 1993, p.10.

7

The 'Pravda mentality':

its influence on preventing us fixing our problems

In the hammer-and-sickle days when Soviet man was allegedly perfectible and Lenin God, their were two adult comics published in Moscow: *Pravda* and *Izvestia*. The resulting *'Pravda mentality'* struck its characteristic triumphalist note 'Uzbek Sausage Factory Workers Triple Production'. This did not actually furnish sausages to the long queue of Babushkas holding string bags in line at the corner shop. The *'Pravda mentality'* reflected the unreality of the 'triumph' of communism. It prevented the confession of error, the fixing of problems, the genuine management of hard choices. If we are not careful, NHS Trusts will catch the virus.

It *is* clear that the NHS is advancing. We are getting better and more appropriate investment, higher productivity, improved process analysis and we are seeing more patients, but we are not yet fixing the detailed problems which really influence the patient's experience, even though we have some systems in place which *ought* to deliver this. In Brighton we are struggling to see and to fix the 'invisible hospital', which patients see and experience, but managers still too often do not. The accumulated detail which has been overlooked still has a very poor impact on service. Many transactions are not viewed as customer transactions, and NHS executives still find it difficult to see details which matter, to implement policies to achieve genuine change, and to follow up in their own localities superb initiatives such as those described in Bill Murray's *Environments for Quality Care.*[1]

I recently spent an afternoon in a wheelchair and on a trolley, an odyssey through the 'invisible hospital' (as discussed in the previous paper). I did so with Bec Hanley (our Patient's Advocate), Mrs Kathy Goddon (a disabled patient, permanently in a wheelchair) and her husband Bill (who is virtually unable to see at all). They ensured that I got as close as possible to the experience of disadvantaged patients, they helped me see those things that are invisible to management. I had to remind myself that what for me was 'managerial tourism' is the reality that Kathy and Bill have to cope with *every* day of their lives.[2]

What happened to me was officially impossible and the systems that we have in place should have tackled the problems in a structured sequence of management priorities. More than a year ago, Brighton Health Care launched its 'Search for Quality and Search for Patient Choice'. We have a visible management programme, team briefing, quality circles. We appointed the first ever Patient's Advocate inside an NHS-provider Trust, and as Chairman I hammer away at the themes that every detail speaks; that every detail is a customer transaction; that every detail matters for the patient's experience; that every event has to be seen from the patient's point of view. Yet the experience described in this article *really* happened. I offer the following notes of my visit to The Royal Sussex County Hospital so that readers may test for themselves their own services, by requisitioning a wheelchair or a hospital trolley and spending an afternoon in their own 'invisible hospital'.

Arriving at accident and emergency

I drive in, but cannot find a dropped kerb so that I can get into the wheelchair from the car. Eventually I am helped in by Bec Hanley. I have to negotiate the slope into the Accident and Emergency Department. Where is it? I cannot find the slope, but when I do it is too narrow and the gradient is too steep. The bays right next to the A&E entrance are reserved for doctors. Why are they not for disabled parking?

Bill, very partially sighted, falls over the car parking space reservers, which are very rusty and not clearly marked. Once in the A&E entrance it is very grubby, with rubbish everywhere. It is not possible to open the doors from a wheelchair – it takes three of us to do it. Why is there not an automatic sliding door? For our slogan is 'Putting Patients' Interests First'!

In a wheelchair I cannot get anywhere near to the A&E Reception desk itself and have to be helped by a volunteer. At Reception there is no privacy as I cannot get near to the desk. There are no induction loops. However, arrangements at the initial assessment desk are excellent.

Into the transit area

Here we are. I claim to be an ordinary member of the public who has lost all feeling in his legs. I am lifted onto a trolley, but there are no pillows. I am stuck behind a curtain, immediately feeling grateful but guilty for the attention I get. There is a horrible noise from the fans and as I stare at the ceiling (the patient's point of view!) I see seven sets of fingerprints, marked in oily material. Clearly, Sir David Cookson's lightbulb-changing team[3] had not bothered to wash their hands after fixing a motor engine. I am warned that there is a shortage of wheelchairs and a shortage of sticks, and if mine is not carefully guarded it will vanish. This could mean that when I leave treatment I will have no wheelchair in which to do so. There are no leaflets, no tape players and no magazines. I am offered tea or coffee. As I lie there I wonder what I would do if I had a heart attack. There are no patient alarms in the transit area bays. Kathy Goddon (one of the advisers) tells me that when she was last there in a transit bay the rain came in on her. Staff are aware of this, but since the ceiling has not been repaired they just move the trolley. I am given a grey bag for my clothes – and expect the advice 'Take this with you to the Undertaker' – it was pretty grim. Kate Ford, the really professional Sister, bleeps the Porters. There is no reply. There is nobody in the Porters' office. She tells me she will just have to keep bleeping. Kate says that the whole shift is a struggle; that they are constantly waiting for things, chasing things, and that there is usually a shortage. The energy of the nursing staff is completely dissipated by this struggle. That day there was between a four and five hour wait on average in the transit area. The nurses took the flack. No one in management had ever done what I had done today.

I cheat, and ask to be moved on more promptly so that I can see more. As I lie behind the curtain I hear a man who is drunk in one of the other bays hurling abuse. Often, they hurl chairs. This is not Russia, but it sounds like it. This is not what we expect on the basis of our idea of what Britain is actually like, and is the NHS not 'the envy of the world'?

If I had really been a frail and elderly A&E patient, I would have been very frightened. Whither privacy and dignity? When you are really ill, you are frightened and bewildered enough, without having to deal with all this. If I had really lost all feeling in my legs, I would now be waiting to see a Registrar. This person would probably be in the Operating Theatre. I could wait three hours, during which time the nurses would just keep bleeping. Nearby there are tatty and peeling 'Why Am I Waiting?' notices stuck up with old sellotape, on the wall. I feel very vulnerable. I wonder whatever happened to the quality drive and the campaign against the 'sellotape culture'? I feel all this, but am not in pain. Here I am in the hospital 'patient park' – for wards can say they cannot take a patient but A&E *must* take them and park them in hope.

I am soon wearing a gown. It is the totalitarian item one would expect in Uzbeckistan. There is a gap down the back, so I am glad I have my clothes on underneath! I ask Kate what would happen if I was desperate to go to the loo and were a disabled user. I would need two nurses to help me get out of bed and get to the loo. What if I could not wait? If I wet the bed I might have to lie there for 15–20 minutes until nurses are free. If my self-control does fail I cannot bleep.

By now the Nurses have discovered that I am the Chairman. I wait for a Porter to move me to the ward. I am told there are not enough of them (but

I soon form the view that we need different kinds of people, and multi-skilled too). After 40 minutes two Porters arrive. They have no name badges 'They aren't important, mate'. The second Porter puts the point with more colour. I ride on past building work and a drunken man in another bay.

In the lift, I cannot reach the lift buttons above Level 7. I cannot reach the emergency button. There is not a directory telling me on what floors departments can be found. I am freezing. The lift stops 4 inches below the floor level. How do I get out in my wheelchair?

I am in bed. There is no buzzer to call the nurse. I have no idea when the doctor will come; the nurses are not warned in advance. Sometimes three separate consultants with their teams of doctors arrive all at once. A card gives me the name of my named nurse, plus a care plan sheet – a very bad photocopy. Why are these not carefully produced and printed? Nobody knows. I cannot see out of the windows – they are filthy. Two friendly and positive young nurses help me to have a bath, and I am impressed by the fact that they always explain to me what they are going to do before they do it. (During this bathing episode I remain fully dressed, and no water or bathing actually occurs!) In the bathroom itself we can hardly move. There are no bath mats and no bath brush. We have to have the door open in order for me to get onto the hoist so there is no privacy (remember, I have lost all feeling in my legs). We need a bigger bathroom for patients here. I ask the nurses to redesign the facility and send this to me. I ring the nurse call in the bathroom and the nurse is there within 15 seconds. There are, however, peeling handwritten notices everywhere.

I can go home

I am told I can go, but I cannot find the way out. In my wheelchair I cannot reach the button in the lift. Still no name badge worn by the Porter and no positive customer care. I leave the lift. There is no sign telling me which floor I am on nor where the way out is. I cannot get down the slope to the main entrance in my wheelchair. I could not get down or up the kerb outside the main entrance on the road.

Out-patients department

Here I am at last (but only because I have three helpers). In I go in my wheelchair. The receptionist asks me sharply and bleakly (like the Beadle in *Oliver Twist*) 'What is your K Number?' I do not know. I am made to feel stupid. Because of my entourage, it is discovered that I am the

Chairman. A patient nabs me, telling me she had to take a half day off work to come for an appointment and was told to come at 4:30pm. This was then changed to 3:30pm. It is now 4:30pm and she has still not been seen. In the toilet, apparently designed for the disabled, there is no grab rail. It is a humiliating experience to use the toilet 'designed' for the disabled.

I am taken back to the main reception. I ask for directions to Pickford Ward (which is in The Sussex Eye Hospital). The receptionist tells me there is no such ward. Wearing the special visual disability spectacles designed for me I experience the most terrifying half hour of my life crossing the main road, and finding my way to The Sussex Eye Hospital.

When we leave The Eye Hospital, Bill trips over some very uneven paving on the front doorstep. I wonder to myself what it is like in the other more inaccessible parts of the five sites we manage, which I visit less often?

These events prompted all sorts of thoughts

First we are trying to shake up the system, without shaking it to pieces, and we need genuinely to applaud those who create our successes, linking this to new pay and reward structures with genuine monitoring and incentives, giving us more and better performance for less. Equally, we do need to confess our weaknesses. Even though we are in a goldfish bowl. We need the local press to be informed and empathetic, so that we can do so without producing devastating headlines. This is clearly hard to do, especially with the Parliamentary question ever possible as the profound ambivalence between centralism and local initiative continues to predominate. We need to see genuinely individual and locally managed change, with purchasers and Trusts promoting innovation and difference. The confession of weakness and the commitment to detailed scrutiny is the prelude and the prerequisite to improvement.

If we are to change, the key messages seem to include:

- it is not sufficient for executives to adjust their blinkers to let in only a bit more light; they must change their ways of *seeing*, combining diligence with imagination, exhilaration and even fantasy 'How do I get A&E waits downs to 10 minutes? I can make a difference. Now.' This is a time for imagination

- at all levels we have to accept (and welcome) responsibility for our actions, and invest in the transformation of service and work from below, with pay and reward, job design, building self-esteem and process analysis. We need to find local levers for change, motivating our people in ways motivational in *their* terms

- we need to stop believing that the only solution is a cheque in the post and we need to get management focused on enhancing performance if we are to justify the inevitable competitive cacophony of Trust triumphalism

- clinicians and others who meet centralist triumphalism with local disbelief need convincing that management adds value in a collaborative culture which *reduces* controls and demonstrates real change for patients (including the measurement of clinical performance).

My wheelchair day offered an almost Faustian sense of reaching out to reality, by experiment, adventure and enquiry. It is part of the stringent, meticulous scrutiny which we are focusing on in the drive to improve service in Brighton. The appointment of our Patient's Advocate, our Complaints Task Force, our Patient Focused Care pilot, our local Reward Strategy, are all part of this, and we know that we do need meticulous, enquiring (even suspicious) analysis *undertaken jointly with patients* of what the patient's experience *actually is*.

For the prestige of the system should not reside in numbers alone, nor in aggregate measures of quality, but in clinically and patient-defined outcomes and the patient's experience of a better life resulting from our treatments.

We need an almost Wagnerian display of alertness, insistence, ambition, ingenuity, determination and Gold-Standard-setting management if changing the 'invisible hospital' is the daily challenge.

Without this management approach the extraordinary accumulated problems of the NHS will remain unfixed, because unseen. Draped in the flag of the *'Pravda mentality'* we will accept underpowered areas (like HR) and we will be unable to enable cultural change. The *'Pravda mentality'*, centralist and vulnerable to its own distortions, places a premium both on controls and marketing. Instead, we need to place a premium on scrutiny and monitored detailed change. We need to see our faults, from the patient's point of view. We need to oppose energy to entropy. We need to endorse the pride of the centre in the reforms of the NHS as a political institution, but locally inspect the patient's experience in response to national leadership. We need to beware of the disabling implications of centralism and work with the practical obstacles posed both by bureaucratic administration and by an inherited, compliant management in a service whose shape is still too much determined by hospital clinicians.

This requires us to uncover the reasons for inaction, and for the accumulated silt of 45 years. These would seem to include personal uncertainty and fear ('Do I dare?'); a lack of scrutiny and meticulous audit on whether policies are actually implemented; the presence of some executives only equipped to find arguments for doing nothing, not something; local opportunity atrophied by departmental boundaries; and the fear both of precedent and expectation. These last two are fundamentals, in hindering follow-through.

Do we fear to act in case we raise expectations which we are afraid we will not have the courage to satisfy? Do we fear precedent, since we will need to do it again? For if we act on one area, we shift the focus of others too. Frances Cornford pins down this executive anxiety illuminatingly in his *Microcosmographia Academia*: 'That every public action which is not customary, either is wrong, or, if it is right, is a dangerous precedent. It follows that nothing should ever be done for the first time.'[4] He also offers what he calls his 'Principal of Unripe Time': 'That people should not do at the present moment what they think right at that moment, because the moment at which they think it right has not yet arrived.' There is, too, the inherited and preferred way of managing initiatives into the margin, by leaping on a bandwagon seen to be inexorably rolling, shouting 'yes', and then reaching for the brakes.

The NHS *is* advancing, but beware the *'Pravda mentality'*. For it leaves people like Bill and Kathy Goddon on the outside, looking in. It leaves the 'invisible hospital' unseen and untouched by executive action and executive eyes. A case, if you like, of out of mind, out of sight.

Is it disloyal (and dangerous, in the internal market) for a Chairman to write such a piece about his own Trust? Some might think so, but unless we admit our faults and discuss them openly – stretching out to understand the disabling factors in our culture – how are we going to change them?

Notes

1 *Environments For Quality Care*, op.cit. See also, my 'Healing the Estate to Heal the Patient: Culture Change in the NHS Provider Unit', speech to the NHS Hospital and Care Premises Management annual conference, NEC, Birmingham, 21 October 1993, published in *The Health Summary*, November 1993, pp.10–11, and, 'Right Place, Right Time. The Relevance of NHS Estates Management to Advancing the Reforms. Or, How Many Beans Make Five?', to the national launch of the NHS Management Executive Estates Report *Environments For Quality Care*, King's Fund Centre, London, 4 February 1993 (unpublished, deposited in the Post-Graduate Medical Centre library, Brighton Health Care NHS Trust). See also my essay 'Quality: what is it? estates management and the patient's experience of NHS services', in *Hospitals and Care Premises Management Conference 1992, Collected Papers*. NHS Estates, Leeds, 1993.

2 Subsequently, eleven months after the event, the national press became interested in the wheelchair tour. See note[1] to 'Where do NHS Chairmen get their information, and is it worth having?' in this book (p.86).

3 See speech by Sir David Cookson, Chairman of the Audit Commission, to the

NHS Trust Federation annual conference, 29 September 1993 at Torquay, reported widely in the national media the following day.

4   Cornford F (1993) *Microcosmographia Academia: Being a Guide for the Young Academic Politician*. Mainsail Press, Cambridge.

This paper was first published in *The Health Summary*, London, January 1994, pp.4–5.

8

Where do NHS chairmen get their information,

and is it worth having?

Where do Chairmen get their information, and is it worth having? Does it really tell them what their services are like for patients, and is it a basis for effective change? What are the incentives for them to take an interest in such lethal issues? And who is looking, and asking, anyway?

These are real questions for (and about) those whom we put in charge of NHS organizations, especially if we are to justify appointing as Chairmen people who know nothing about it. For we need them above all to influence the improvement of clinical practice, acceptability and effectiveness.

In fact, it does increasingly seem that Chairmen are not the only ones who do not know. For the system has never been managed on the basis of information. Indeed, except for financial decisions there has been little call for information with which to manage the hard issues – notably, clinical performance. Trusts that want to improve clinical performance cannot do so unless they know what it is. A key role of Chairmen is to get these questions into play, to get answers that mean something and to get Chief Executives to do something. Consensus, deference and collusion are cosy blankets, but they will not drive a motor in a market.

When Chairmen ask what special contribution they can make and whether their presence makes *any* difference, they need to think about the information that they are getting about patients, about their service, from whom and why.

Forests fall daily to provide the paper to print executive letters. Internal reports on finance, activity and other alleged monitoring flood in. The paper maelstrom is unremitting and relentless, but what is it really like out there?

As Chairman of an Acute Trust (and, before that, a Health Authority with a budget of £100 million) I often wondered how to find out. It struck me that being 'next to the action' was not the same as being in the 'thick of it', as are the staff.

When I look back on nearly four years as a Chairman in the NHS, I wonder if I <u>ever</u> stood a chance of getting at the truth of the patient's experience. This was one of the prompts for my 'wheelchair tour', when I went through my own A&E Department as a 'patient' as a way of trying to get in the thick of it.[1]

However, I now think that no NED is yet being enabled to do that. In part, this is because the centre is not clearly asking for it to be done. In part, this is because some NEDs are well known to the staff ('Watch out – here he comes!'). In part, this is because of the style in which many tour their hospitals – with an entourage reminiscent of *HMS Pinafore*, 'accompanied by the admiring crowd of sisters, cousins, and aunts that attend him wherever he goes.'[2] The official justification for their appointment, too, isolates them. They are said to be there to offer an independent view, an independent voice. They are not supposed to get their hands into the detail, and they do not manage it unless they are very determined indeed. For this is 'wrist-slap' territory.

The difficulty is partly that the NED does not know what he does not know. It is partly because he finds it difficult to discover the questions to ask. He often finds it hard, too, to judge if an answer is duff or incomplete. At Brighton Healthcare NHS Trust, for example, I had this true (and truly 'Yes, Minister') conversation.

Chairman:	How many operations did we cancel last month?
Senior Manager:	Not many. We're doing well. Only eight.
Chairman:	Yes, we are doing well. But surely that is only a figure for elective, cold surgery? What about the cancellation of emergency operations in the middle of the night? That is when we are staffed by Junior Doctors. And when Consultants are 'On-call', but the Juniors are reluctant to call them out. Indeed, I'm told that in some hospitals around the country consultants might make it clear that they won't be called out, by all sorts of little signals. So, how many emergency ops do we cancel?
Senior Manager:	Ah.

The new Audit Commission report, *The Doctor's Tale: The work of hospital doctors in England and Wales*[3], reiterates one of my boringly regular statements, that many NHS executive directors do not see the 'invisible hospital' that patients see and experience. They accept the idea that 'It's always been there', or, 'It's not <u>so</u> bad, is it?', or, 'It's too big to change', or, very commonly, 'You can't expect *me* to tackle the docs'. All comments that I heard from top boys.

It is clear that we are getting better at communicating goals *down*, even though no-one on the shop floor generally seems to want to know, but how does information come up? When I put an invitation into wage packets inviting staff to tell me two or three things they would fix if they could, executives seemed astounded at the dozens of practical ideas (in fact, 309) that came from staff. We invested £1.6 million in them. The most notorious comment was about the mixed ward, which had a loo, but no door. It only had a curtain, which did not close. Why had no-one ever informed a NED on tour, and why had no-one noticed? Indeed, why had no executive noticed on our proudly proclaimed 'visible management walkabouts'? Why had no staff member felt empowered to report it, or actually to get it fixed? Classicists would share my disappointment. *Solvitur ambulando* – the problem is solved by walking around. Why is this not true?[4]

Chairmen and NEDs need to think about where they get their information. What do people feed *up*, and what is it in the nature of organizational functioning that gets information suppressed? How can Chairmen hear of needs, problems, demands, moans and groans, and get problems dealt with? If they cannot hear it from staff, how can they hear what is happening to patients?

Suppose there is an unhappy patient at the bottom. It is the nurse and the junior doctor whose life is made harder. How does that information, or the snag in the service systems that it flags up, travel upwards, to an executive director, let alone to the Chairman? It does not come from the ward sister, nor from the junior doctor. Both may be part of the problem. Even if they are not, they must go through the correct management system. They have access only so far up the management chain. If there is a responsive, patient-sensitive ward sister who sees the problem and wants change, *she* has to go to the clinical director or to the business manager. Does the buck then stop there? Perhaps the clinical director or business manager will take it to their director. Maybe. What is the incentive to do so? Is not the organizational incentive for *each* of them to present a view of the problem that makes it look as if they have got it under control – as they *ought* to have!

So, even if – and it is a big if – an executive director gets at least a diluted idea of what is going on, they will always want NEDs and the Chairman to think they can manage the place, even if there are problems, and even if they cannot!

Look, too, at when the Chairman is out and about – 'Here he comes!'. Perhaps he goes every Wednesday, or perhaps he prearranges departmental visits. Or is he accompanied by an executive director? If so, what is the signal there? Not many staff members prefer to tell anyone what is happening in their work when placed in that situation.

How many non-executives know what to watch for, what to ask, or what they are asking? And are they sensitive to the staff situation with regard to their Manager? In my experience, the insistence on Anno Domini as a retirement-Sergeant (when Trusts were set up), removed from the service the most valuable experience of those who did know and understand. Few of the new non-executives I have worked with subsequently have the know-how of the older, streetwise, sensitive (but over-retired) non-executives, alas.

So how can we get any value from the NEDs walkabout? One way to get value is to ask staff 'what is the most irritating thing that happened this week?' You get answers like 'No pillow cases'. Ask then 'What did you do about it? What *difference* did you make?'. Which takes us back to what Chairmen and NEDs need to be asking themselves, and why they need information to impact on change and to action the purposes of modern management.

Where *do* Chairmen get their information, and *is* it worth having? In whose interest, too, is it to prevent them getting it?

Of course, not all want to know, or to ask. For some Chairmen know that to ask is perhaps to find out, and then they would have to be responsible for doing something about the information. For being a Chairman or an NED is too often all about local status. Like First Lord of The Admiralty, Sir Joseph Porter KCB (in Gilbert and Sullivan's *HMS Pinafore*), they do like to be 'ruler of the Queen's navee'. But, equally, they prefer to be 'hardly ever sick at sea.' Chairmen (typically called something like Councillor Alfie Peardrop, B.Com., a figure from local industry) too often adopt the manner of the naval luminary. When the breezes blow – in the words of Gilbert and Sullivan – they generally go below, and they will continue with this naval manoeuvre until the centre signals a change.

The Chairman's real role is, surely, to ensure that the organization raises its standards of performance. The centre needs to do a lot of thinking about the incentives for Chairmen to get this job done. They are not there yet. Indeed, a quiet life pays. It is then no surprise that they respond instead to Sir Joseph Porter's advice:

> Now landsmen all, whoever you may be,
> If you want to rise to the top of the tree,
> If your soul isn't fettered to an office stool,
> Be careful to be guided by this golden rule
> Stick close to your desks and never go to sea,
> And you may all be Rulers of the Queen's Navee.

Few Chairmen do find out what is really going on. The most devastating evidence for this assertion is in the newest Audit Commission report,[3] with its devastating 'action checklist'. This shows that we are still not managing the NHS at the most rudimentary level, and that neither Chairmen nor Chief Executives have noticed! The Commission shows that the most basic processes still need proper clarity and control over who does what, why, how and to what effect. The report demonstrates basic areas on which we do not have a grip and to which we do not pay attention. The availability of case-notes at out-patient clinics, and the surprise that operations are conducted in their absence; uncontrolled radiology costs; the absence of job plans for medical staffs, and the lack of monitoring which permits fixed clinical commitments to be missed with regularity – all show poor control of medical staffing on a large scale.

What is to be done? Alan Langlands Chief Executive, NHS, has asked all Boards to discuss the report at their next Board meeting. Not a difficult challenge, but will this be enough? Local management is clearly concentrating on survival in a pre-election period and believes that there has been sufficient change. However, it is clear that change has hardly touched the fundamentals. Yet another Board discussion led by a Chairman with no incentive and no determination for change may not be sufficient. Who will monitor what is then *done* to ensure that Chairmen and Chief Executives (while ruling the Queen's Navee *sic*) work effectively on a proper basis of knowledge to tackle the systemic and cultural problems to improve clinical performance, acceptability and effectiveness? Will market forces, or the genuinely empowered patient, be the winds that are allowed to fill the sails and to change the course? How will Chairmen be asked to report back to the centre on their boardroom debate, and what action plan does the centre expect to be put into place? Patients should ask their local Chairman, and say they would like to know. Wouldn't he?

How realistic is it to expect Chairmen to be animated, with a sense of direction, to insist on the implementation of change, to take chances, and to say that ideas matter? How realistic is it to ask them to link day to day events to a coherent set of principles as the only basis for a strategy that anyone outside can understand? How realistic is it to expect a local NHS Chief Executive, who needs the job, to take risks, to express convictions and to associate his career with challenge to powerful and unmanaged special interests?

It is not sufficient to ask for managerial skill. It will not be forthcoming unless there is clear and determined political will. If the political will is not there to back the non-executive, then it is too much to expect the salaried executive to jump.

Mobilizers are exceptional and unusual, even when the political will is evident. The paradox of the Tory radical challenging established, professional (and Conservative) interests is perhaps an historical oddity. Prudence and caution has a place, but it is not a reliable philosophy. Success in the end is measured in the accomplishment of goals; consensus risks being directionless. If the NHS wants different styles, attitudes, and role transformations, it needs to send messages both to Chairmen and to

Chief Executives. It is to the service itself that we need to look for the new generation of managers. They will be thrown up by the professions as we design a new doctor. Much of the best change is doctor led. Much of the best implementation needs to be insisted upon by Chairmen. Backing has to be consistent and explicit.

Of course, we can turn to the literature of political science for the conventional debate about the alternative styles of leadership, focused on the paradigms of 'persuasion' and 'confrontation'. Each carries with it characteristic risks. Consensus sounds useful, but it is associated with a conscious bipartisanship which can protect special interests, involve the appeasement of pressure groups, and the avoidance of tough decisions. Its emphasis on consultation, on incremental change, is associated with the demonstrated ability of important pressure groups to veto change. Its emphasis on unity and harmony, using the managerial tag 'getting the balance right', can result in the sacrifice of strategy and of long-term objects to short-term contingencies. Political management in the Health Service (under any political party) tends to require consensus management from Chairmen. This is not only to achieve ownership within; it reflects political ownership without.

One recent (non-Tory) commentator, Dennis Kavanagh, in a study of Mrs Thatcher's alternative, mobilizing style has said 'A political consensus, and associated concepts like hegemony, folkways, political culture, rules of the game, and so on, also represents a mobilisation of bias. It favours certain interests and directs attention to certain issues and procedures while neglecting others. Here is what social scientists now call "a second face of power", one that shapes the political agenda.'[5] Mrs Thatcher famously stated this directly 'For me, consensus seems to be the process of abandoning all beliefs, principles, values and policies'.[6]

Radicals with both optimism and energy have criticized the sacrifice of policy goals to the compromises which can be required by the apparent need to accommodate pressures exerted by the professionals. They can rely on another recent academic commentator, who has said of the risks associated with this emphasis 'Public policy is simply equated with finding the least controversial course between the conflicting interests of vociferous private groups. It is not a doctrine of government; it is a doctrine of subordination.'[7]

It is clearly necessary to get the pace and balance right. Politics is about reality, not least when there is a slim parliamentary majority. However, we do need to think about the conditions of work which enable 'doers' to be forceful, decisive, resolute, persistent, principled implementers and facilitators of change. We cannot remodel the world with words alone.

It is still too easy for Chairmen to 'go below'. It is still too difficult for the Chief Executive who *needs* the job to be sure that he will get the backing if he *does* the job.

Notes

1 See my essay 'The Invisible Hospital', in this book (p.65). For the long-term consequences of the wheelchair tour see also Clark S (1994) Vulnerable, afraid and humiliated: How the hospital boss felt when he became an undercover patient. *The Sunday Times*, 24 April; Swain G (1994) A Breach of Trust. *Daily Mirror*, 26 April; Hall C (1994) The Brighton Amputation. *The Independent*, 9 September; Macdonald V (1994) Champion of Patient Power to Fight on. *The Sunday Telegraph*, 11 September; Limb M (1994) One for the Record. *The Health Service Journal*, 15 September; Clark S (1994) What the Hospital Boss Saw. *Reader's Digest*, October (reprint of *Sunday Times* article); Lilley R (1994) A case of blurred vision. *The Guardian*, 5 October; and (1994) Roles of Honour. *The Guardian*, 28 December. Also Macdonald V (1994) The Men Who Killed Sir Lancelot Spratt. *The Sunday Telegraph*, 20 November.

2 Gilbert and Sullivan, *HMS Pinafore* (1878). All quotations from *The Complete Plays of Gilbert and Sullivan*. W.W.Norton, New York and London, (1976).

3 Audit Commission report, *The Doctor's Tale: the Work of Hospital Doctors in England and Wales. HMSO,* London, 1995.

4 See Brighton Health Care NHS Trust booklet (written by Pauline Sinkins) (1994) '*Things to Fix'*, an Initiative in Using the Best Ideas of Brighton Health Care Staff to Help Patients, Staff and the Organisation. Brighton, March.

5 Kavanagh D (1990) *Thatcherism and British Politics, the End of Consensus?* 2nd edn, p.7. Oxford University Press, Oxford.

6 Speech in 1981 in Australia, cited in Kavanagh, op.cit.

7 Chapman B (1962) *British Government Observed,* p.61. Allen & Unwin, London.

An extract of this chapter was published in the *British Journal Of Health Care Management,* **1**, (No.4, May 5 1995, pp.181–3, entitled 'The Role of Chairmen and the "Invisible Hospital"').

The NHS and its performance

One goal down – let's get two in the second half.

Traditional terrace refrain

Sed quis custodient ipsos custodes (What about the vigilantes? Who is going to watch over *them*?)

Juvenal, *Satires*

"'Whatever is is right' an aphorism that would be as final as it is lazy, did it not include the troublesome consequence, that nothing that ever was, was wrong.'"

Charles Dickens, *A Tale Of Two Cities* (1859)

9

Top of the league:

or, will your club be relegated?

This June the Management Executive will publish the first six individual provider League Tables, based on 1993/94 performance.[1] This is an incremental approach and is an important new initiative. It is clear that this dog will bark – press interest will be huge – but will it bite? Surely, it must because the material will be in the public domain, and the public interest can sometimes only be protected by publication and open scrutiny.

The League Tables start with six valuable (though hospital-centred) measures. It is probably important to start with issues that the public can understand easily and get a handle on. It is obviously desirable to assemble public understanding of how the service works. These new indicators will enable us to see how a particular hospital delivers some of the basics.

What is it we are being asked to do to irrigate the secret garden? We are to participate in individual provider League Tables, to be published in June, based on 1993/94 performance. This is an incremental approach. The NHS Management Executive Letter says the tables are for the use of the general public, a commitment given by the Government in the Citizen's Charter.[2] The Audit Commission will validate the data collections system to check that this is free from error, robust and properly documented. Chief Executives must sign off the figures personally. Six initial indicators come into play. Five relate to hospital services and will identify each provider, but not yet each clinician, by name. The sixth covers the speed of ambulance response to emergency calls. The tables will cover the performance of the provider over the year, apart from three items collected under the Patient's Charter monitoring system, which will be updated on the basis of fourth quarter 1993/94 results.

The Health Service has agreed data definitions as a genuine basis for comparison, an attempt to base development robustly and to cut off the inevitable retreat by those who score poorly into the defence that the method is faulty. Consumer groups have helped test the presentation of the tables, to make sure that they can be used by Joe Public, who may know nothing about our internal workings. Clearly, the material has to be really real to Joe (and to Josephine) – *real* like the kids, the mortgage, the holiday, the weather.

I greatly welcome the League Tables, but we must be careful about them. They must not substitute a political exercise which apparently 'names names' on the softer issues for *really* naming names on the hard issues that hurt. The first six indicators matter, but they are soft data which is easy to get and easy to give. They must open the gate to the harder issues: the quality of care, the outcomes of treatment, cross-infection, re-admission rates, and the actual naming of individual clinicians, with an analysis of their performance across a range of essential indicators.

There are a cluster of issues that the initial indicators raise. Let us look at them through a quality eye-glass.

A & E: patients assessed within five minutes of arrival

Here, fundamental organizational issues hit us dramatically, on trolley waits, A & E admissions and what Brian Edwards once called 'the struggle to find the hidden bed'. There is a conflict between public preference and our definition of appropriate behaviour – the 'inappropriate self-referral'. And other fundamentals are brought into place when we really scrutinize A & E. It is not only about measuring assessment time, is it? It is not, either, only about doing it in a warm, friendly way. It is not only that there are probably too many A & E departments. The questions prompted by the indicator surely include: What is primary care access like? (and other forms of non-hospital support, for example, crisis care with mental illness), where people need to be picked up in the community with crisis support. Why cannot patients get to a GP 24 hours a day? Why can we not supplement existing diversion schemes within A & E by using more GPs there? At Brighton Health Care we have a GP scheme, but East Sussex Health Authority, very disturbingly, are hesitating to continue to fund it. Should there be open access to A & E, or only via a GP? If we discourage the right of self-referral or even charge for inappropriate self-referral, what would the public say to that? Perhaps 'You killed my child by deterring my 999 call'? Or, if people feel unwell, would 24-hour open GP access reduce pressure on scarce resources. Some 50% of 999 calls bring patients who are sent home without treatment.

We are told it is good practice to give people immediate assessment in A & E. OK. Now let us get the *quality* issues into play, to get at what is required. How do we measure what we do in assessment and what should our purchasers be asking us to do about it? Do we have any outcome data on A & E assessment? Do we compare initial and final assessment. Do we have details of who carried out the assessment? Do we have satisfaction data from patients on the initial assessment and the result? What is our programme of continuous improvement? Would it be more appropriate for the whole structure of A & E assessment to be changed, for it to be done by a nurse *and* a GP? What are the costs of failure in an area where, often, you cannot do the job again?

Out-patient appointments

To be seen within 30 minutes of appointment time is a customer care issue. You want to feel as if you are in a private clinic, comfortable, your time valued as an individual, a scarce resource, attended to in a timely way, your experience valued and thoughtfully delivered, and in an environment emphasizing the arts.

All this speaks of an organization that gives good service and that sets up its management systems and focuses its recruitment and training around what the customer wants. But this still does not tell you much objectively about the quality of care you are getting, and the quality of contact you have with the professionals. The initial indicator offers the chance to break it down further. Break it down by consultant teams. Ask what proportion of out patients goes through the cycle of out-patient care without ever seeing a consultant. Ask when is your trust to move to a consultant-delivered service (as in the Calman Report recommendation), and even when we do move to it, break that down once more by asking what is the actual leadership role of consultants in seeing out patients. This is an issue for time resource management. It will vary from specialty to specialty and critically affects quality. In ophthalmology, we have greatly enhanced our service and productivity by nurse screening. In diabetes, in some Trusts, consultants see only the follow-up cases; juniors see the patients the first time. This is an area where compliance is no longer helpful in the executive management toolbox.

We have to ask what appropriate contribution our most highly paid employees make to the quality of the out-patient visit and how they are influencing the quality of out-patient experience, and how do we *measure* that? We should ask them to tell us the standards they set, ask them how they can show we are getting value for money from the inputs of their teams. We need to get this into play with the Clinical Performance Improvement Unit in your Chief Executive's office. Brighton will be glad to share what it is doing with you – we need to stand shoulder to shoulder here, on this fundamental shift. A simple indicator – to be seen within 30 minutes of appointment time shows us that we have hardly started to get to quality measures. And, incidentally, how do you feel if you are seen within 30 minutes but wait three hours for transport home? Who owns *that* experience? And what about the patient's wheelchair? It was there on arrival. Where is it now?

Day surgery

The measure of elective episodes (planned and booked) by selective procedure

Clearly this is linked to keyhole surgery and minimally invasive techniques. It is one of our areas of greatest momentum, apparently offering the most alluring gains: shorter hospital stays, less pain, tiny scars, quicker recovery. Equally, it is emerging as an area of greatest query, anxiety and complexity. It highlights our accountability, that we are open to question, that everything is on record, that we are here to get knowledge and give it away. The Secretary of State's forthcoming comprehensive new guidelines for keyhole surgery will ensure that doctors are all adequately trained, experienced or closely supervized, alert to the dangers of new techniques. The new training programmes at the Royal College of Surgeons are essential.[3] We need to look hard at subsequent measurement and quality indicators. If this is the route for 70% of all our operations by the end of the decade, we need signposts that the public can check. It is the 'my daughter' test again. Where would you send yours? The needs of keyhole and open surgery are very different, and it may be that the people that we are to retrain are not suited to it at all. This is not an area for retrained, sawbones, muscle men, but for delicacy, empathy and the deftness of the clockmaker. We may need to take a step back first and to ask if we are recruiting the right people, designing the right doctor and training doctors appropriately in the first place. We need to be sure that a surgeon working with a two-dimensional camera image of a three-dimensional operation is not being asked to take unacceptable risks. Equally, we need to get the data to offer patients informed choice and counselling before they accept the keyhole gallbladder operation, the 'simple' sterilization and the new operations that technology and drug innovation offer.

'Length of stay' tables prompt their own caution. Many smaller hospitals will have much longer lengths of stay, particularly in care of the elderly wards, by contrast with acute hospitals. The trend of earlier discharge from acute to post-operative rehabilitative care in local hospitals, needs to be given a weighting. It is equally clear that local conditions vary widely; the tables will call forth explanation and public debate as this is documented in the League Tables.

Waiting times for admission to a number of specialties

The percentage of patients by selected specialties admitted within three months and within twelve months of being listed

This is an issue of resource use, management competence and individual (but still anonymous) quality assessment. The day-case procedures covered a cataract extraction, inguinal hernia repair, arthroscopy of the knee and laparoscopy with sterilization. Inevitably, it is an initial push at the door, relatively general, aggregate rather than individual, but until now, the door has been like the exit in *Alice in Wonderland* 'tiny, at toe not eye level and only available for action after a stiff drink ("Drink Me!") and a swim in a pool of tears.' Purchasers and Trust Boards need individual waiting times for each consultant, by specialty. They need to compare the performance of each surgeon within the specialty, and, a short waiting list might be as bad as a long one. Few mind queueing for Kiri Te Kanawa but no-one is much surprised if a concert hall welcoming heavy metal band, Mega Brain Dead, is empty. Bad restaurants do not attract queues. We need to measure and publish the number of referrals to individual doctors, their throughput and their patient-determined and clinically measured outcomes.

Clearly, waiting times for admission need to be handled with care. Short waiting times may be a signal that a surgeon is perceived by knowledgeable local GPs to be incompetent. He or she may be failing the 'my daughter' test. He/she may no longer be getting the difficult referrals. The waiting time for the first consultant appointment is probably the most crucial measure. In some disciplines, notably orthopaedics, they ought to prompt radical purchaser action (to set up hip factories with a public service test of monopoly) and we need, too, fiscal incentive to prompt private provider expansion. (25% of all hip replacements are now done privately.)

Operations

The number of patients not admitted within a month of second cancellation of operation

When I first asked how many operations we cancelled, I was told 'Not many, Chairman. Only 8 last month.' But surely you are only giving me the *elective* operations? 'Ah, yes.' So what about the emergency operations cancelled. 'Ah.' Why are *any* operations cancelled? Is it the hospital's fault, or the patient's? If it is the patient, is it a communications issue? We know our capacity. We know our trauma and emergency workloads. Seasonally adjusted. Where do we go wrong organizationally? Should we be cancelling <u>any</u> operations? Why can we not give a Golden Guarantee to give an elective patient a firm date, nine months in advance, and pay for it to be done elsewhere if we do not deliver? Why do purchasers not insist on this? In Liverpool, medical elective beds are ring fenced. Why do we not all do this?

This indicator throws up more questions than answers, not least who does the cancelled operations, who does the nighttime work, and with what results? We know what is behind much of this. Why cannot consultants make a reality of the on-call system? Why cannot we manage beds properly? Why cannot we plan discharge properly? Why cannot we get it into pre-admission planning? This is an area for nurse leadership.

Ambulance speed of response

A significant number of ambulance services are not meeting this standard; they are putting patients at risk. There will be no competition for ambulance services if they have to be run strategically, but why not competitive tendering from private and public services? This is all about an army of paramedic fast motor bikes to achieve patient stability very promptly. If competition is not acceptable politically, we have got to be able to change the management of the public service of these key requirements. And why not a tougher target for the motor bike, followed by an on-time arrival by the ambulance?

The challenge to management

How will these new League Tables help us? The test will surely be whether they help drive purchasing, contestability and patient choice. Whether they offer a challenge to management, which must be in jeopardy, if discovered in persistent failure. Whether they empower staff and patients and prompt us to set 'Gold Standard' guarantees that bite us, not patients. Whether they help get us effectively into primary care purchasing and into more sensitive mental health care. Whether we respond by really studying the clockwork, getting inside the organization, analysing and changing processes and shifting resources to the efficient provider.

The system must use the League Tables to prompt change, initially to improve our *internal* systems since competition is still mostly around the margins, but they must also prompt the recognition that the revolution required in the NHS – to get to a scientific, rational, evidence-based service; to bring the organization into a modern form and to get to genuine customer-centred, patient-driven care – has hardly started. They ask us to bring in a culture of managerial excellence, to complement clinical excellence (which is still sold hard, but hardly verified). They ask us to build a performance organization, where 'suspicious scrutiny' is funda-mental, to change attitudes and behaviour, insist on pace and style of working, in an ambitious enterprise culture of monthly scrutiny. This is to go from unmeasured 'quality' to performance management in a market, being prepared to be vulnerable as well as strong, and being driven by the real experience of our staff and of our patients. The development of comparative League Tables challenges the 'rationality' of planning, too. Surprisingly, that sustains its adherents, at least until the audited reality of what planning has produced is fully understood.

Dilemmas, and public understanding

Inevitably, there are some dilemmas. The Hon. Mrs Lindy Price, CBE, Chairman of Powys Health Care Trust, has pointed out that the publication of these League Tables may reinforce in the public's mind, that the only care *worth having* is in hospital. And that 80% of care is in out-patient and community care practice (with the ratio of funding being the absolute reverse). The advance of medical technology and expertise enables patients to receive treatment previously given in DGHs in local community/cottage hospitals, in GPs' surgeries and even in patients' own homes; for example, in Brecon War Memorial Hospital, patients are now being treated for cataract removal on a day case basis – unheard of even 4 years ago.[4]

It is essential, as the League Tables develop, that they swing our eyes back to the necessary focus on primary care from the now deviant obsession with hospitals. Initially, the risk is that they reinforce the myth that the NHS is about hospitals, or even about beds and in-patient bed numbers, but they help us pose other essential questions: What about access to a GP 24 hours a day and enhanced primary care? What about access to non-hospital support in a crisis? Will publication enhance patient choice? Will publication help us focus resources into primary care and assist primary care purchasing. Surely the answer is 'yes'. If we are to progress here, we need the information available so the public can know what to expect and can exert pressure on the GP and say 'I'm not satisfied'.

The gap between what we need to measure and what we are measuring, is brought into focus by the reality of the first six League Table indicators. The gulf between what we know and what we need to know and act upon is more visible, where formerly it was unseen. We need to respond to these League Tables – to stress that pace matters and that the market can work. I hope Brighton will do so. Accordingly, I asked our Chief Executive, Stuart Welling, to bring forward in the public part of our Board Meeting on 12 May, quality indicators to supplement some of those – such as individual consultant waiting times for admission in all specialties – which we publish already.

We need to know:

• the number of referrals to individual consultants, their throughput and their patient-determined and clinically measured outcomes – six months and one year later

- outcome data on initial assessment in A & E, comparing initial and final assessment and patient satisfaction

- details of who carried out the initial assessment

- an analysis of why any operation was cancelled

- the alternatives we offer patients whose operations are cancelled

- our potential to ring-fence elective beds and to give a Golden Guarantee

- to publish complete data in an illustrated 'Who's Who' on the expertise, skills and experience of our consultants and the supporting clinical and practice teams who back them up. Their qualifications, where and when they got these. How they update these. What university departments they are accredited by. What is the cut-off point at which any patient will be beyond the skills of our hospital and must be referred on. Which clinicians are using the latest techniques, how are they trained in them. Our success rates and how many peri-operative deaths we have by specialty. Our levels of day surgery now, our targets, the protocols being used and how these are updated

- cross-infection and re-admission rates by specialty, and the functioning of the infection control team on hospital-acquired infections.[5]

On all this, Trust and purchaser Chairmen have a dilemma. They are here to be cultural change-makers but also to ensure that business plans are achieved. Their legitimacy comes from their place in the local community and as a proxy for the patients' interests. We want open and full publication of as much data as possible – required or not by the League Tables. It falls to the Chairman to lead the Board to insist on this point of view and to ask the Chief Executive to manage the consequences – including the impact on bottom line.

The NHS has to become a performance organization and a truly democratic and accessible body. We must break down the mystique of an untouchable culture where only initiates speak to initiates. We must create an open system, debatable and open to question by anybody, by people in the street, in their terms. League Tables help us to say: wherever you go, you will get good treatment. The League Tables help the public participate in their own care, by identifying where the best care can be delivered. They show that it can be delivered everywhere by good management and leadership. For we are locating accountability where it properly lies – with management – and celebrating competence. There are many success stories. It is clear that significant management improvements are improving performance. We are also helping to see where service is less good, and where improvements can be made, for improvement depends on open comparison, and on learning from one another.

It is too convenient for us to talk about 'quality' in a general sense. The new era of the Health Service is not only about *the vision,* but about making the vision work, making it real for every man, woman and child that uses the NHS. We have to make quality real and integrate it into the daily grind of service. This is about particulars and specifics, making the details work, converting the vision in the particular work of getting down to business. This is forcing us to make some really serious decisions about the detail of how we deliver sensitive services. We are regrouping ourselves around our customers (our patients). We are focusing on the public as our starting point and trying to give our staff starring roles with the public.

We are putting the old, inward-facing culture behind us. We stand at a crossroads. There is a great deal at stake. We have drawn the new map. We have described the new territory that lies ahead. We have decided the strategy for getting there. We have heard the rallying cries. Now we have to make the journey real. Our goal should surely be to make every single 'transaction' between a member of the public, whether a patient or not, and the NHS as sensitive, as satisfactory, as it is possible to be. This is about the individual experience of every patient. This is not only about what we said we would do, but about what is actually happening. This is the only true measure of whether we are getting there or not. The League Tables are an important step on the road.

The *Daily Telegraph* on March 31 1995, reported that a fox led a pack of hounds up a mountain and left them stranded on a ledge at Patterdale, in the Lake District. They were later winched to safety. Critics will say these indicators are the wrong fox, leading the public to a stranded edge, but they are surely the latest stage in a process of building an objective picture of NHS life which is much concealed, not least from themselves by the passion and commitment of executives who do not see the 'invisible hospital'.

The NHS cannot be a sovereign entity outside the command of the growing culture of accountability and to that extent the Patient's Charter and the League Tables are conceptual landmarks. Clearly, neither is a comprehensive scheme, but they do ask us to compete not only against others but against ourselves and they prompt further development in moving us from an organizational framework to a *managed* service.

This is at the heart of the challenge. It goes back to the basics of the 1983 Griffiths Report on accountability and individual responsibility, where no one was accountable or responsible for anything.[6] We are edging along the windowsill to get some measures of quality. Purchasers and Trust Boards need to be much more ambitious. Let us stop ducking the issue: we are talking about life and death. The key facts at the heart of the secret garden: which doctors, which procedure, which competence, which outcome? These are not known by doctors about one another, nor by any other key players. We do not pass the simplest schoolboy or schoolgirl test: 'Compare and contrast'. This is not a challenge to whether doctors work hard or devotedly. It is an issue of outcomes, not a measure of effort. Doctors' performance must be under our perennial gaze. We have to get doctors to attend to effectiveness with seriousness, to be prepared to be retrained and re-accredited. The role of managers is to work with them on what we do, on the quality we get, on the relationships with those with whom they work, on the standards to be achieved.[7] And, of course, all the data we collect and publish will be meaningless unless purchasers act upon it.

Notes

1   *The Patient's Charter: Hospital and Ambulance Services. Comparative Performance Guide 1993–1994.* NHS Executive, Leeds, 1994. The second set of tables were published in July 1995.

2   EL(93)64, *League tables of performance.* NHSME, Leeds, 20 July 1993.

3   For a detailed discussion see John Spiers and Roy Lilley, op.cit.

4   Private communication, April 1994.

5   See *Journal of Hospital Infection's* editorial, issue 25, 1993; HAIs have an estimated cost of £115 million per annum in the UK and 950 000 lost bed days (1987 figures). It is suggested that one in three infections could be prevented, reducing patient morbidity and mortality and freeing up hospital beds. Is ICT to remain a firefighter or will sufficient time and resource identify those aspects of hospital practice which significantly contribute to infection and which require change? Would League Table indicators kick-start this development? Will health authorities start periodic surveys of HAI in selected clinical areas, such as intensive care and surgical wards, monitor trends and reflect change in practice? What are the areas of most concern which are valid for inter-hospital comparison? The key next step is to challenge clinical anonymity.

The Maryland Quality Indicator Project offers a cluster of other indicators which should be integrated into the Patient's Charter for publication. See 'The View From Brighton Pier', in this book (p.120).

6   Griffiths R (Chairman)(1983) *Report of the NHS Management Enquiry.* DHSS, London.

7   An important commentary on attitudes and management is Mary Donn, 'The Patient's Charter: Achieving Objectives Through The Framework'. Address to English National Board Study Day, 8 June 1992.

This chapter is based on a section of my 'Secret Garden' speech, which is in this book as 'From medical mystery to public rationality' (p.46). It seemed more useful not to include the material there, but to place it here and link it to additional material based on a paper I wrote for the Secretary of State's office in June 1994.

10

Performance, the flag to fly:

NHS Trust scrutiny, and setting standards that bite us

All ideas have their moment. Today, the key challenge is how to build a *performance* organization that will be patient-led. Trusts, who seek a flag to fly by making the patient's experience and wants pivotal, will see that 'suspicious scrutiny' is fundamental. It is, too, a positive alternative to the triumphalist 'Pravda mentality' to guide Trust management for performance improvement.

My day-in-a-wheelchair experiencing the 'Invisible Hospital', which patients see, but managers still too often do not, focused us not only on operational management but on our learning style, on our ways of working, and on how to translate not only proclamation to policy, but policy into proven practice. How, too, to pass bad news upwards but act on it at the lowest possible level. This is to see how the clockwork really works, what the real issues are, and to action the problems that arise when the 'invisible hospital' and the patient's experience is really scrutinized for change.

In the socialized 1960s, comprehensive 'educators' taught Britons that the highest ideals of public life could be delivered by scorning the alien sins of action, decisiveness, competition, measured risk, profit, and effective follow-through. To substitute equality for quality, directives for diversity, and centralism for choice, we all joined hands together to step over the finishing line joint-last.

In the resource-aware, patient-focused 1990s we offer Britons the seductive idea that the highest ideals of public life will be fulfilled by the performance organization that values action and private sector *attitudes* without which we will never achieve fundamental change, enhanced and proven performance and choice. Thus, the expectation of taking responsibility and running things, to insist on pace and style of working, which calls out a forthright determination to succeed and is clearly valued as an executive route to the top. For the change is to an ambitious enterprise culture, shifting from a culture of annual record to one of monthly scrutiny, to become a developmental organization in an unpredictable market-place. An identity as a performance organization will take us from merely fulfilling low expectations, which we have taught the public to expect (with little choice or leverage), to setting standards which surprise them. This is to go from unmeasured 'quality' to performance *management*, in a market which will enhance value in ways which 'rational planning' will not deliver.

We live in *our* decade, energizing an organization saying vibrant new things: make experience open and visible; know yourself; be prepared to be vulnerable as well as strong; be open; take risks; know that quality is never done; and be driven by the real experience of your staff and patients, which we need to link in the process of learning and change.

The NED's pivotal cultural role

Here, the NED is supposed to have a pivotal cultural role, although we are finding in practice that too many are too weak. They must secure their contribution (and their local legitimacy) by keeping firmly in view the higher goals of the individual patient's well-being and experience of our service.[1]

Executives, too, to their credit in Brighton, have not hidden in the possible claim that a meteor had struck on the wheelchair-day, but that otherwise the sky was clear. Evidently, the unsettling experience was repeatable every day, and we admitted this to one another.

Nor did executives appeal to our traditional and sophisticated prevention systems that deter, defer, or deny enterprise by consensus, committee and procrastination. We did not misfile the marching orders, but set an action plan. The clear message there is that accountability and contract-renewal is about performance, not merely punctuality. The focus on performance and review impacted immediately, for example, on a new programme of lavatory inspection (and an audit to find out how many we had, where, when cleaned and who used by). If motorway cafes can do it, and invite a call to management if standards fall, so, surely, should we.

Setting 'Gold Standards' – guaranteed

Clearly, scepticism of the '*Pravda mentality*', that says 'all is well, leave it to us', gets your head above the parapet on quality. It forces the pace on the core business targets, triggers incentive, measurement, pay, reward, multi-skilling, to see how to get more and better for less. This is to welcome a state of perpetual agitation, movement, energy and change. It is to ask the organization to transform itself, working with an enlightened medical team and with wide staff understanding. It is to specify that an effective service organization will set out standards and ask to be judged by the public. One way to take this seriously is to set watertight and explicit 'Gold Standards'. *Real* guarantees, with sanctions that bite us. We all have mission statements, lists of critical success factors, quality maps/chains/ charts, but how do we make them lock into gear? Or are they merely *vinum daemonum* – the wine of devils? First, we need to find meaningful standards about really fundamental things, give an absolute guarantee and apply sanctions: public contumely, reduced purchaser faith in your ability to deliver what you say you can do, or a cash fine where *you* pay for work you guaranteed to be done by someone else if you did not deliver it as you guaranteed.

'Gold Standards' would address the issue that causes us so much difficulty, where, even with goodwill, we agree policies but do not ensure that they become real, that everyone attends to them. We are trying to *personalize* all services, and much of what my wheelchair odyssey showed was officially impossible. Yet it happened. Guarantees are the 'Patient Charter Plus' next step to change, and the waiting-list promise is an opportunity. Why not guarantee that we will give everyone on our elective list a definite date six months prior, and do the operation on that date? We know we have an 18-month absolute ceiling. We know our capacity. Why not put real people's names into the work charts, and pay for work elsewhere if we fail to deliver? This guarantee would re-emphasize the requirement of performance, the private sector respect for pace, and for taking one's client's time and anxiety seriously.

Pace matters, yet we are weak at focusing detailed change at a lick. We are not always superior to the snail. It was John Clare the poet who, in 1825, noticed 'a snail on his journey at full-speed and I marked by my watch that he went 13 inches in 3 minutes, which was the utmost he could do without stopping to wind or rest'. Do we always reach out to the utmost? Is the incentive there? DH Lawrence reminds us that 'hell is slow and creeping and viscous and insect-teaming', and it is visible from 'The Wheelchair', where we see the results of management toying with air whilst planning plans. Instead, at Brighton we hope to embed change in patient-focused (or integrated) care, and to insist on 'suspicious scrutiny' of the patient's experience.

Trusts have to manage the concurrency of corporate development with service development at the operational level. 'Golden Guarantees' would cost us money, and hurt. Yet, like the unfunded three percent wage award, they would force change and take the patient seriously. There are many guarantee targets to hand. We could guarantee that every in-patient would see a doctor every (or every other) day, and ensure we know who this is. We could guarantee an active courier service with welcomers *seeking* arriving patients. We could stop challenging patients to find their way around, and find it for them. We could guarantee to advise the patient in advance of the identity of their named nurse and the clinician in charge of a patient's care. We could take the opportunity, too, to ask our local community to help put in place the guarantees *they* want, the things that really matter to them. A coupon in the local paper ('Tell Us!') would manifest a Trust's desire and anxiety to really do something in this way.

Doctors, above all others, need to make clear the standards of performance by which they expect to be judged, with these agreed standards forming part of their contract and with targeted improvements agreed by a regular review process and linked to pay.

Changing behaviour and attitudes

Commonly, we seek to recapture the initiative by new systems, structures and policies, but good or bad practice towards patients depends on behaviour and on attitudes, not on systems or policy documents. As usual, it is all about people. Clearly, some people treat patients better than others in their peer group. It is clear that we are right to be concentrating on 'culture'. That the primary focus should be in the area of behaviour and attitudes towards patients as directly perceived by patients in particular in their personal contacts. It is all very obvious, but it is precisely what is overlooked and lost in institutional settings. Helping people to see and change attitudes is our single most difficult task. It involves the sort of basic shift of perception that most of us will go to almost any length to avoid. It is clear that this is a very difficult area in which to bring about change, or we would have done it ages ago. One difficulty seems to be that the poor response or poor behaviour towards people in a seeming subordinate or dependent position has a great deal to do with early learning, and which is untouched (or, indeed, reinforced rather than eradicated) by the organization one has joined. This seems to be a difficulty held in common in local government, the police force, state education (except in the vital new Grant Maintained Schools and City Technology Colleges) and the NHS.

Of critical importance is the evidence of good, alternative, senior role models and the carefulness, too, with which newcomers are selected and socialized into the role they assume. Organizations need strangers – NEDs have given us greater leverage. So, too, must a new breed of executive – creative, pioneering, unapprehensive, confident, positive – who can actually implement policy and develop it on-the-run from first principles and test it by patient-led values. Personnel and nursing directors are especially vital to cultural change, and must be seen to count in the set-up while working with the 'fresh-eyes' of new staff, who they recruit because of their appropriate frame of mind and style. To get to efficient, effective, patient-focused, patient-led care we need, too, to underpin these underpowered areas, if we can find the people equipped to do it. We are only just starting to unravel the management consequences of the general proposition that market pressures will prompt performance, and that local Trust status will legitimize energetic, new, sympathetic action. The key to Trust survival (in the coming world of merger, re-profiling and acute service review) is location, but public support will count in mediating, enhancing or restricting change, as we strike the balance between maintaining the here-and-now and looking forward.

What would you fix?

A key part of the here-and-now is the patient's experience and staff knowledge, which we need to link creatively both to quality and to performance. This requires us to take staff knowledge seriously, not platitudinously. The NHS swarms with unread paper yet the one piece that everyone unfailingly studies every month is the wage-slip. We can use this doorway into action. In October Brighton Health Care inserted a specific invitation into 4300 wage-slip envelopes, saying 'Please tell me the two or three things you would fix if you could'. Performance management can only succeed, as Sunderland car workers have shown, under Japanese tutelage, if it passes responsibility outwards, applauds and rewards behaviour that gives concrete expression to its cultural values, most especially asking to be told, advised, and helped. Our staff believed 'fix it'[2] was a genuine invitation and several hundred ideas were submitted, identifying needed and mostly very practical changes. The ideas are pure gold. We told all staff, by *personal* letter, that *all* ideas would be investigated, their impact assessed, their cost identified, with an action plan, a cost and a completion date specified. Equally, a proper and detailed explanation would be published if an idea did not then seem workable. This is to take professional communication skills seriously, too. A public staff meeting, attended by the entire Board, will debate a published action guide. This is the start of a new learning style, to change how we do what we do based on what staff see and know but management still does not. It is the 'invisible hospital' made temporal. It should now take us into genuine process-analysis, to release staff and patient knowledge (engaging our Patient Access Group further) for quality, change and 'Gold Standard' performance. Just as we want the centre to be lean, cheap, silent and strategic, so, too, do we want executives to be enabling, facilitating, listening, as tools not tractors.

Process-analysis is flip-chart stuff: a facilitator, a team in a room, and three questions: 'Tell me what you do' (the job description emerges); 'Tell me what you *really* do' (the practical variations materialize); 'Tell me what you *would* do if we let you. Now I am going for a walk. See if you can fill the flip-chart in in an hour' (the pure gold emerges).

We need to see that the people who do our work confidently say that they like what they do; understand why they are doing it; that they know how; and let them alone both to do it and to come forward with ways to do it better. Only in this manner will we nurture a *performing* organization and ensure that things that ought to change have changed. We know, too, that we have *both* to release staff energy and vision and to save money, improve service and use fewer and better-paid staff more efficiently. We need staff commitment to this problematic but essential process of development. Taking their ideas, knowledge and experience seriously is a fundamental if we are to do more and better for less by abandoning traditional approaches to work as well as reducing top-down control management.

The performing organization will have a genuinely open outcomes focus. It will ask its doctors to take explicit responsibility for standards of performance and for after-care scrutiny. It will be in the process of disease management, interested in the currency of measurement and managing, and go from negative to positive tensions — working with staff, patients, and especially medical professionals to signal that *performance* is *the* core value, and that precedent is not to be feared.

No Trust will be able to build a meaningful monopoly. Only unwise management will believe that they can. The best move is to pass 'Go', collect the £200, and to land on the 'performance' square. This is the moment to make the leap.

Notes

1 Insomniacs will know that there is more dull, dim and fairly pointless writing about NEDs than on most NHS topics. The useful commentaries are listed in note 8, in the chapter on The Invisible Hospital in this book, (p.65).

2 Commentators on corporate governance can be both stimulating and soporific. An outstanding example of the first is Sir Owen Green (1994) Corporate Governance – Great Expectations. *Pall Mall Lecture*, Institute of Directors, London, 24 February. See also the judicious commentary by David Hunter (1993) No more corporate. *Health Service Journal*, London, 9 September; the report of the Corporate Governance Task Force, *Public Enterprise Governance in the NHS*. NHS Management Executive, Leeds, 1994; Wall A (1994) Corporate Governance. In *NAHAT NHS Handbook*, 8th edn. Macmillan Press, London; and West M, Sheaff R (1994) Back to Basics. *Health Service Journal*, 24 February, pp.27–9.

This article was published in *The Health Summary*, London, March 1993.

11

Facing the customer
and asking to be judged:

or, what does the market want?

The key to accountability is to face the customer and to ask 'What problems do we have in giving the market what it wants?'. This should be the focus of all we do. We are here to get the statue out of the marble.

The core of the accountability debate is surely to welcome central accountability to the customer, but to shift responsibility for effective delivery to the NHS organizations out there in the localities. That is the only way to deliver the health gains for which Parliament is accountable. The cultural imperative is for these local organizations to achieve the health gains and to set higher standards for themselves by which local people can judge them; and we should expect them to use the powers they already have to do the job. Accountability, subject to fine scrutiny, but with the opportunity to show drive, style, vivacity and results.

This will, and does, press them into strategic thinking and an implementation strategy which gets them into proper demand management to deliver change. The contract culture asks us to say what we stand for, and how we will show that we are winning. These are remarkable changes in a society generally listless about competition – the best regulator – business or risk.

The post-1945 welfarist consensus settlement is shifting too; we are asking if our expectations of the NHS are still appropriate in a society where aspirations, incomes and standards have hugely changed since 1946. In balancing priorities, we are asking what we can expect to see delivered by the NHS, and to be accountable for getting it done – all with the least possible interference from the centre appropriate for accountability.

What is the positive balance to be between overt community stewardship, local transparency and initiative, and central direction? In this discussion will the intermediate tier be the advocate to sustain change or the adversary of Trusts? To what extent will it turn on the style, or turn off the oxygen?

Saying what we stand for

It is purchasing that gives us purchase on accountability. Purchasing is not about contracts, of course, but about the questions that are asked before the contract is signed. Essentially accountability lies in assessment, health gain and the leverage to get it from producer activity; to attain clear objectives for better health, with performance ratings linked to published targets. Purchasing not by the acre, but by the close-ploughed furrow, identifying the issues and doing something about them, with informed patient choice de rigueur. The heart of it is surely about setting high and local standards and about saying 'This is what we stand for, this is the kind of organization we are. This is who we are and what we ask to be judged by. Check it out. Test us. See how we do. Compliment and complain more. Work with us to strive to do better. Help us to help you.'

This is all about quality and outcomes, about frame of mind, about managing attitudes and behaviour, about demand management, about boards getting executives into production management, about utilizing all assets (for example, by patient-focused care) 365 days a year, and having the appropriate information to manage the key variables. Dump the belief that capital is the solution to all our ills, come away from the notion that quality is mainly a matter of resources. Manage better what you have got.

Changing attitudes and behaviour

The Patient's Charter asks us to compete against ourselves and to expect comparison with others. This point of view makes us focus on critical questions. What does your Board ask to be judged by, aside from what it is told it will be accountable for? Is there an explicit Board agenda on the critical success factors which are your core commitments, and for which you set a standard? How does the Board judge its own performance? Not only by the essentials we should expect as the norm – financial probity, activity control – but by cultural issues, which are new. How do we bring about changes of attitude, management and inspiration to deliver the service orientation of the Patient's Charter – involving the whole hospital? Does the Board ask: how do we change custom and practice; how do we work effectively with the 'twin Mandarinarate', the executive management and medical staff; how do we get a much more dynamic Board, managing from a position of knowledge, functioning as a corporate whole? And how are we to improve staff morale and empowerment within themselves and bring about a mind set of continuous improvement and sign up everyone to the Trust agenda, with a passion for their Trust.

The contract culture implies a real commitment to service; as if there were a real sense of jeopardy; as if the customer really could go away. Once this is the genuine focus, some of the most difficult issues come into clearer view. In addressing them, tone of voice, language, a pragmatic, flexible, non-confrontational style are essential. There are key issues about doctors (and about medical manpower planning, training and management), which pose very real dilemmas for them and for scrutiny and accountability. They find themselves in a world they never expected, where change is very fast. They recognize the fundamental point that resources are finite and involvement in managing choices will optimize original values, achievement and outcomes. This is a problematic partnership for change. It has huge potential for clinicians and managers to help manage the market with purchasers, but it is a situation where special pleading is not a viable currency. Clearly, without doctors, you have not got a system.

It is encouraging that increasingly, we have got the doctors. For too long we have been taking a journey through a tunnel of time like one of those old Bette Davis films where a fast train runs on rails right out of the screen, with the date 1946 whizzing repeatedly beneath the wheels.[1] That indelible lettering is finally fading. Legitimacy is draining away from old attitudes.

Systems like merit awards look increasingly odd, and previous control by doctors of what valid information is, and what the currency of professional accountability should be, is clearly shifting rapidly. Really accountable purchasing will have to incorporate knowledge of what works in order to change practices; to ensure the specialization of clinicians to achieve better outcomes, measurements and monitoring. This implies the reform of remuneration and contract, changes in the structure of hospital medical teams, and the continuous injection of more competition, including a proper market in consultants. The challenge to offer incentives for change is immense.

Medical management is, of course, an issue at the national systems level, but it is a Trust issue too, and one on which we will ask for central support. The whole system needs more management and incentive, more control, more penalty. There are not many Dr Deadwoods. It is the fine doctors whose commitment to the management process we most need. All professionals in society are being asked to give a new account of themselves, of their conduct and their use of resources. To make a commitment to the total strategy of their organization, to share management and join an 'industrious revolution'. Doctors are at the fulcrum of accountability. They control outputs and outcomes. They control costs, which impact across the whole budget. Persuasive leadership can bring them on board, with a shared agenda and commitment to accountability. This can be thin ice, but was it not Edmund Burke who remarked 'I mean no harm, not a bit'?

The key is demand management – getting more from the same resources. We must ask how much work we could do, how productive we could be, how we could get the work done with the best possible care with the medical staff budget we now have. The answer surely should not be the one we get now. The Trust movement says 'be care-driven'; set in place an accountability framework to get this done locally. Setting standards is basic. Asking to be judged is fundamental.

A prismatic example of these new opportunities is activity management, which identifies what we will do week by week, with case-mix. Why cannot we put names and addresses of real individuals into those grids, guarantee the date of an operation six months in advance and meet that at least 85% of the time? Why cannot patients have a care plan which books them into the system, tells them where and when they will be admitted, which care team they will see, what will happen and when they will come out? Why cannot we manage emergency loads better? Why are there so many emergency postponements? Why three hours to get emergency patients to theatres? Why not one hour door-to-bed, rather than 0–10 hours in A&E? Extra money always helps, but these issues are not entirely resource-dependent; they are responsive to organizational change.

All these are accountability issues. I believe they are about changing the culture by defining what our responsibilities are and gearing the system to deliver them. It is a shift from administering a federation of NHS cultures, accepting old standards and levels of performance, to a system which asks management to control resources, to set and deliver new standards and to be judged by them. We will be sensitive to the difficulties, of course, but take the initiative and say this is what we are going to stand for. It will be done through demand management, through how patients are managed, through staff utilization, through *organizing* to take a quantum leap.

Notes

1 My childhood excitement at the magic of the shining steam engines of the LNER running through North London from King's Cross, with their literary, historical and sporting nameplates (and their faraway destinations) has occasionally tempted me to make railway references in articles, speeches and interviews. This has produced, in the words of a film critic in *The Guardian*, 'The relentless chugging, the enclosed space, the weird passengers who are not what they seem and are apt to disappear, the sudden plunges into dark tunnels ...' Anon (1995) Ticket to Ride A Trainspotter's Guide. *The Guardian*, (Screen Section), 17 April.

This article appeared in *The Health Summary*, London, June 1993, pp.11–12.

12

The medieval knight stirs:

doctors, awake!

It is not our job *deliberately* to look for unpopular solutions to impossible problems, which produce outrage and alarmed sensitivity! Yet we *are* making progress – with doctors, with the BMA, with the British Association of Medical Managers (BAMM), on buying best processes, on ensuring effective purchasing, on querying and changing clinical practice, on setting incentive into play, and on thinking creatively about patient audit of services. The key message to the BMA is: join hands with us to lead this!

On better management of clinical effectiveness we are seeing many swallows. They will, I believe, give us an 'outcomes summer'. Professor Peckham's R&D Programme, the Clinical Outcomes Group, the work of the Cochrane Centre in Oxford, the leadership from Professor Alan Maynard, Director of the Centre for Health Economics at the University of York, the work at the Nuffield Institute at Leeds and the *Effectiveness Bulletins*, the recent Clinical Guidelines issued by the Department of Health: these are all giving us momentum and a science-based programme for change.

Of course, there is a lot of suspicion and wariness, but we *are* seeing the permanently immovable actually beginning to shift. As the novelist Candia McWilliam says 'as though the stone knight on a tomb, were waking and beginning heavily to stir in his burdensome carapace'.[1]

None of this is about confrontation. It is a partnership issue, about extending ownership, about switching people on, about implementation with credibility. The key is a joint approach, between purchaser and provider, between Trust Board and doctor, between doctor and patient. All this must be doctor-led, and constantly patient-referential. I believe this is actually happening, too, as we have seen with Brighton's experience in establishing the first-ever Clinical Performance Improvement Unit in the NHS. We are moving towards purchasing best processes and clinical proficiency. We are seeing a psychological shift genuinely to believe in responsiveness to the customer/patient. We are beginning to generate indicators of quality and audit by patients. All this is becoming part of the routine drive, management and monitoring of the service, with the patient-perspective as a routine part of clinical audit, ensuring that clinical and patient-audit meet.

These need to be *natural* processes, the norm for what all best professionals do normally. We should all set out our improvement goals and say how we are going to achieve them. We need to define the right set of professional targets and have a rigorous follow-up process. We need too, I believe, to look at the education of doctors and teach management skills, communication skills and business skills to junior doctors so that all we learn goes back into the training loop. We need, too, to invest in managers' training so that we know how to use the knowledge we have for the routine development of practice. We also need to talk more about how to make progress in purchasing *effective* care. There are three big issues:

- what interventions are cost-effective and proven to work, and do we do them?

- how can clinical behaviour be changed to respond to the research data, and to demonstrate that we do best?

- how can we ensure that patient and carer opinion punch their weight and help shift service delivery?

This is about the BMA and the Royal Colleges working in partnership with us, to educate peer leaders, to regularly re-accredit places, policies and people, and to join hands to achieve effective change including how to learn from patients on a systematic basis. It is, too, an invitation to the Health Service to say that we take patient opinion *seriously*; to say that we are *all* committed to using these mechanisms to improve standards.

What is all this really about? It is to seek to achieve *effective* clinical practice, *truly to believe* that our patients are the owners of the service, and that truly to satisfy our customers is *a requirement*, not a purpose alone. Surely, it is about the leadership of the organization, about why we are really here, and about the cultural luggage that we have carried with us and that we now need to sort out and much of which we need to leave behind. For we are arriving at new ways of doing and seeing; at the professional level, with the emphasis on effective practice, and at the level of the patient's experience with the emphasis on asking 'Can what patients want really drive the system?' We need to think about how we can develop this, and to go beyond the crude and rather unhelpful satisfaction measures which we now superficially celebrate.

In all this we need doctors' leadership of change and we need to find incentives for doctors to *want* to lead change. We need, too, to ask what do the customers value and do we deliver it? What contribution can 'patient and carer audit' make to better practice and more effective outcomes? How can we explicitly engage the patient and the carer to help us assess the quality of the outcome? How can a user's perspective be successfully incorporated so that desired outcomes are addressed, assessed and delivered better?

The crux is patient audit and advocacy. We need to work at how we think about getting information to patients. How do we learn to listen? How do we build shared decision-making? How do we change service planning? How do we build active consent and accommodate dissent? And how will this work influence purchasers, who have the responsibility to be sure that an intervention is actually providing benefits. For we need to know that interventions are not only scientifically shown to be *capable* of providing benefits but are *actually* providing benefits in real situations for real individuals. We think we are purchasing best processes, to achieve best outcomes, but what do patients tell us about the results? Clinical audit does not tell us. Indeed, it is a disappointment of clinical audit that it has not opened up medical practice to query and confirmation, nor is it integrated into wider NHS management.

We are seeking to develop a new culture of scrutiny and measurement, and we need, too, an informed debate about the patient's experience. The Royal College of Surgeons *Patient Satisfaction with Surgery Audit Service*[2] seems to me to be a very important initiative. It provides surgeons with detailed consumer feedback on their services, to provide important indications of the effectiveness of their work. It asks that the patient's experience of the process of care and the evaluation of the success of the outcome of care be fundamental to quality. We see, here, the medical profession moving towards recognizing that modern medical practice must be an equal (or much less unequal?) partnership between doctors and patients. It emphasizes that doctors are providing the scientific and clinical input into decision-making and that patients are the experts on their own personal situations, and their desired outcomes from treatment. The questions asked of patients implicitly look at how choice and information can promote better care. The BMA's current work on medical ethics under Dr Fleur Fisher is an important aspect of this work, too.

Over the past three years, with nine hospitals and 800 patients, a survey design has been developed and validated using some 70 questions. These address the specific features of the *surgical* rather than the 'hotel' experience. Two questionnaires are used, distributed immediately post-discharge and after an eight-week gap. Elements of structure, process and outcome are identified from the *patient perspective*, identifying any shift in patient rating of a service over the period of care. The audit is designed to help surgeons improve services. Summary data is provided by ward and by surgical 'firm', in the form of confidential audit and with the anonymity of the patient protected. Here is an opportunity to go into longer-term analysis of the results of clinical intervention, and, indeed, the RCS is now inviting commissions for audits from surgeons, with 400 eligible patients per consultant proposed as a basis for contact over a year. Data is presently collected on the surgeon, the ward surgical team, and the out-patient and ancillary services.

Here is a major opportunity for Trust Boards to engage *every* surgeon in patient audit, and for purchasers to accredit consultants in these terms. Here is a lever for all purchasers to set in place a quality control, as a requirement of a 'preferred provider' profile. Here is one basis on which we could involve patients in purchasing decisions, their contest-ability and their validity across a range of patient-determined measures. These value-options, with scoring measures, are available, too, as we think about purchasers putting incentives into place, to give reality to patient audit, and to render the data in an appropriate way that is designed and respected by doctors. This innovative audit offers the possibility of building a comprehensive measurement of the patient's experience. This is surely an important element of appropriate contracts between purchaser and provider, and of an appropriate contract of employment between Trust Board and clinician. Innovation, too, should confer prestige.

Patient satisfaction and audit which focuses on quality of life issues may matter most where a patient is a long-term patient, as in mental health. It has often been pointed out, too, that people are often mislead in their expectations of acute care, and that if people knew what the consequences of surgery actually were they would not have had it. Since outcomes are not always what people expect, we need to measure the surgeon's performance by asking the patient if the outcome is what he had been given to expect in the original consultation. This would really be to value what the patient thinks is important.

Good firms, clinicians, GPs and purchasers should welcome this openness.

Dr Adam Darkins[3] has pointed out (in his work on videodisc guidance and patient advice) that most health issues are not dealing with long-term illnesses, not dealing with life and death issues, but are dealing with quality of life and choice. Patient audit and patients' views of quality of life matter most. There should be indices to measure this, but this is not happening widely yet. To make it happen we need to work with patient groups, with CHCs, with an audit of GPs and of referrals, and with a post-intervention audit. If much of health is a consumer product, then consumers need access to impartial information which is consistent and believable. Outcome evaluation in *advance* is an important element, and, as Adam Darkins has pointed out, on a practical level if you ask a patient on a ward what advice has been given on outcomes you will probably get very varied data – from the GP, from the consultant, from the junior doctor, from the student nurse. Systematic patient literature, with advance consultation and advice, should include a discussion of likely outcomes. Independent audit needs to grow alongside advocacy counselling, too, and in helping us to find out what all patients want, to help them make decisions about their own care.

This process could help us impartially produce new levers that purchasers should introduce into contracts.

These developments would help us consumerize medicine objectively, and not by Government dictate. Patient information on likely outcomes and appropriate care seem likely to change demand and to release new resources. This could contribute to the de-politicization of health care, which is vital, as no government anywhere can deliver all possible health care. If clinical interventions are to be shown to be effective, be known to work, and deal with real problems, then patients must help define their appropriateness. People must tell us what they want from their care. If managers or politicians decide to deny a service, this is defined as 'cuts'. If patients lead us to change services, we will be in new territory. This does, too, get us back to the market, as it would be local people helping to make the real choices. By engaging patients in audit and choice, our patients will help us unlock changes, with *their* point of view driving the system.

The Patient's Charter has been critical to this development. For its emphasis on scrutiny and performance is moving patients from being grateful to being demanding; from being passive to being heard; from being talked to, to being listened to; from being ordered about to being able to say how *they* want to be treated – and when they *do not* want to be treated. Our next step will surely be to move from 'quality' in general to set *specific* criteria for what we do, for how good the audit has to be, and how we develop it *with* patients and carers.

This is about the equalization of power. Here, we need doctors' leadership for change. We need to find incentives for doctors to lead patient audit *with* patients and carers, and we need disincentives. For if a clinician is not accredited, if he or she is not doing patient audit, then they should not be insured. If they are not insured, they should not be able to be accredited. If they are not accredited, they should not be able to work.

If we are to make progress on building health status, and to achieve better costs and quality, we need to go on measuring progress and, as Don Berwick has argued, we must learn without blame.[4]

We need to build skills in purchasing, together with constructive purchaser/provider forums on quality standards in which we engage patient and carers consistently and permanently. This will be to use measurement to help learning, to build a learning environment, to build a performance organization, and, as the Brighton 'two or three Things to Fix' campaign showed, if you admit what you do not yet know and what you need to learn, you can creatively involve patients and staff in ways never tried before.

In answering the three big questions ('What interventions are cost-effective and proven to work and do we do them?' 'How can clinical behaviour be changed to respond to the research data and to demonstrate that we do best?' 'How can we ensure that patient opinion punches its weight?'), we need to buy best processes, to drive re-accreditation, and to engage patients in audit. We need real clinical guidelines that are knowledge-based. We need incentives to change behaviour and sanctions for failure. We need to invest in managers' training, to know how to use the knowledge we have – including clinical managers.

This is to look for popular and effective solutions to problems that have every possibility of creative solutions, to make real progress. The stone knight on the tomb *can* rise, breathe, and fight in the interests of patients. Let us sharpen the sword on the stone of patient knowledge and engagement.

Notes

1 McWilliam C (1994) *Debateable Land.* Bloomsbury, London, p.18.

2 This innovative concept which could take purchasers much closer to genuine knowledge provided by patients was developed by Mr H Brendan Devlin CBE of North Tees Health NHS Trust, a doctor who has supported many innovations for the improvement of the NHS. Purchasers have been shockingly slow to adapt, and at the end of 1994 only eight NHS hospitals had joined the project. On the methodological issues see Dixon P (1993) Some issues in measuring patient satisfaction. *CCUFLINK,* December, pp.6–7, and Michie S, Kidd J (1994) Happy ever after. *The Health Service Journal,* 3 February, p.27.

3 Dr Adam Darkins, Medical Director at Riverside Community Health Care, London (who has also worked as a doctor in the USA) deserves great credit when working at the King's Fund College, London, for encouraging the NHS then and since to take seriously the potential of the interactive video disc for empowering patients as shared decision-makers. See Darkins A (1994) Shared Decision Making in Health Care Systems. In *Proceedings from the Annual Research Conference 1994, Profession, business or trade: Do the professions have a future?* The Law Society Research and Policy Planning Unit, London, pp.73–8. See also Ellwood PM (1988) Shattuck Lecture, 'Outcomes Management: a Technology of Patient Experience. *New England Journal Of Medicine,* **318**, pp.763–71; Fries JF *et al.* (1993) Reducing Health Care Costs by Reducing the Need and Demand for Medical Services. *The New England Journal of Medicine,* **329**, (No. 5), pp. 321–5; and, MacLachlan R (1992) An Out and Out Success? *Health Service Journal,* 19 November, pp.26–7.

4 Berwick DM (1994) Quality and Outcomes: How Do We Compare?. Speech to *National Association of Health Authorities and Trusts Annual Conference,* Brighton, 22 June.

This essay gives the text of an address to a workshop at NAHAT's Annual Conference, Brighton, 23 June 1994.

13

The view from Brighton Pier:

will improvement sink or swim?

Before my premature discharge into the community by Brighton doctors, since when I have had time to re-read *David Copperfield,* I established the first Clinical Performance Improvement Unit in the NHS.[1] Naturally, like Dickens (in his last preface to *David Copperfield*) 'I am a fond parent to every child of my fantasy'.[2]

We are here to make sure that we do what works, that we know what that is and how to measure it, and that we do not do what does not work. But how do we know? My intentions were to prompt the Trust to ask the right questions and to respond to discovered answers, as well as to involve patients in formulating the right questions and in assessing the answers.

The right questions would seem to be: what is the quality of patient care in our hospital? are we doing the right things? how do we *know*? how do we compare with the best international benchmarks? how do we know? indeed, what comparative knowledge of cost and clinical effectiveness do we work with at all? and how does that work back into targeted and measured improvement? what do we do with the knowledge we collect? and what relationship does that have to the generation of local questions about why what we do is done, and what could and should be changed?

The NHS reform processes focused us initially on cost-containment and on 'efficiency', but we are now starting to enquire within. We need to become better at defining what our problems are, and at defining appropriate solutions, both at the level of policy and at the level of individual patient treatment as we seek to make sure that we provide cost-effective care. We need, too, better methods and models for developing a cost-effective system both of evidence-based medicine and of evidence-based policy.[3]

We spend £112 million a day on the NHS, but with a seriously inadequate knowledge base. There are few well-designed clinical trials. Few initiatives are piloted and evaluated properly. We utilize and co-ordinate the research community inadequately. We know very little at all about the cost-effectiveness of the diagnostic and therapeutic interventions available, either at the secondary or the primary level.[4] Purchasing is not yet evidence-based, nor is central government policy. Indeed, too much purchasing is provider-led, validated by special interests. Reliance on effectiveness alone may itself be inefficient.[5] Since the majority of medical practices are unevaluated, practitioners themselves are uncertain about diagnosis and treatment, which is the source of major variations in observable practice.

Alan Maynard has recently put it like this 'The art of medicine requires practitioners to exercise judgement against a background of a seriously inadequate knowledge base about the effectiveness and cost-effectiveness of treatments. Where there is knowledge of cost-effectiveness, practice takes time to alter. The twin issues of what works? and how to translate cost-effectiveness knowledge into more efficient clinical practice are both acknowledged and ignored by policy makers. Everyone knows about this ignorance but policy makers seem reluctant to confront it directly, preferring instead to reform the structure of health care systems on the basis of ignorance. It is remarkable that such system reforms and clinical practices are dominated by the twin forces of unsubstantiated assertions and gross ignorance of the cost-effectiveness of alternative strategies!'[6] It is perhaps no wonder that only a non-executive Chairman ventured where most executives fear to tread, and where powerful interests exercise both direct and indirect power to ensure that this remains the case.

Yet the necessity *is* to enquire within, and to ensure the clarity and energy of the management chain. We need customized change, not general 'outcomes' talk. We need an internal drive, and not only externally applied inspection (although we need that, too). We need to assign clear responsibilities for action; to set expected levels of performance; to analyse (with reference to benchmarks, on an externalized and comparative basis) what is discovered; to explain and to 'trend' the data; to identify and give a time frame to possible improvement; and then to act to get it done. It is a requirement, too, to report to the Board, and to the public and its purchasers. Then, to start the cycle over again. All this is a major investment in information, especially on the increase in length and quality of life ('patient outcome' – on which, of course, there is little agreement on measurement, and on how to use this to inform purchasing). Clinical audit and accreditation, do not do this; they are a disappointment and do not involve patients in the design of standards and audit, in measurement, and in inspection.

There is an international context for all this. We must connect with the international knowledge base. Best practice must be international best practice. Internationally, we know that there are several lines of evident difficulty about the rationality and effectiveness of medical interventions. There is no justification, for example, for us to be behind the United States in the frame of mind we adopt in thinking about these problems, and taking action on them in the local hospitals for which we are responsible.[7] We know that practising physicians in the USA are increasingly becoming involved in generating and disseminating new knowledge about what does and does not work; for example, the work led by Dr Scott Weingarten at Cedar-Sinai Hospital in Los Angeles.[8]

It is an unfortunate characteristic of the British liberal to be very illiberal about American advances. There, doctors are taking part in helping to build national databases and major regional databases on chronic and acute conditions.[9] They are learning to interrogate the literature and on-line data as a matter of course, and to take individual responsibility for improving the database. There is movement to try to make progress with the collection of data at ward level, which a visionary like Dr David M Eddy urged in 1993.[10]

Nine months after I left Brighton I was thrilled to discover that the Northern and Yorkshire Region of hospitals in the NHS is offering important leadership and supporting many of these perspectives. They are the first NHS Region to support the Maryland Hospital Association Quality Indicator Project. They are pioneering an approach to audit and quality improvement in which over a thousand hospitals, mainly in the USA, voluntarily participate and receive quarterly data. Both clinicians and management are involved in the interpretation and the analysis of the indicators. I wish we had known about it at Brighton.[11] The Maryland Project is market led, prompted by the pluralistic organization of health purchase and provision in the USA. External accreditation of hospitals by the Joint Commission on Accreditation has long been in place there, although still focused on an assessment of structures and processes, and with insufficient patient focus.[12] The project emphasizes the key question. Ask not only *can* this hospital provide high quality care. Ask the *real* question: *does* it provide it? The comparative data generated by the project, using indicators valid and comparable over time and space, is necessary for a useful assessment of standards of care in a particular unit, to enable these questions to be asked and to prompt answers with any useful practical meaning. The project offers acute hospitals a wider context for the cycle of continuous improvement. In the USA it has highlighted problem areas, encouraged further analysis of treatment processes, prompted changes in services, and seemingly led to better outcomes.

Two points seem very striking. First, where are the patients? Where is the patient focus, and the systematic engagement with the patient's point of view – crucial if we are to give our actions *definition* in terms of the patient's values – has not been a primary axis. The project recognizes this and is now addressing it. Here, the initiatives of which I was a patron at Brighton (the Access Action Group; the College of Health work with patients; actually paying ex-patients to give us their time to study whether our changes worked for patients) could have been and should have been linked to the project by local management.

The second point is that an initial effect of inclusion in the project by the first British hospitals has been a recognition of the inability of present NHS information systems to provide outcome-based indicator data. The development of hospital information systems has been improved by the project.[13]

One challenging locale for engaging with the patient's perspective is the maternity delivery room, and it is of particular interest as a forum for patient values, preference, and decision-making.

Caesarian section rates are one of the key Maryland indicators, and a cause of both international and national concern, but, so far, the patients' values and preferences appear not to be a fundamental influence.

Clearly, cultural attitudes to Caesarian births vary greatly; for example, the Maryland Hospital Association in 1989 was reporting an indicator for Caesarian sections of a hospital mean 23.9%.[14] In July 1994 I asked for the Brighton figures. The national rate for England and Wales was 12%. Brighton in 1993 was 17.2% and in 1992 16.2%. The information unit reported to me 'This is higher than the national rate, presumably because of the catchment effect of the Trevor Mann Baby Unit' – a regional neonatal unit.[15] The worry is the word 'presumably'. The other worry is how it would be appropriate to consult with parents about a section, and whether we should, and in what circumstances, in addition to the choices offered by *Changing Childbirth*.[16] The issue for patients is that once a procedure is offered, they are already in the system and it is often too late to choose. Patients need to be able to know in advance the hospital's policy on the positive management of labour, its criteria for selection for emergency Caesareans, to decide where they prefer to have their delivery. The issue for hospital management is to know what they do, and to have comparative indicator data to check whether they should.

Again, in the USA these questions have been clearly put and it has been demonstrated that a programme of stringent management with a requirement for second opinions, objective criteria for the four most common indicators for a Caesarean section and a detailed review of all sections (and of individual physicians rates of performing them) seems likely to impact on the rate substantially, without adverse effects on the outcome for mother or infant. 'Presumably' does not achieve this.[17]

Obstetric care is frequent, ongoing and involves more than half the population. It is an area where the frequency and type of care can appropriately involve patient preference as well as provider choice of management and purchaser policy. The relationships between outcomes and processes of obstetric care are often easily quantifiable, too. There is ample room for understanding the reasons for the two most common procedures, Caesarean section and hysterectomy, and for modifying their frequency if the appropriateness of the procedure(s) is questionable, as the New Hampshire enquiry demonstrated.[18]

Patients, doctors, hospital management and purchasers need to influence what is the 'right' rate and the appropriate use of this surgery, both for itself and as an example of what might be achieved more widely and across the spectrum of choices. Caesarean section is a complex area, but one where the issues can be clearly formulated and in language that expectant mothers can understand, discuss and influence – not least in the debate about when a section is a valid and even life-saving procedure. A Caesarean section is major surgery and rates vary widely.

The Maryland Project examines guidelines for the induction of labour; whether clinicians know what other clinicians are doing and which guidelines each are following; whether there is a consistency of approach in any unit. It asks what are our Caesarian rates, why are they higher/lower than we thought, what is the quality of our decision making, are our decisions consistent and appropriate, what can we do if the answers cause us, purchasers (and patients!) concern?

In Colorado, as a development of the Maryland Project, there has been established the Colorado Quality Indicator Project, where 21 hospitals are voluntarily testing measures of hospital performance for their comparability, validity and feasibility for collection and release as meaningful information for the public to use.[19] Its work on Caesarian sections is significant, in clarifying the reasons why section rates vary and the benefits that may arise from an increase in vaginal deliveries and the development of an informed choice for parents and physicians. Colorado has the lowest Caesarian section rate in the USA, at 16.3%; the US national rate in 1992 was 22.6%; the highest State was Arkansas, with 28.4%. *Healthy People 2000*, the health care goals document of the US Public Health Service, recommends that by the year 2000 the national rate of Caesarian section be lowered to 15%. Even with a low rate, the health authorities do not assume that it is the right one. 'Presumably' is not the lexicon employed.

Colorado research suggests that rates vary due to clinical judgements (including mother and physician impatience at 'abnormal' progression of labour; fetal distress; maternal age and other 'complications', as well as for non-medical reasons including medical liability concerns, insurance coverage, patient preference, availability of hospital support services, hospital protocols, organization and guidelines). Since this is an area of medicine weighted by unrealistic expectations, it is one in which clarity and openness with the public is vital. It is, too, essential to describe the processes of care, if quality is to improve, and if purchasers are to develop strategies to change Caesarean rates. It is the case that Caesarian rates are higher cost deliveries, have a generally higher risk to mother and baby, and are often unnecessary – all reasons why we need increased surveillance of provider activity.

This is, too, a good arena for testing whether practice actually changes when guidelines are promulgated. For guidelines for medical practice can only contribute to improved care if they succeed in moving actual practice closer to the behaviours the guidelines recommend. The evidence is not very encouraging. Management has to be alert to its responsibility to assess the effect of guidelines, not least by checking discharge data which reflect actual practice. A major Canadian enquiry concerned with Caesarean sections and the question of whether practice guidelines guide practice demonstrated that awareness of guidelines, and agreement with them, was significant, but that knowledge of the content of the recommendations was poor. The study concluded that guidelines for practice may indeed predispose physicians to consider (!) changing their practice and behaviour, but that unless there are local incentives (and the removal of existing disincentives) guidelines may be unlikely to effect rapid change in actual practice. It can take decades to achieve change.[20]

My purposes at Brighton were non-executive, but to prompt executives and clinicians whose job this was supposed to be to do the appropriate work. This was a time for thinking and for reading. All this was, of course, a prerequisite to investment in improving clinical practice based on standards and guidelines which follow the assessment of the appropriateness of procedures, and to ensure that actual practice then changed. The assessment of the individual competence of the clinician is a separate but parallel enterprise. The availability of information to guide the patient in the choice of referral and in the choice of procedure is a principal objective of public policy, and in the USA it is a consumer imperative.

There are a number of basic premises guiding this general enterprise. First, clinical quality and effectiveness can be measured, to the advantage of the patient and the doctor. Second, the rationality and effectiveness of current provision is challenged by a large body of recent research which shows inappropriate intervention, geographical lottery, unacceptable variation in practice and avoidable death. Third, clinical leadership is essential if clinical colleagues are going to achieve improvements. Fourth, positive incentives are required to make this happen: financial, professional and the pleasure and pain of publicity. Fifth, major investments in IT and in the understanding of how to manage data for improvement are needed: both executive management and clinicians need help. Sixth, it is fundamental to encourage and facilitate the expression of patients' preferences, not merely on a consultative basis, but as paid inspectors and contributors to policy. Seventh, investment in effectiveness research must be co-ordinated and increased. Eighth, all of our data about diagnosis and treatment must be interrogated along the axis of effectiveness. Ninth, long-term patient tracking must become a reality. Tenth, the data generated must be used, both for providing care and for improving understanding of how to produce better care.

We still know too little about what does and does not work. We still know too little about why doctors disregard new knowledge about both, and thus fail to improve their clinical practice and impact on major variations in diagnosis and treatment. We do not collect standardized data on patients, so we cannot incorporate it into a national database which could be called up on screen by every doctor sitting alongside every patient.

Dr Robert H Brook, an American physician, wrote in 1991 in a landmark article 'Incorporating such data into a national database would result in what is admittedly a body of non-experimental information. However, after adjusting for differences in patient severity and co-morbidity, it would be possible, based on data from patients with newly diagnosed conditions, to develop and test clinical hypotheses that link what physicians do to patients (process of care) with what happens to them (outcome of care).'[21]

We are very far behind in the measurement business. If doctors are to know what works, and purchasers are to buy it, we will have to get to ward and GP level IT. We need to see and record who our patients are, their conditions, what we do, what happens, what it all costs, what are the intermediate and long-term results, which only they and their GPs can report. We need to map and analyse the benefits, harms, and costs, tracked over time. We need to assess our difficulties with value judgements and surveillance procedures. The analysed data needs to be available to all, and to be used in future clinical interfaces with patients when considering alternatives. We need to approach quality quantitatively. Eddy is right. This needs to be doctor-led and data-led. Doctors need to know. They need the answers.

We owe it to British patients to have a programme which collects data from all patients and all doctors who provide care to the patient. That is, if we are to determine what does and does not work so that in a shared and informed partnership with the patient, we can enable a joint decision about treatment to be made. It is, indeed, surely the doctor's responsibility to give time to generate and share this knowledge. How to do it should be a fundamental part of what we do in medical schools.[22] So, too, do we need to involve patients in deciding on the most relevant measures of physical, mental, and social health – what matters to them – and how to report back on what difference our interventions made to their lives. Such a programme would be a trident for advance: care might become more appropriate; technical competence could improve; the patient's perspective and the uniqueness of his knowledge could be engaged. Each of these components of quality needs to be accurately measured. We know that we have good ways of measuring the first two; we need much more useful ways of measuring the third than the crude and unhelpful satisfaction survey. Clearly, there is a big issue for Government: the geographical lottery of who gets what and where, and the problem of inappropriate interventions, consume significant sums of public money which could be targeted more effectively if we had the data on which we could rely. As the interactive videodisc programmes that we have already demonstrate, demand falls when patients have a choice and can discover that there is such a thing as inappropriate care.[23] Indeed, the phrase 'infinite demand' might leave the language.

Essentially, it is purchasers who want to buy procedures that work and to identify the improvements they require. Guidelines are needed so that the clinician can decide under which clinical circumstance a procedure is appropriate. Here, knowledge of effectiveness must be linked to purchasing mechanisms so that clinical practice changes, not least in eliminating unnecessary procedures. Positive incentives matter. Indeed, Robert Brook has even suggested that fellowship status might only be conferred on physicians who provide services that are medically appropriate more than n percent of the time.[24]

It is entirely reasonable and proper for doctors to say that such a programme will take time and money. Clearly, neither purchasers nor government can will the ends without providing the means. When I was Chairman at Brighton I initiated that discussion both at the centre and with the principal purchaser, but the 'resources' call must not befog two points that must be held up in public with Arctic clarity. First, it is the Board's responsibility to behave as a Board of Directors. If NEDs are not there to support such a point of view, what possible use are they to the public they are put there to serve? Second, purchasers have to get data on outcomes collected (including what patients say they are), and conduct enquiries on measures of process, comparing them with international standards.

We need to make a reality of public information and local consultation. We need to tell the truth. What we find out about unacceptable variations in practice and outcome, what we discover about appropriate or inappropriate interventions, what patients tell us about the effect we had on their lives – these are the essentials we should report in our Trust documents. Happy little photos of nurses smiling by beds; a jolly little pic of the Chief Executive sitting behind his desk; an impressive scene with the Chairman 'on his rounds'; columns of finance chat in the Annual Report do not do the job of telling patients whether they should allow themselves to be referred to us. This knowledge is needed, to build social consent and to enlarge the involvement of patients in decision making. The knowledge, too, will help us isolate and engage with those determinants of health status (which are outside the control of the individual doctor – social, genetic). In each of these fundamental areas of public policy America is in the speedboat but we are in the punt.

If better outcomes are to be in charge, purchasers should now ask every provider to establish an improvement unit, and refuse to buy from any that decline to do so. For a Clinical Performance Improvement Unit offers a genuine opportunity to hunt the outcomes fox, to shift from 'best efforts' to guaranteed improvements, and to set improvement targets that can be published, measured and compared. St Augustine of Hippo wrote that he knew perfectly well what time is, provided that nobody asked him. If they did, he was lost for words. We need not be so; for, clinical effectiveness, like time, can be measured, and so, too, can be improvement.[25]

The initiative to establish the unit in Brighton asked the BMA and other professional bodies to join hands as partners in change, to learn from patients, to set improvement targets, to take *explicit* responsibility for standards of performance and for longer term after-care scrutiny. There is an important opportunity, not least to enable doctors to perform to the highest standards and to help lead NHS management. The best leadership from doctors is changing clinical and working practices. The focus on improving outcomes is a route to collaboration and understanding, which itself needs to be reinforced by doctors and managers training together as managers.

What is emerging is the model for a 'Modern Major General' – a modern Chief Executive, whether purchaser or provider. A credible and useful model for real change asks each to deliver Dickens' demand in *David Copperfield* 'Let us have no meandering'. The Chief Executives need to: identify and document clinical protocols now in use and their results; ensure that all work is clinically 'patient' and cost-effective; scrutinize and manage the processes by which new treatments and new technologies are adopted and evaluated and check on who is trained and allowed to do what. They need to get at the processes of clinical decision-making to improve outcomes; incorporate consumer views and experiences as long-term results for patients are assessed by and with patients as patient values are integrated into service delivery; provide effectiveness information to consumers so that they can be assisted to make informed decisions, participate in decision-making, and recognize the uncertainty in clinical decision-making. They should publish as much as possible, as often as possible, as clearly as possible, and set out the improvements aimed at and publish the targets. Next, get all this into executive performance contracts! Really make it happen, not merely adopt a 'policy document'.

The reader will recall that in *David Copperfield* the hero's father called his house 'a rookery'. This provoked Miss Betsey's derision, noticing that when there was not a rook near it Copperfield's father still took the birds on trust because he saw the nest. If this were the Brighton case, this would be a sad avian analogue.

The Brighton Clinical Performance Improvement Unit has the potential to help purchasers carefully to separate random variation due to chance, or due to variables beyond practitioners control, from variation attributed to the quality of processes followed by practitioners and to investigate patterns which need change. This could get us to *real* analysis of process, of what really goes on. So the hope of real improvement of performance critically requires changes in the methods and systems of clinical work, if we are to change the historic performance of existing clinical processes.[26] For the quality of outcomes management is fundamentally about documenting current processes, about subjecting individual performance to continual scrutiny, and ensuring that relationships between processes and ultimate outcomes enhance health status. The most useful framework of accreditation needs to be a dual framework, too. First, at the professional level, and, second at the level of the patient's experience.

This itself requires doctors to be open about shared decision-making with patients, and about what can and what cannot be achieved. The challenge to the Chief Executive of purchaser and provider is considerable. It requires alertness, insistence, and decisive follow through. It requires a genuine belief in enterprise, and in ingenuity. It places a value on imagination and empathy with the user's point of view, essential to the successful delivery of the values of public service in an informed democracy built on informed choice and with improvement the objective.

One key to all this is to pay people locally for what Government strategy and purchasers' contracts want to have delivered locally, tie a reward to the required changes in practice and performance so that we get it. Suddenly, the social revolution of the past 18 years, which has changed the lives of miners, teachers, railway signalmen, and local authority workers, is lapping at the steps of the professional staircases. The professions have benefited hugely from these social changes, but still plead exemption from them when asked to change how *they* work. This is a penny that must now drop. The NHS's leading expert on medical manpower practices, Dr John Yates (Head of the Inter-Authority Comparisons and Consultancy Unit, Health Service Management Centre, University of Birmingham) has, indeed, now queried whether some of the currency in circulation is counterfeit.[27]

If an outcomes focus is to be routine and to drive the system, we need incentive in place so that knowledge impacts on practice, on management and on training. Chief Executives have to *believe* this is necessary, not merely be driven by general election results. Purchasers, too, have to adopt a developmental role. As providers become self critical, both in understanding the cost-effectiveness of their services and in encouraging the evaluation of benefit and the constant querying of practice for improved effectiveness and better outcomes, purchasers must look at known areas of clinical variation, and on establishing a learning environment locally in a joint change-management programme.[28]

A service consuming £112 million of confiscated taxation each day does need to act upon the huge unknown variations both in activity, in resources, and in quality – not least to make optimum use of existing resources. Assessing and improving achievement, enhancing rationality, are fundamental to the achievement of optimal and demonstrable benefits, and to what doctors are supposed to do.

The idea of Brighton's Clinical Performance Improvement Unit was to *blend* management, professional, patient and carers perspectives in identifying and delivering best practice, as measured against international benchmarks and local views and preferences. It is the contract culture that should enforce these and reward their achievement, and ask what is the Chief Executive *doing about it*?

A focus on outcomes and improvement is the key to rapprochement between doctors and management, but it requires us to measure and publish the comparative performance of doctors against the targets *they* set together with patients. Then we will know *they* mean it. It is the Board who should be receiving the data, taking it seriously and acting upon it.

We need rooks in the nest, as Miss Betsey urged. Not, to adapt the avian analogy, a mere cuckoo in December.

Notes

1   See the Brighton Health Care NHS Trust Public Board paper, 'Improving Clinical Performance: A Proposal to Establish a Structure for Delivering Improvement in Clinical Performance'. The alert reader will note the coded language and appreciate the background of pull and push and the areas of compromise and hesitation. The document, however, offered an opportunity.

2   The Penguin Books edition, London, 1985, edited by Trevor Blount, reprints this preface.

3   See Thomson R (1995) The Maryland Hospital Association Quality Indicator Project. Address to conference on *The Patient's Charter and Quality*, London, 11 May. The author is Senior Lecturer, Public Health Medicine, University of Newcastle.

4   See Maynard A, Bloor K (1995) Primary Care and Health Care Reform: the Need to Reflect Before Reforming. *Health Policy,* **31**, 171–81.

5   See Maynard A (1995) *Health Care Reform: Don't Confuse Me With Facts Stupid!* Paper given to the Four Countries Conference on Health Care Reform, The Netherlands, 23–25 February. (Forthcoming, in conference proceedings.)

6   Maynard, ibid.

7   Professor Michael Peckham, Head of the NHS Executive R&D Programme, is leading British initiatives. See "Famous for 15 minutes?", Annabelle May interview with Professor Michael Peckham. *The Health Service Journal*, 17 February 1994, and in "R & D Towards Knowledge-Based Care". South West Thames Public Health Report, 1994. Also, *Research and Development in the New NHS: Functions and Responsibilities,* Department of Health, NHS Executive, Leeds, January 1995.

8   See Weingarten S (1994) Research, Development and Implementation of Guidelines for Inpatient Care Using Outcome Measures: A USA Experience. Address to *The First NSW Health Outcomes Conference*, Sydney, 12 August.

9   See Faltermayer E (1992) Health Care: Building the System we Need. Cover feature, *Fortune* magazine, 23 March; also, 'Peering into 2010'. A Survey of the Future of Medicine. *The Economist*, London, 19 March 1994.

10   See David M Eddy, op.cit.

11   Richard Thomson's presentation drew this to my attention. Another example of the need for the leadership by public health doctors to be paramount!

12   See Roberts JS, Cole JG, Redman RR (1987) A History of the Joint Commission on Accreditation of Hospitals. *JAMA*,**vol**, 936–40.

13   Richard Thomson, op.cit. Ten in-patient and five day-case/A&E indicators are in place with new indicators being developed. The in-patient indicators are: hospital-acquired infections; surgical wound infections; in-patient mortality; neonatal mortality; perioperative mortality; Caesarian section rate; unplanned readmissions; unplanned admissions following day-case; unplanned returns to special care unit; unplanned returns to the operating room. The day-case/A&E indicators are: unplanned returns to A&E within 72 hours; patients in A&E more than six hours; cases where discrepancy between initial and final X-ray report required an adjustment in patient management; patients who leave A&E prior to completion of treatment; cancellation of ambulatory (out-patient or day-case) procedure on day of procedure. See *Maryland Quality Indicator Project, Newsletter*, Issue 2, May 1995, Northern & Yorkshire RHA, Harrogate. Also Kazandjian VA, Wood P, Lawthers J (1995) Balancing Science and Practice in Indicator Development: the Maryland Hospital Association Quality Indicator Project. *Int. J. for Quality in Health Care*, **7**,(No.1), 39–46.

14   Richard Thomson, op.cit.

15   Internal Memorandum, Brighton Health Care NHS Trust, 10 August 1994.

16   Department of Health (1993) *Changing Childbirth, Report of the Expert Maternity Group*. HMSO,London.

17   Myers SA, Gleicher N (1988) A Successful Program to Lower Cesarean-Section Rates. *The New England Journal of Medicine*, **319**, (No.23), 1511–16.

18   Kazandjian VA, Smith BD (1993) The Impact of a Cesarean Section Protocol on Hospital and Physician Activities: a Case Study of the State of New Hampshire. In *Measuring and Managing Health Care Quality*, supplement no.2, August, Aspen Publishers, USA.

19   *Colorado Quality Indicator Project, Special Report, Issue: Cesarean Delivery*. Denver, November 1994.

20   Lomas J *et al.* (1989) Do Practice Guidelines Guide Practice? The Effect of a Consensus Statement on the Practice of Physicians. *The New England Journal of Medicine*, **321**, (No. 19), 1306–11.

21   Brook RH (1991) Quality of Care: Do we Care? *Annals of Internal Medicine*, **115**, (No.6), 486–90. This brilliant and humanist article prompted me when I discovered it in April 1995 to think through some of these ideas with greater clarity. I have drawn on his work with gratitude. His footnotes supply the evidence and references for the extensive body of work on which I comment. I am grateful to Dr Adam Darkins for drawing my attention to the article. See also, Lawthers AG (1995) The Future of Quality in Healthcare. *Journal of the Association for Quality in Healthcare*, **2**, (No.3), 83–97.

22   See my article (1995) Training Should Be More Diverse. *Healthcare Management*, London, May, p.7.

23   See Darkins A (1994) Shared Decision Making in Health *Care* Systems. In *Proceedings from the Annual Research Conference 1994, Profession, business or trade: Do the professions have a future?*. The Law Society Research and

Policy Planning Unit, London, 73–8. See also, Spiers J, Lilley R (1995) *How To Be A Street-wise Patient.* Forthcoming, and Fries JL *et al.* (1993) Reducing Health Care Costs by Reducing the Need and Demand for Medical Services. *The New England Journal of Medicine,* **329,** (No. 5), 321–5.

24   Robert H Brook, op.cit.

25   St Augustine of Hippo. I owe the reference to Paul Davies, 'Time Beats the Clock', *The Guardian* (On-line section), London, 20 April 1995, pp.8–9.

26   See Donald M Berwick, 'Quality and Outcomes: How do we Compare?', speech to NAHAT annual conference, Brighton, 22 June 1994.

27   John Yates, *Serving Two Masters: Consultants, The National Health Service and Private Medicine.* op.cit. See also his subsequent book *Private Eye, Heart and Hip,* op.cit.

28   An invaluable story of a 'growth stock' in this area is Ellif Scrivens, *Accreditation Protecting the Professional or the Consumer?* Buckingham, Open University Press, 1995.

A very brief one-page extract from this paper appeared in *The Health Service Journal,* 9 February 1995, entitled 'Is Brighton Set To Rock The NHS?'.

14

It takes two to quango:

or, who is in charge and why?

A precocious young Victorian boy with golden ringlets is reported to have seen Queen Victoria in all her pomp and glory, and asked his father: 'What is a queen *for*?'

If the problem is, *what is an NED for*, we are talking about power and cultural change.

Above all else, the role of the NED is to raise expectations, especially by improving relationships. They are also there to fulfil the 'political' role of holding the executives to account. It is the NED who must ensure that the policy of the Secretary of State is delivered, with the Board the key forum of discussion, power, decisiveness and action.

My discussion of the roles of the NED seeks to unravel how fundamental relationships really work, observed day-to-day, rather than how they ought to work in theory. I rely on what I see, in reality, day-to-day.

It is the *whole* Trust (or purchaser) Board that is accountable to the public, to the staff, to the State, and who should answer affirmatively to Lord Beaverbrook's question 'Who's in charge of the clattering train?' The executives and all others must be held accountable to the Board. I leave aside whether or not the Board structure and membership is appropriate, save to notice that it is a complexity and special tension of those Boards that one half hire and fire the other half. It is a difficulty, too, that the heavyweight clinical directors do not commonly even attend the Board meeting. Clearly, this impacts on the Board's capacity to make explicit ultimate accountability and to ensure the existence of *regular* controls and analysis. This creates special dilemmas, too, for the medical director who *does* serve on the Board.

A major function of the NEDs is to find and motivate *special* people as executive directors, for it is special players that put into play special service and provide the unexpected. It is these that NEDs must work *with* and for change. NEDs, too, need to be informed and knowledgeable about the NHS, or they can be caught out by missing key linkages. At the same time, they must not be sucked into the system. They must be in the NHS world, but not of it. Their contribution will only be secured if they keep firmly in view the higher goal of the individual patient's (and visitor's) well-being, wants and experience of our services.

My own view is that the whole Board is in charge, but that within it NEDs have very particular and independent roles. The Board is the forum for decisiveness, and the focus of executive accountability. A key issue is: how do we draw on the benefits of what we hope are the new NED's assertiveness and skills, and at the same time protect the *separate* roles of Chairman and Chief Executive from the dangers of collusion within?

How do we get across the swaying rope bridge that spans the ravine between achieving cultural change and the risks of the over-reaching NED? How do we ensure that the NED function in corporate governance (and, therefore, due distance) is effective, and serves both Ministers and the public while enabling NEDs to give energy to cultural change and to insist on enterprise? Experience shows, too, the risks of dangerous liaisons: if a Chairman and Chief Executive collude in joint kingship we have a dangerous model that disables the Board. Equally, without new NED drive and insistence, we will not see the changes we require.

We need clarity and understanding based on what really is happening, to understand the ecology of power in the boardroom, in NHS Trusts and purchasing authorities, if we are to select between desirable and undesirable change. This is about analysing clusters of power, the relationships of a federation of cultures, and it is about understanding the diffusion of power, which is often subterranean, its mapping problematic. It is essential to keep the patient's perception central to all we do – including the *patient's* definition of urgency – and not be misled by triumphalist temptations when we proclaim the (very evident) successes of the Health Service reforms. We need 'suspicious scrutiny' of all we do, if we are to create the performing organization and to help the staff to lead change by process analysis and team-led action on the basis of continuous improvement.

The cultural challenge NEDs embody is going to prove irresistible, since it reflects broad social trends on accountability, openness and the changing nature of successful organizations.

Clearly, we need to research what they actually achieve. It is very difficult to measure influence, to calibrate the effectiveness of control, to identify the formal barriers to change, especially when words are often merely at the surface, with the real driving motives of people much more complex.

The enormity of the cultural changes we require of the NHS, if we are to overcome huge institutional inertia and vested interest (often proclaiming itself as 'national interest'), imply a much less narrow definition of the NED role than convention allows. Even though we lack much of a research base on how NEDs behave, they seem to be one of the most unforeseen but substantial benefits of the NHS reforms. The best argue that people have to be in charge, to stand the consequences of their decisions, and to take the pain if performance falls short of expectation.

The NHS reforms have set in train three major shifts to which all of the powers that be (or would like to be) must respond. The challenge of the NHS reforms is to deliver these three intermeshed and revolutionary shifts.

- First, *a scientific revolution* to demonstrate and ensure best practice based on research evidence and which ensures that practice changes in response to it. To get into the measurement business, seriously and at last, to get us to evidence-based outcomes in clinical and community care. This means exploring new ways to manage professionals, and asks Boards to intrude into the interdependence (if not collusion) of clinical and executive directors in a service where some top management has been compliant and where the shape of the organization has been determined by hospital clinicians.

- Second, *a social science revolution* for organizational fitness, to reshape our organizations and our management in response to the market developing *as a market,* and in response to our shifting understanding about the nature of successful organizations. We must produce the *performing* organization. This is to shift from control to collaborative styles, to motivate, to reward, to improve, to generate workforce effectiveness, better use and control of resources, by changing work structures and systems, as with the experimental implementation of Integrated (or Patient-Focused) Care at Brighton, and, which we need to test and measure as we develop it. It is critical to commit to doing more, better, and for less. Pace matters, too by transforming work, by transforming us as individuals, and by changing the way we do things together. This is the *performing* organization, not merely the *learning* organization (in which beware process), which enables us to learn how to change as we do so but to *ensure* performance results. We need an organization that can go on changing in response to the wants and aspirations of people, inside and outside, to think differently and to go on thinking differently. Such a shift might resolve our immediate problems, too, as we learn from that process of change, and *prove* better performance.

- Cultural change requires grafting. Executives need to get off of their pinnacles and start to listen. They need to leave their caves of anxiety. They need to use *every* opportunity, *every* practical project, *every* functional development, to *ensure* that it is infused with the new values, to make sure that changes are not divorced from them; for changes have got to mean something – indeed *everything* – to both manager and worker. This is *not* the soft stuff – it is the key core issue for competitive advantage. It is where the added value is found. It is what <u>every</u> high-achieving modern business knows. Are we going to take it seriously, and change our behaviour? Or merely talk about it?

- Third, *a revolution in customer-culture*, built on recognizing the essence of customer transactions, in both clinical and non-clinical needs, with incentive for better performance and its measurement, too. This is to believe in the customer, and in a dynamic culture in which we deliver, not because the NHS is an obedient organization, but because we genuinely believe in consumer sovereignty. The consumer culture which does not mean you merely stop people being annoyed, but which genuinely pleases the customer.

- We must seek to sensitize every customer transaction, every contact, at every point where delicacy, dignity, privacy and respect is fundamental, and we must enable it to come through. Our new sense of jeopardy, that the customer might hit back, or go away, is a vital new element.

Basic questions of power and authority, of reward, commitment, ownership, leadership, openness, communication and access to information, are at the core of our potential to transform service and work, by transforming an administrative system into one of enterprise. The NEDs' work is pivotal; they are a proxy for the customer and should seek to see the service in every detail from the patients' and customers' point of view, and then to *require* change. It is they who must say that the NHS can no longer live in its own different cultural world, but has to make service personal to the individual, as it is in the 'outside' world where we all otherwise live. We need to be aware how damaging it is (to patients and to its own institutions) for the NHS to have a sequence of interactions with a customer which are consistently just a little bit off. In the airline business a dissatisfied customer tells eleven people – according to British Airways research. What do our patients tell their friends?

NEDs are there to put obvious but new questions into play: 'What concept do you have of service recovery after failure, to get better next time? Or could you, like a failed airline, be grounded for good? Do you raise or lower patient expectations? Would you *choose* to go to your local hospital? Do you surprise and impress your patients? What prompts do you give your staff (and what incentives) to remember in giving excellent service? Do you *always* give *special* service? How do you *know*? Is your service quality declining or being enhanced? How do you know?' Purchasing leadership, especially, is key here, and purchasing NEDs need to be selected as change-agents.

In all this we have acquired the language of customer service and 'delivery', but is it yet a power in the land, or, like Russia's two generals, Janvier and Fevrier, does the executive system wait for time (and the political weather) to take care of the intruder – assertive NEDs included – with business-as-usual still a future prospect? I doubt it myself, but skilful

NEDs must still squeeze more from the hands they have been dealt without becoming executives themselves.

Non-executives, too, have a role in shaping the structure of the service by ensuring that the service does not mislead *itself* about the purpose of the reforms or become preoccupied by functional issues.

Good, bright, able, positive, but long-serving NHS company men and women still seem to find the adjustment to the new world very difficult, even when they want to change. In the past week (prior to delivery of this speech) alone I have had a striking example. An apparently radical Trust executive director described market testing to me as a threat not an opportunity, even though it is clear that without market testing you do not know what service you have got!

This executive, and colleagues like him, are people who are responsible and passionate for the NHS. They evidence the passion that thousands feel – passion for which most companies would kill. One challenge for NEDs is to help direct, guide, maintain and convert that passion into the path of major change so that (in Sidney Webb's words) we can show people, as he said, how their arguments lead to our conclusions. For it is not opposition, but alchemy, that we seek.

Organizations need strangers. NEDs are the unexpected, unforecast, extra gain of the reforms – lively, committed, able, experienced, and with entirely new cultural values and expectations. Few of these NEDs have travelled steerage-class.

Good organizations and good managers served by good Boards have some readily identifiable characteristics. Many non-executives are reinforcing the better Chief Executives in bringing these key factors into play – many of them are new values in the NHS.

There are 'Seven essentials of new NHS management man and woman':

- *vision* – the ability to project an image into the future of where the individual believes the service could be

- *motivation* – a need for achievement, and the ability to succeed by setting realistic goals under a structure to achieve them

- *openness* – the ability to accept information, ideas and guidance from others

- *calculated risk-taking* – the ability to evaluate risk and plan a strategy to reduce but accept it

- *opportunism* – the ability to perceive opportunities for business development within the operating environment (market awareness)

- *responsibility* – an acceptance of personal responsibility for performance rather than explaining success or failure by external factors (luck; chance)

- *creativity and innovation* with imagination the core of the competitive cutting edge of any business, but not yet much valued in the NHS.

Non-executives offer many if not all of these qualities, although I do not assume all NEDs are businessmen or women, nor need to be so. They should be selected as change-makers as well as for professional skills. They need to insist on forming a new regime. This is not about better carpets alone. It is about shifting attitudes, using and influencing power, dramatizing new values. It is newcomers, outsiders, who are helping the service to see for the first time.

Non-executives, too, must be insider-outsiders. They are inside the tent. They have to remain unsocialized by the NHS. They should not let their energies be dissipated, nor be inducted into the system. As Jung puts it 'follow your bliss'. For it may be that the only way the organization *can* haul itself around is by the distinctive contribution non-executives can make.

Non-executives need Olympian and heroic qualities, at a time when we are all having to work at new roles. Line managers are becoming corporate executives; medical directors are becoming Board players, representing *medicine* not medics; Chief Executives are wanting to learn and to grow, but not be consumed by a Chairman; Chairmen are wanting to insist on new points of view, and on measured monitored change, without becoming a Chief Executive. They must be relied upon to understand their role and know how to discharge it. NEDs too, must be able to review how Chairmen perform.

Boards are seeking, too, to engage, inform, advise and hear the public, but are uncertain what to do when the public tells it things which it does not want to hear. Vitally, they are trying to discover what the public wants (which we discover in the market) rather than giving it what it needs (which planners decide), and to find ways to deliver from these new perspectives.

All this is to say that the effective functioning of Health Authority and Trust Boards, and the success of NEDs (without the necessity of mutual suspicion) is a key national issue in a system which is both managerial and political.

The new Codes of Conduct and Accountability which came into force from 1 April 1994[1] make it clear that the role of NEDs is to be significantly strengthened and their responsibilities made more explicit. These roles are being more precisely defined, with clarification of the essential purpose of monitoring executive performance, and this perspective is fundamental to a Board's definition of its role. The success of NEDs is a test of the polity of the nation, of the design of the organization, of the effectiveness of a

Government structure. NEDs are non-elected appointees of the political system (though not necessarily political appointees); they represent the community and need legitimacy within it. They are aware, if you like, that *it takes two to quango.* We see on the dance floor the NED and the executive director; the local Board and the Centre; the Health Authority and its locality. Deftly guided by Al Pacino,[2] not General Patton, new steps can be learned, practised, and beautiful. If the NHS is to decentralize but maintain accountability, these change-makers must shift energy from a centralized system to local, credible, known and effective operational management. They link the centre and its strategy to local legitimacy, local sensitivity and local visibility, and they demonstrate that the old medical masonic culture and other NHS structures, where only initiates talk to initiates, is being brought into public scrutiny. Thus, we can get to an evidence-based outcome-focused system, where improvement is the aim, incentive the guide, security and quality the result.

NEDs are not here to give away ten year pens, important though these are. They are here to see that the Board make dynamic judgements about what to do, and then to see it done; done in the spirit wanted, by the date wanted, with the result wanted. For it is not what the NHS says it is, but what it does, that counts. Non-executives survey the field from a special quoin of advantage, as strangers.

To be effective independent minds they should not lose confidence in what they know because they do not know what all those words ending in '-oscopy' mean. A key role is to slay the dragon 'Fear!'

What can a non-executive know? All in nature agree the conventional roles of non-executives and these are easily rehearsed. They are virtually or actually mandatory, and they read, of course, like Whitehall minutes. But minutes are not enough; a machine is required to make things happen.

The public expect NEDs to predominate in issues of corporate governance, probity, openness, what we used to call honour. These are the basics of the proper conduct of business. The conduct of Board meetings, the functioning of the Audit Committee, the Remuneration Committee, the Company Secretary role, and the Board list of areas it reserves to itself for decision are essential. However, still the fundamental question is: 'How much can any NED really know about what is happening in a major business, and how much can any NED be expected to do?'

Some, like William Rees-Mogg,[3] have argued that nobody who is not working full-time for a major enterprise can have any real understanding of it except at a level of strategic generality, and in one or two areas of their specific professional training. Even a full-time executive is, of course, dependent on the efficiency and integrity of the reporting system, which Chief Executives have to ensure is appropriate. One key is the shape, timeliness and relevance of adequate and useable information. Certainly, it is clear that non-executives cannot hope to run a health authority nor should they seek to do so. They have a duty to take strategic responsibility with the Board as a team, to make absolutely clear what the measure of success is to be, and to satisfy themselves that the organization is being well run.

They need to define what 'well run' means. A key test is whether *individual* responsibility for management decisions can be established, and to that end (in part) the shape of the Board agenda is significant. It is the Chairman's responsibility. He should require appropriate executive reports and a Chief Executive commentary; plan a core agenda; separate matters for information, report, and action, and hold a 'cultural' watching brief.

The present and immediate challenge is, in developing the market as a market place, that NEDs have a clear role in ensuring that Boards make both purchasing and providing work. This means leadership, clarity of thought and courage, pursuing the hard agenda. For the danger, if leadership is not there, is that the market will be run from the acute units and Trusts by the consultant body and compliant managers, as it has been for so long, restricting community shifts and outcome management. We do have to get hold of the momentum problem in purchasing, or it will slip back. This is, I think, especially true for an activity like purchasing which is least likely to capture the interest of the public. Purchasers have no shrouds to wave.

On leadership, it is not sufficient to be very able to be a Purchasing Chairman. They have to be tough and demanding. They must be appointed as change-agents. The key imperative is for Purchaser Chairmen and Boards to be tough, demanding and communicating. If purchasing is to go forward we need to recognize that this is where the opportunities are for the brightest; this is where leadership needs to be; this is where the management of public understanding needs to be most creatively led. We do need providers who think with a purchasing mentality – that is a gain – but we need *purchasers* who think with a purchasing mentality, and especially those who say 'we only want to buy if...'.

Inevitably there is tension. We are noticing the end of the system of avoidance of enterprise, analysis, openness and competitive measurement, and we are leading the service away from endorsing the highly developed NHS culture of consensus and compromise, which strongly militates against achieving some of the most difficult and conflict-producing implications of the reforms.

The prismatic area where all the light splits into its constituent parts is outcomes management – the attempt to get an evidence-based, rational service. If doctors are not prepared to follow best practice, and if purchasers do not buy it, they are digging a pit for their organizations and themselves since litigation is likely.

This returns us to the first of our necessary revolutions, to the rational shift to a science-based, evidence-based service.

The governing idea must be quality. The key question is 'Is purchasing going to influence the practice of medicine?' Is there a rational basis for it to do so? Can purchasing really be based on hard knowledge? We know well, for example from the NCEPOD studies[4], that a number of lines of evident difficulty are revealed by research into medical practice. Medical decision-making produces major variations in practice patterns, inappropriate care, huge variations in physicians *own* perceptions of likely outcomes, and a wide range of uncertainty.[5] All this has worrying implications for informed consent, expert testimony, and the use of consensus methods to develop practice guidelines. Let us admit it: this kind of scrutiny, after years of clinical audit, has not been pressed forward by executive directors into management action and control, yet it must be.

If, in my view, NEDs are to speak for patients, these outcome issues are core problems that they must ensure the organization addresses.

I began with the notion of power as a relationship, not a possession, and I have tried to explore some key relationships, testing their efficacy against the three revolutions we need; an evidence-based service, a *performing* (as well as a learning) organization, and a customer-focused culture. My conclusion is that in addition to the Cadbury remit[6] for corporate governance the NED is *culturally* pivotal, crucial and achieving. They are taking their places in building new ways of seeing, new expectations about doing, and new relationships to achieve effective change. *It takes two to Quango,* but the music is pleasant. The influence of NEDs has grown, is growing, and ought not to be diminished.

We should be providing an informed choice that people *would* pay for with their own untaxed money if they had the opportunity – as in the real world of service outside the NHS – rather than let them receive poor service just because it is a tax-funded service which is individually beyond account, and from which relatively few have an exit.

With the active and insistent support of the new NED we can achieve the three revolutions: a science-based openly outcome-focused service, an organization that facilitates better quality, more outputs, and at lower cost (with constant learning and change) together with a genuine consumer-culture of enterprise and customer-focus.

Please take your partners for the Quango!

Notes

1   *Codes of Conduct and Accountability*, op.cit.

2   As in the film *The Scent of a Woman*, not as in General Patton, no dancer.

3   Lord William Rees-Mogg (1993) Whose Hand on the Company Tiller? *The Times,* London, 1 November.

4   Campling EA, Devlin HB, Hoile RW, Lunn JN *The Report of the National Confidential Enquiry into Perioperative Deaths, 1991/1992 (1 April 1991 to 31 March 1992)*. The National Confidential Enquiry into Perioperative Deaths, London, See also Editorial (1993) End Results. *Health Service Journal,* London, 16 September.

5   See, for example, David M Eddy, op. cit.

6   *Cadbury Report*, op.cit.

This is a shorter, previously unpublished, version of a speech given to the International Communications for Management Conference on 'The Role of the Non-Executive Director within the NHS' at the Hyde Park Hotel, London, 27 January 1994.

15

Inside the clockwork:

signposts and icons for change

Signposts assist change and icons illuminate the path. If we are to realize the fullest potential of all our staff, and to create a genuine patient-focused performance organization, we surely need both, and, as in all history, cries out the need and then comes the echo with a solution!

Two iconographic signposts are British Standard 5750 and the Investors in People programme. Both offer seven essentials for successful change:

- they make us look inside the clockwork of our organizations – how do they really work, in detail? What is our self-portrait and how do we compete best against ourselves by putting ourselves under pressure?

- they offer an independent, external audit of what we do then

- they oblige us to set standards, to commit to them, and to ask to be judged by them, and never to let ourselves off the hook

- they get us into real process analysis and help us find ways to learn what our staff know could be done radically to improve our services

- they start us on the road to measuring quality, not merely asserting or boasting about it

- they give us practical ways to set in motion *continuous* improvement

- they require transparent, vocal, communicating commitment from the top of the organization.

The cultural context of BS5750[1] and of the Investors in People[2] programme is the imperative of change. Change always puts me in mind of Wagner, whose music has purpose, momentum, noise, direction, and the complexity of cultural struggle. It was Woody Allen who said he could not listen to too much Wagner; it made him want to go and conquer Poland. We need an almost Wagnerian display of alertness, scrutiny, insistence, entrepreneurship and enterprise – of ambition, ingenuity and determination. We need flair, imagination, empathy and style, and, critically, we need targets and measurement if we are to change our health organizations, and if we are to work with the talented managers in public service who have passion, commitment and drive but who are not accustomed to a culture of scrutiny and measured improvement.[3]

What is it this could deliver? Measures of quality, clearly, and by that we do, of course, mean effectiveness. Targets and incentives, to light the flame in the heart of every staff member. The organization stretching to surprise the customer. To change the 'invisible hospital', which the public sees and experiences but managers still too often do not. And to set us on the path to Gold Standards which we promise, and meet, or pay to be delivered on our behalf and on behalf of the patients.

Critically, too, these standards ask us, as does the Patient's Charter and the forthcoming League Tables, to compete against ourselves as well as against the contract competitor.

The vital element of the Investors in People programme is that it stretches the organization, and that an external auditor says whether or not its benchmarks have been met. Here, the leadership of Roy Lilley and the Homewood NHS Trust has been inspirational. The delivery of the project has been concrete and explicit: the yield for the staff – caught doing things right – and for the clients, has been verifiable and particular. To the NHS they say – here it is, Investors in People. Take it up. It gets the energy and empathy and knowledge of everyone into play.

There is no need for any of us to behave like a mouse with gloves on, instead, let us get to action stations. With decisiveness, effective follow-through, and with everyone taking responsibility. To deliver quality, not equality; diversity, not directives; choice, not centralism. This is to value action, pace, and private sector attitudes which are fundamental changes where fundamental change is wanted. The job of us all is to face the customer and ask to be judged; to let the unexpected in. The key for management is to face the staff and ask to be partners, not in the socialized sense of all joining hands together to cross the finishing line together last, but in the enterprise sense of setting standards for development together.

The Patient's Charter, in asking us to compete against ourselves and to expect comparison with others, focuses us on critical questions, as do BS5750 and Investors in People. What does your Board asked to be judged by, aside from what it is told it will be accountable for? Is there an explicit Board Agenda on the critical success factors which are your core commitments, and for which you set a standard? How does the Board judge its own performance? What does it have to *do* to deliver the critical success factors (rather than merely list them)? This is to deliver not only the essentials we should expect as the norm: financial probity and activity control, but the cultural issues, which are new. We need to bring about changes of attitude, management and inspiration to deliver the service orientation of the Patient's Charter and to change custom and practice. This is to work effectively with the 'twin Mandarinate' – the executive management and the medical staff. It is also to find practical ways to improve staff morale and empowerment within themselves, to help bring about a mind-set of continuous improvement, to sign-up everyone to the Trust agenda with a passion for *their* Trust. This is to recognize that we have been taking a journey through a tunnel of time, like one of those old Bette Davis films where a fast train runs on rails right out of the screen, with the date 1946 whizzing repeatedly beneath the wheels. That indelible lettering is finally fading. Legitimacy is draining away from old attitudes.

Essentially, we are seeking to improve service development. This should rely on what patients want and what staff know. It gets you to look at the clockwork. A key part of the here-and-now is the patient's experience and staff knowledge, which we need to link creatively both to quality and to performance.

Investors in People and BS5750 get your head above the parapet on quality. They welcome a state of movement, energy and change. They ask the organization to examine itself and to transform itself. They specify that an effective service organization sets out standards and asks to be judged by them by the public. One way to take this further is to set watertight and explicit Gold Standards – real guarantees, with sanctions that bite us. We need to find meaningful standards about really fundamental things, give an absolute guarantee, and apply sanctions. Gold Standards would address the issue that causes us so much difficulty – where, even with good will, we agree policies but do not ensure that they become real, that everyone attends to them. BS5750 and Investors in People, if embraced properly, do not leave easy exits. They also imply that systems, and structures alone do not do the job, but they establish an attitude of mind which changes behaviour and focuses on service and behaviour. Here, of critical importance is the evidence of good alternative senior role models and Homewood is a very successful role model for us all.

There is also the general question of transparency, openness and measurement. This is really all about the attitudes of people-to-people and it is about taking the patient's experience seriously, scrutinizing it in detail as an experience, and discovering the patient's point of view. Sensitizing every customer transaction is to sensitize every member of staff. We need to link staff knowledge and patient experience creatively both to quality and to performance, and a key requirement is to take staff knowledge seriously. For the prestige of the system should not reside in numbers alone, nor in aggregate measures of quality, but in clinically and patient-defined outcomes. Critically, this means finding measures for quality.

I am not paid to lead a quiet life, and negotiating with doctors is not a cosy pastime. It has been likened to herding cats. Well, cats vote for tin openers. Doctors do not easily vote for outcome measurement, but Brighton is leading the way. In my view, this information should be published, and we will, I believe, go from anonymity to the naming of names, and from there to more re-training, accreditation, and competitive tendering. It is about *your* daughter.

We need a concerted effort here to end secrecy. Too much is off the record. We need to get to knowledge, and give it away. We need informed consumers, purchasers, and most of all informed staff at every level to build on our strength.

The NHS has truly to become a democratic and accessible body, available to all. It has to break down the mystique of an untouchable culture where only initiates speak to initiates. To become an open-system, debatable and open to question by anybody, by people in the street. The issues now are public accountability, proven quality and better experience for patients. This is the door that we have to get through. Investors in People and BS5750 are well-crafted keys. Staff motivation and commitment are clear benefits, together with independent assessment and approval and they are essential to the integrity of measuring a quality system. It is in the nature of health care that we can never say 'we've done it', but the continuous improvement in processes of change from the shopfloor up are hugely assisted by these externally assessed standards. They are signposts and icons. We should embrace both of them.

Notes

1 BS 5750. See *Managing in the '90s: BS 5750/ISO 9000/EN 29000: 1987*. A Positive Contribution To better Business, Department for Enterprise, London, November 1993, an executive guide to the use of quality standards.

2 See *Investors in People*, Sheffield, Department of Employment, 1991, and The Manpower Services Commission White Paper, *New Training Initiative,* 1981. Also, 'Investors in People: An Early View of NHS Experience', HOST Consultancy paper to NHSTD conference, University of Reading, 14 December 1993; Lilley R, Wilson C (1994) Change in the NHS: the View from a Trust. *Personnel Management,* May, 38–9, and Finn R (1994) Investors in People: Counting the Dividends. *Personnel Management,* May, 30–3.

3 It is exciting to see what the best managers can achieve, and especially when the winning team includes a patient; for example, The Leicester Royal Infirmary single visit neurology out-patients clinic entirely reorganized for patient benefits, which was a justified winner of the European Healthcare Management Association/Hewlett-Packard Europe Award in 1994. Hilary Pepler, Chief Executive, North Mersey Community NHS Trust appointed one person with a one line job description 'Perform Symbolic Acts' – the rule was to empower staff to do something that staff knew needed to be done.

4 See note 4 to 'Where do Chairmen get their information, and is it worth having?', in this book (p.86).

This paper was previously published in *Health Manpower Management,* **20,** (No.2), 1994, 33–4. It was prepared as an introductory speech from the Chair to the Conference 'People and Quality: Quality and People', Forum Hotel, London, 28 March 1994.

The NHS patient

He who is conceived in a cage, yearns for the cage.

Yevgeny Yevtushenko, *Monologue Of A Blue Fox On An Alaskan Animal Farm* (1967)

At the centre, in Whitehall, old attitudes and the old guard prevail. The only heads that have rolled have been among the revolutionaries themselves ... The guards are in charge of the escape committee.

Sir Peter Kemp (formerly Second Permanent Secretary, The Cabinet Office/Office of Public Service and Science) (1993) *Beyond Next Steps: A Civil Service For The 21st Century*

16

Patient-focused care:

taking care to the bedside

The Patient's Charter is having a major impact on the quality of NHS care, and on the patient's experience of that care.

Now there is a new concept, Patient-Focused Care, which fits the purpose of NHS Trusts of responding to the individual needs of the patient.

The patient-focused approach is based on the fundamental assumption that everything a hospital does, including its physical layout, should be centred on the needs of the patient. Patient-focused hospitals are being developed in the USA and also in Australia and in the UK there are a number of hospitals implementing such an approach, funded, and actively supported by, the NHS Management Executive. These are: Kingston Hospital NHS Trust; Hillingdon Hospital; St Helier NHS Trust; Cambridge Community Services; Brighton Health Care NHS Trust and Northern General NHS Trust (self-funding).

The patient-focused approach is based on a radical review of how hospital services are organized and staffed with the patient's point of view as the focus of all we do. The aim is to decentralize and bring the majority of routine services closer to the bedside, performed by cross-skilled, multi-trained practitioners.

The approach is based on the findings of research carried out in several hospitals which showed that current hospitals are highly specialized, compartmentalized and fragmented organizations and that to improve efficiency and provide optimum care, the whole care process must be redesigned. Research in Brighton showed nearly 300 different job categories being performed by staff of around 4600 WTE (whole time equivalents).[1]

Traditional hospitals in Britain have tended to be administered for operational and organizational convenience, with departments and wards organized in terms of medical specialisms. The technology of the day meant that equipment was expensive, highly complex and cumbersome and tended to lack portability, so it required highly specialized staff and was centrally sited.

The computer revolution has changed our potential and we are enhancing the quality of all we do.

A survey of ten hospitals showed that medical and nursing staff spend several hours a day walking around hospitals on activities not dedicated to patient care. The average junior doctor walks about seven miles a day. This approximates at least two to three hours a day when the doctor is unproductive. In Brighton we have discovered that 50–55% of nursing time is spent on non-direct care activities, nearly all of which needed no nursing qualification.

In addition services are not arranged around the patients; very often patients have to travel around the hospital site for X-rays and blood tests, which is inconvenient for them and wasteful of staff time. Nursing staff are a valuable resource and represent the largest item in the hospital budget. A patient-focused approach provides nurses with an opportunity to expand their skills through cross-training ensuring that the best use is made of their professional skills and patients receive the best care possible. Nurses are multi-skilled professionals and should be doing more of the work that doctors and others currently perform. Improvement in the hospital layout and simplification of processes would ensure that time spent by staff on activities unrelated to patient care would be reduced to a minimum.

Findings from US hospitals, which have adopted this approach, show an increase in staff morale and reduced sickness, absenteeism and staff turnover. The average number of individuals coming into contact with a single patient during an average stay of five days is 45, which demonstrates the complexity of care. It requires a great deal of effort to co-ordinate such a large number of individuals, and the scope for communication breakdown between care-givers is considerable.

In a patient-focused hospital, on entering the hospital the patient would be assigned a named individual (care co-ordinator) who would be responsible for co-ordinating all aspects of patient care. A multi-disciplinary care-plan would be prepared for each patient, identifying which tests would be performed and on what days. Co-ordinators would be assigned to patients throughout their stay to ensure that the patients' and doctors' needs were met and to monitor the quality of the treatment.

The entire process would be under the supervision of medical staff, to create new 'patient pathways'. For a patient being admitted to a patient-focused hospital this would be as follows:

- on entering hospital, patients will be assigned a named individual who will be responsible for co-ordinating all aspects of patient care
- patients will be treated in expanded operating units, with their own theatre and intensive care facilities and grouped by commonality of care requirements and not necessarily by clinical speciality

- a multi-disciplinary care-plan will be prepared for each patient, identifying which tests will be performed and on what days

- care co-ordinators will be assigned to patients throughout their stay to ensure that patients' and doctors' needs are met and to monitor the quality of treatment

- care co-ordinators will ensure that all the necessary tests are carried out, the results received, and that discharge planning is started upon admission.

The aim is to provide as much care as possible in an operating unit to ensure maximum utilization of resources and empower care-givers. Patients should benefit as a result of the greater continuity of care and more responsive treatment.

Management systems must reduce undue complexity, which wastes resources and bewilders patients; for example, more than half of all biochemistry test requests are for one basic test – blood urea and electrolytes. In the average hospital this takes 60 steps, carried out by 11 individuals with results being returned within 18 hours. This complexity is damaging to patient care and results in slow turnaround times.

Patient focused-care involves everyone; it is organized around wants, not presumptions or professions and is about being aware of innovation accepting it and seeking to manage it thoughtfully.

We do not know very much at all about how much patients value various initiatives which we have put in place. If we have a certain limited amount of money to spend, should we put it into new treatment facilities or better wallpaper? For example we do not know how much patients value the following:

- seeing fewer people during the course of an average stay

- travelling around the hospital less

- waiting less time for out-patient appointments

- having shorter lengths of stay.

We are taking various approaches to obtain patients' views, including the following:

- interviewing patients and/or relatives

- surveying patient attitudes by asking GPs to ask them questions

- running focus groups of patients

- using standard patient satisfaction surveys.

Two things are of particular interest here. The first is that patient satisfaction surveys highlight a much lower level of satisfaction for the question 'Do you feel your treatment was successful?' than for general questions about satisfaction (which probably are distorted by the gratitude factor).

The other area of interest is that we increasingly believe that we have to assess the views of different patient groups with a similar clinical condition, since overall responses do not tell us much. Patient-focused care is very helpful here since we are for the first time grouping patients with similar needs and values, and considering their care in a holistic way. For example we are asking gastroenterology patients in some detail what they liked and did not like. In the NHS this is revolutionary.

It requires more than ever, a new management style; much less territorial compartmentalization and more focus on common goals. In developing this new management style we have identified a cluster of change themes, all of which are central to the 'learning and changing organization' – in any service or industrial sector. To be where we believe we can be in the future, we need to :

- substantially improve communication flows and use them more effectively

- lead change from the front rather than push from behind

- develop our ability to work together in teams, regardless of professional discipline and levels of seniority

- channel our resources effectively and efficiently to the point of need

- actively push decision-making down to the most appropriate level to reduce bureaucracy and increase quality

- spread best practices and use these to plan care from admission to discharge with the care events being actively managed and co-ordinated across the various departments

- give the patient more control over all aspects of their stay

- ensure the right person is doing the right job with the right training, is clear about their responsibilities, and receives recognition for good performance

- streamline and rationalize our organization and processes

- provide welcoming, comfortable and safe facilities that are easy to get to and find one's way around

- provide all services required by the specialities and improve their location, scheduling and use to provide maximum effect on patient treatment and minimize inconvenience

- develop leadership and management skills in our people.

This is a major challenge to the NHS. We are glad to be leading the development of patient-focused (or integrated) care.

Notes

1   The detailed research data cited here was made available to Brighton Health Care by Arthur Andersen Consulting, and health care workers interested in following this up could do no better than to contact them. See *Transforming Healthcare Delivery*. Andersens Consulting, London, 1993. The data concerning Brighton was internally produced by the preparatory work undertaken there. See Welling SJ (1994) Patient Centred Care – A New Approach in a Changing Environment. Speech to Australian College of Health Service Executives National Congress, Perth, 27 July; and Langan J (1993) Kingston Hospital and Patient-Focused Care. *The Health Summary*, May, 5–6.

This article first appeared in the AT&T Istel Healthcare Magazine *Viewpoint*, 1994, pp. 17–20.

17

Patient-focused care:

or, with one bound is Jack free?

The key challenge is: how can we best manage the total process of patient care for maximum beneficial outcomes, and take what patients tell us they want *really* seriously? It seems clear that patient-focused care is the way that the NHS will now progress, if we really are at last to take service seriously and to focus on what actually happens to patients. This is part of a wider radical agenda which places accountability – and the governance of Trusts – out there, in public light.

Its focus is on outputs, not only on inputs; on costs and benefits; on action being put back in the unit, centred around the team; on really involving everyone – even those in the boiler house. Its focus is on practice and performance; on power, and its changing use; on whose writ will run, and for whom; on organizing around wants, not round presumptions or professions; and on being aware of innovation, accepting it, and seeking to manage it thoughtfully.

Patient-focused care focuses, too, on the core issue of standards: how can we set standards which tell us if we are winning? The pilot projects stress local, field-level, creative initiatives based on a point of view, not on a blueprint. Patient-focused care is a philosophy, for which each of us needs to find or adapt a method and a local practice. It gives a coherence to all that is happening around us – a model of a viable future for service development with the patient's experience the touchstone.

Also it offers positive hopes of fixing the unfixed, and seemingly unfixable, problems, including major adjustments to professional boundaries and relevant (which means flexible) contracts.

But with one bound Jack is rarely free. Patient-focused care *is* a newly minted currency; new NHS legal tender; and it *may* circulate widely. Certainly, it looks like an authentic coinage – offering 'more for less', with the Queen's head on one side and St George slaying the dragon on the other. *Who* could *resist* it? But, as with all new coins, it is met with delight by some yet with proper caution by others. Does it work? Is it the real stuff? Will it really circulate *outwards* from the Chief Executive, for delegated use by everyone down there, who is actually delivering the service?

New coinage. We hold it up to the light. We bite it between our teeth. We hit it on the table. Does it sound right, ring true? We test it in the acid of practice. Some of us bank it. And we hope the new currency will not end up (like Tsarist War Bonds, Leninist Roubles, or even Confederate Dollars) framed in glass in our bathrooms.

It is a very considerable challenge that we have to resolve. Do we trade in it, and will it deliver our values better?

There are many questions. We need to ask how much it is necessary for us to change to get what patient-focused care seems to offer us. How fast must we change? Is it necessary to change everything? What will we do when purchasers bear down on us and insist on finding out in detail what kind of place we run, and what it is like to be a patient with us? Will patient-focused care really help us then?

There are immediate gains from taking it seriously. First, it builds our understanding of what we do now. It encourages lateral thinking about what we do and could do: how we deliver services, and whether we meet the wants of patients and our own expectations. Second, it gets questions asked about the problems of the present organization, and it stresses that it is self-critical organizations which prosper. Third, it prompts the query as to whether patient-focused care will deliver, in practice, the rights and rhetoric of quality in the Patient's Charter. It should, since it is driven by choice, performance analysis and quality. And it is Trust driven, rather than centrally driven. To deliver its benefits, just as with those of the NHS reforms, we need to enable the maximum freedom for provider opportunism that we can maturely negotiate in a tax-based, cash-limited system. We need a world where there is less top-slicing, less secret back-pocket management, more pound notes in purchaser circulation, and the purchaser-provider split maintained right up to the Secretary of State's door.[1] Money-back guarantees? Fine. But we will need access to capital in a sensible system of planning based on business case, please. And let change be driven down the purchaser contract line, *not* down the telephone line to provider Trust Chairmen and Chief Executives.

We each want to do it locally. That is the point of Trusts. We do not want a national fix; we need to make patient-focused care work locally, as, for example, the Central Middlesex NHS Trust have done under the leadership of Dr Martin McNichol, who has made arrangements with clinicians that work. We each want to ask whether we want to invest in patient-focused care, whether it is appropriate for patients in our community and our particular organization. The impetus for change is to ask: does what we do now work well? If not, will this help?

A core issue is outcome data. How do we know whether what we do works? Do we need to change the guard? Dr Stuart Whittaker, of the University of Stellenbosch, has posed these questions and we have to take them seriously.[2] What impact are we having *now* on the health of our communities locally? What impact would patient-focused care have? Will it really deliver health gain, or give us much the same, but for less cost? To get a longitudinal basis of health information over a long time is itself a very difficult problem. Indeed, the whole concept of health-information and of how we interpret it, is in its infancy. Yet both *The Health Of The Nation* and patient-focused care ask you to look at the community in its totality. What factors impact on its health? What tells us if we are winning or not? Do you, before you go for patient-focused care, need to think about these indicators at the start, and to say what would count as success, what would measure what you are doing? We can agree that we need standards which we can use to assess what the indicators are showing us. We know this is very complex. In my view we need to start by measuring what we do now, procedure by procedure, clinician by clinician, and to publish it. We know how to check some of this, and there is a great deal of informal data which we need to formalize.

It takes special organizational characteristics to drive and enable cultural change and service delivery: leadership; staff commitment gained through understanding; the ability to demonstrate that change is in the interests of patients; clarification of the benefits – the 'end vision'; a strategy for overcoming the barriers which retard the introduction of change; a realistic timetable; a competent change project-manager; and adequate and identified funding. A commitment to pace will be critical.

These changes take a very long time, and require a *huge* effort. It takes substantial money, and although money follows innovation will there be enough of it if we all want to do it? And, of course, patient-focused care is just one change competing with many others – *The Health of the Nation, The Patient's Charter, Opportunity 2000, Project 2000*, junior doctors' hours, and Community Care.

Patient-focused care requires, more than ever, a new management style: collaborative, not controlling; involving, not directing; offering real opportunities for the redesign of work and for the organization to learn to listen to patients and to itself; much less territorial compartmentalization; more focus on our common goals.

The change-maker, the team-leader, and the make-up of the team, are all vital. For success, creativity and interpersonal skills are as vital as the professional background of the change-maker. The control of pace is essential, but do we have the change-makers if we want a large number of patient-focused care projects?

What about the staff? How do we present it to them? They are more likely to believe in it, and not to close ranks, if they are secure in their jobs. Is it another threat? We know we want to tackle the low-pay culture. What is *their* incentive to change? Staff will ask how patient-focused care will impact on finite resources and on existing services. It will be necessary to discuss how fixed costs can be delivered more cheaply than now and what purchasers will pay towards the cost (and pain) of change.

Training is *the* key, whatever you decide to do. To make progress we need to see clearly what we are getting wrong; to commit to process-mapping and continuous improvement; to ask staff for their ideas, to listen and motivate. Then we have got to specify what we want in full and open discussion with the staff to whom we offer the training for them to achieve the goals. The NVQ programme is a model. All the analysis generated preparing for patient-focused care shows that the NHS does not use its workforce well – and the reforms require us to manage, even to sweat, all our assets better.

Achieving ownership is essential, if we are to get the changes in productivity, work practice and performance. The issues of the professionals and power are central. How does patient-focused care involve and motivate them? Does it narrow or enhance what doctors do? Does it give some of what they do to others? Is it true that if you have not got the doctors, you have not got the system? How are we going to tackle this? The work at Central Middlesex on changing attitudes and moving away from traditional professional boundaries is both informative and encouraging.

Notes

1 Early in 1993 the debate continued about the so-called 'intermediate tier', and whether the NHS reforms could credibly and properly be implemented if RHAs supervised both purchaser and provider in one building on two sides of the same corridor. In this debate I preferred to be on what turned out to be the losing side. The reduction of RHAs from 14 to eight, the pressure to centralize, the retreat from local pay-bargaining, and the maintenance of Civil Service establishment numbers in the Department of Health reinforce my point of view. It is not a happy picture.

2 Dr Stuart Whittaker, contribution to discussion on the first day of the two-day conference, for the second day of which I took the Chair.

3 Bill Latimer of Arthur Andersen Consulting, speaking on the first day of the conference. The partner in charge of patient-focused care projects and the project leader for the 6 month £300 000 Brighton set-up period. Much of my understanding of patient-focused care is due to talking with and working with Bill, and to discussions with Professor Eric Caines CB, who selected Brighton as the seventh patient-focused care pilot project when Personnel Director of the NHSME. Brighton Health Care NHS Trust makes no mention of patient-focused care in its printed application for Trust status; the project arose from later discussions between Professor Caines and myself. Brian Prytz, then Brighton's HR Director, was influential and able in helping to create the project. Conversations with John Smith, then a Vice-President of Booz-Allen

Hamilton and a leader in patient-focused care development in the USA and the UK, were influential on our thinking, although his then firm were occupied on trial sites elsewhere.

4 Bain J Farris, President and CEO, St Vincent's Memorial Hospital, Indianapolis. One of the leading patient-focused care hospitals in the USA, and custom-designed for it. For the development of patient-focused care and hospital re-engineering, see Ahlquist G, Greene A (1989) *Hospital Mergers:Cure Or Disease?* Booz-Allen & Hamilton, London, and Greene A (1994) Performance, Productivity, and Managing Costs: the Successor to Patient-focused Care. Hospital Process Re-engineering. *The Health Summary*, January, 6–9; (1994) The Successor to Patient Focused: Hospital Process Re-engineering. *Advanced Hospital Management*, 1; (1994) The Lean Mean Caring Machine. *Healthcare Today,* April; with Woods P (1994) Behind The Myths. *The Guardian,* 13 April; (1994) Generic Engineering. *Nursing Management,* 1, (No.1), April; see also Lathrop P (1994) *Restructuring Health Care.* Macmillan, London. Andrew Greene and Eric Caines addressed an evening 'fringe' meeting at NAHAT's Annual Conference, Brighton, 22 June 1994: transcript of main points entitled *Customer Care – Cure For A Sick Hospital,* from Booz-Allen & Hamilton, 18 July 1994. For up-to-date information see the Network Newsletter published by the Centre For Health Services Management, University of Nottingham (prop. Professor Eric Caines), and two workbooks, *First Principles* and *Clinical Protocols,* published by The Centre, June 1995.

This previously unpublished material constituted my opening and closing remarks to the second day of the NHS Management Executive Conference *Patient Focused Approach: Future Directions, The UK Perspective,* which I chaired at Hinckley, Leicestershire, on 9 February 1993.

18

Listening to patients:

a decent proposal

I see my job as being a representative of the patient. I think that is the source of my legitimacy. I want all of our staff to take that view, too. We have been extremely fortunate in Brighton to be selected as one of the two NHS Executive Patient Advocacy pilot sites. We have been fortunate, too, in the support we have had from John Shaw and his colleagues in the Management Executive, from Brian Edwards when he was Chairman of the Patient's Charter Advisory Group, and from Philip Hunt as Director of the National Association of Health Authorities and Trusts. In fact, the idea of the Management Executive launching the pilot studies was cooked up by Brian, Philip and myself over coffee after one of the Patient's Charter Advisory Group meetings on which we served together.

The Patient Access Group which Tim Williamson has led at Brighton has ensured that the question that has to be asked has been put: that is, 'What is all this like for patients? How do we know?'

The Patients Advocacy pilots are typical of the thoughtful leadership and creativity at the cutting edge which is typical of Philip Hunt's leadership of NAHAT.[1] That has been a most important contribution to making the service more patient-concerned. Bec Hanley, too, is a most unusual person and we have been extremely fortunate to have her join us from outside the NHS after a successful career as an advocate in Local Government. For this critical reason: organizations need strangers. They need their vision, they need their energy, they need their independence and they need someone who is constantly asking the question: 'Why do you do it this way? Is it logical? Why don't you change it? Would it then produce better patient care?' It is also the case that the only way we are going to transform service is from the bottom up. Transforming work is about engaging every member of staff, in detail, about what they do. It has been one of the skills of Bec Hanley that she has engaged staff with this initiative.

What is our working definition of advocacy? I cannot improve on the definition which was sent to me by Richard Wiles, of the College of Health:

- advocacy is a term that in the Health context was initially used in relation to certain disadvantaged groups (e.g. ethnic minorities, people with mental health problems) but is being increasingly widely applied

- the principle underlying patient advocacy is that, at the time we use health services, most of us are very powerless (lacking knowledge about alternative treatments, lacking confidence, in an unfamiliar environment, in pain) and are therefore very inefficient consumers. Advocacy is intended to provide people with support that will enable them to act as assertive consumers

- whilst there is an enormous variety of advocacy schemes, the common feature is that they are independent of the staff providing treatment or care, and either enable service users to articulate their own wishes, or provide someone who will speak on their behalf.[2]

In a word, this is all about raising standards and improving performance, and if it is not, we might as well all go home. I have left support and the detailed issues of how patient advocacy works in Brighton properly to my executive directors, but there are however particular things a Chairman can do to help. First, I have made absolutely sure that Bec Hanley gets access to all information, all personnel, all numbers and all data. Some of these are papers that only Board members normally see, some of them that only Chief Executives and Chairman normally see. That has been a relationship of mutual trust and mutual respect, and it has worked.

It has worked without falling into a difficulty that we need to avoid which is this: it is most important that the Patient Advocate is not co-opted into management, and is not thought of as a line manager nor tempted to be one. This does raise the question of how does the organization pick up on the issues that the Advocate identifies that need attention?

The core question is how do we get to manage the total process of patient care for maximum beneficial outcomes? *Provable outcomes,* and to take what patients tell us really seriously as valid and special knowledge; to take *service* seriously, and to focus on what *actually* happens to patients; for purchasers to be good purchasers, whose decisions will stand up to scrutiny and contestability; and for providers to be effective providers, whose customers will continue to support us; acting together in partnership to raise expectations and to raise them a good long way.

In the past, the NHS has taught people to expect little, and then we have delivered it. Are we changing? The test surely is for the individual to be able to answer wholeheartedly and enthusiastically 'yes' to the question 'were you *specially* treated?'. And for the purchaser to give a similarly enthusiastic 'yes' to the question 'did we get the outcome we wanted and that we forecast when we made the purchasing decision?' Part of this is to help change patients knowledge and understanding, and to *learn* from *them* too. At Brighton our presumption is that patient involvement is vital if health care is to be a genuine therapeutic relationship; if services are to be truly patient referential and for this not merely to be rhetoric. We have to test the service by what people say they want and what they tell us in face to face interviews, most effectively in their home. *If* patient involvement is to be genuine, *if* we are to have genuine informed consent, *if* we are to have real understanding, *if* patients are going to be enabled really to exercise choice in a therapeutic partnership, much of that has to happen *before* the clinical episode. Not only after the clinical episode when the difficulties arise.

There is, of course, no simple answer to these complex issues. I think it is most important that we are trying different approaches, but one thing that we have in common is that we are learning to see the invisible hospital. That is the hospital patients have always seen, but managers very often do not – It's always been like that.' 'It's God-given, you can't change it.' 'I can't make a difference.' 'Why are you grumbling – you're lucky to have it.' This is a key question. Maintaining a sense of outrage is essential for all of us. Some of us want to do more. Some of us believe we can do more. Advocacy is one of the ways to give staff permission to try to do more, because it is making the system more transparent. We are getting inside the clockwork. We are seeing how to change it, and we are improving communication which is not about talking at all. The essential of communication is constructive listening. Advocacy adds a new emphasis to that.

Philip Hunt asked me to say why initially I was committed to advocacy as a Trust Chairman, originally in Brighton Health Authority and now in the Trust. The NHS needs entrepreneurs. It needs providers to take quality to the market. We need to enhance the market profile of the Trust. Purchasers must be the top cat. We must make services less faceless and more public. We must challenge the 'I can't make a difference' culture. We must challenge the 'It's not my responsibility' culture. We must challenge 'It's a priority, so I'll put it on the end of a long list'. And we must change a provider-driven service where 'People are lucky to get it, they can take it or they can leave it'.

The environment matters too. The public judges us substantially by whether they get the food they choose and is it cold; whether the ward is comfortable, warm and attractive; whether people are pleasant to them; whether ethnic needs are taken seriously. And, most scandalously, recently the gender bias of service which is intolerable and must change. So we are trying to put, are we not, a purchaser mentality into provider units; to see the invisible hospital and to change it. Together with purchasers, in partnership asking how do we put systems into place to take the patient smoothly and effectively through the service?

What does this do for the individual patient, and for staff? First, it means we are stopping treating individuals as 'done to' objects and we are starting to think about them as individuals. We are correcting, in so far as we can, the imbalance of knowledge and power about the complexity of treatments and we are having a look at medical myths which may or may not be justified. We are improving interpersonal and written communication. We are recognizing that the individual's knowledge is valid and that medical definitions of outcomes are unsatisfactory without a patients' view of outcome. We are emphasizing that maximum accountability to the user and the customer is essential if we are to build a more effective service.

This is all about our moral lives. It is about human issues and commitments. It is about the NHS and public service values. It is about our commercial responsibilities to run effective organizations, to maintain successful employment, and to grow and bring quality to the market. I have a commitment to a preference for being influenced by individual wants. I prefer that to a 164-page Central guideline document, because I think the result is security, successful individual outcomes and both staff and patient satisfaction.

It also puts something else into the system, which I believe we still lack, and of which we need more, and that is a genuine sense of jeopardy: that if we do not perform better the organization is not secure; that customers could go away, and that we have got to sort out what is wrong to get it right first time to meet customer wants – *not* needs (which we presume) but wants (which we discover). Bringing the Patients Advocate into the system has, I think a number of other important messages. First, that outsiders have a value. Second, that they have helped us to find new ways to involve people like Tim Williamson and patient groups. And that we have got to make this really real in everybody's lives: real like their holidays, real like their mortgages, real like their children. *Really* real. Not strategically real or organizationally and theoretically real, but really real in detail.

Patient advocacy reveals a number of other cultural points too, that people who do not necessarily write to MPs, sit on committees, join patient's forums, have a lot to say and need to be helped to be heard, and that giving a voice to the voiceless and a choice to the choiceless is not only to work with the underclass, although clearly they need more help than most. There are many middle-class people who are intimidated and find their Health Service difficult to use.

I do not think we should exclude them either. We want assertive patients and we want to help the naturally *un*-assertive patient, especially. Their knowledge is special. We need more of it. It is a benefit to us all and I think there is an issue of how we encourage the un-assertive patient to speak. Whether they are only credible if they speak inside an organizational framework or whether they can become credible as individuals who say 'I am entitled'. Especially when consumer groups may be rather less successful than they think, and indeed when you look at the CHCs, they vary hugely and not always to the advantage of local patients.

So I think patient advocacy is already producing tangible gains: functional analysis 'Why do we do it this way?'; new management disciplines 'Here's how we can do better'; better communication; better work, and better quality. And it prompts the notion that the possession of clinical knowledge is not in itself sufficient to serve patients responsively.

The emphasis on the NHS being driven only on medical knowledge is itself disenfranchizing, not only to patients but to staff. It also (does it not?) prompts us to ask 'What impact are we having on health status?', and how are we to use audit and outcome analysis at the management level and at the individual clinician level to check what we are achieving? How are we going to get outcomes into the management mainstream?

Patient advocacy has a prismatic role in splitting up the light into its parts. All these catalysts for change are focused by patient advocacy, and this is not about quality assurance; it is surely about quality *control*. Actually getting your hands on real levers with real wires that create real change.

I would like to say a few things about the social and cultural context in which we are asking Advocates to work. Is not this part of a whole shift to the development of the market *as a market*, and of public and service understanding of the benefits that the market can bring? Advocacy is one element, as is the Patients Charter, that asks us to make explicit promises and deliver them. Then there is outcome discussion. Then there is patient-focused care. And, crucially, there is the NHS becoming a purchasing organization which is blurring the boundary between public and private providers. Purchasers are increasingly uninterested in the history and the antecedents of a provider, of how long the buildings have been there, how many have got royal warrants and crests and heraldic signs. They are now interested in what purchasers are actually doing for patients. Who should employ the Advocate? I think advocacy should be an agent of purchasing within the provider. The provider has got to help the purchaser have an agent, to be fully informed and work inside the provider unit to create systems that actually get detailed change for patients, and to ask the question 'What happens to patients when I send them to that organization, and how in partnership can I build systems so that together we can do better?'

If we are to make a distinction between private and public sector providers how would a private sector provider (increasingly attracting Health Service money) respond to that? To get purchasing really moving, too, I think we need purchaser League Tables. We need tendering. We need performance indicators. We need contestability of purchasing decisions. And we need the Patient's Advocate to be a critical link in helping those developments and in testing how effective they are.

All this is to think about the Health Service developing as a market. We have, too, a serious problem in society about welfare dependency. We are achieving an enormous amount through the Welfare State but there are negative problems, too. I do not want the patient advocacy to increase dependency. As Beveridge put it 'The State, in organizing security, should not stifle incentive, opportunity and responsibility'. Let us not move to a situation where people say, not only 'Have you got a good Social Worker?', but 'Have you got a good Advocate?'. Let us use advocacy to build the *independent* patient, able to get more from the system themselves, and not to be more dependent themselves. Patient advocacy should not encourage the notion that our health is the State's problem alone. It is not. It is ours. The individual's health is his or her job, too.

Let us use advocacy to test whether other initiatives like patient-focused care are genuinely patient referential. Do they give patients what they really want? And are we answering questions that we *think* patients ask or are we actually analysing what they *do* ask?

All this, I think, is starting to put the patient at the centre of all that we do. It is saying that we are getting to a Health Service where the State is the buyer of the services and not necessarily the provider of them. The Patient Advocate should surely be a key figure on the purchaser's payroll if we are going to continue to open more doors and more windows than were first thought likely?

Are we really getting changes? We are beginning to grow new sensitivity and a sense of jeopardy. We are beginning to understand that poor service means patients may go away. We are beginning to face the moral issues of delivering better quality and proving it. But do your staff *really* believe that a part of their Trust and its service may be *really* in jeopardy if they do not perform better? That there is no cavalry. That there should be no cavalry. Do your managers *believe* this? Are they *really* changing? Do they *really* believe that a telephone call and a letter and a smile at reception is a customer transaction? That it will really impact on patient care? And really impact on their financial strategy? And do your staff further down the line understand that the way they behave towards patients is a strategic and a financial as well as a moral issue? I do not think we are <u>yet</u> getting enough genuine change. I think we have to encourage it. I want to see more Patient's Advocates. And also I want to see managers responsible for the difficulties that Patient Advocates uncover, to feel the breeze.

It is *not* 'nobody's fault', it is often managers fault. And what is the message to the Health Service when big white chiefs responsible for some of the greatest disasters in public services since the Second World War do not see heads roll. What is the message to Porter Bloggs who is in difficulty over relatively small problems? I think that is a major issue.

Patient advocacy opens a number of substantial issues about how the market is to grow, about how we are to involve patients with choices and voices, about how purchasers are to be assertive (and tested), and about how providers are to respond. If managers do not respond, *they* surely should feel the breeze. Why not let them? I am told regularly, when I want to query the performance of an individual manager, 'Chairman it's a team. It's a *team* we are all in this together'. I'll buy that, but on this condition. When executive contracts come to the end of their fixed term, why not ask competing teams of managers to tender for performance?

Why not ask for competing teams of managers (from both the public and the private sector) to tender for the delivery of the contracts that the organization is winning, and why not hold them accountable for that delivery? To actually say we mean it. We mean it for patients. We are getting to change and you are here to deliver it, and if you do not deliver it, it is very unfortunate but the patients are more important than managers, so 'Goodbye'.

Notes

1 NAHAT has published two reports on the Patient Advocacy pilot projects. See McIver S (1993) *Investing in Patient's Representatives.* NAHAT, Birmingham, 1993; and the same author's second report (1994) *Establishing Patient's Representatives.* NAHAT, Birmingham, 1994. See also Hanley B (1993) *The Patient's Advocate Project: Year One.* Report to Brighton Health Care NHS Trust Board July, and Barnes J *et al.* (1994) *Obtaining the Views of Patients and Carers: Guidelines.* Brighton Health Care NHS Trust, April. 'Inside the clockwork: signposts and icons for change', reprinted in this book (p.143), is of course a commentary on these issues. See also an address by one of the most thoughtful of current commentators, Robert H Sang (1994) *The Ethical Implications of Independent Advocacy.* Report to the Fourth International Conference on Public Service Ethics, Stockholm, July; see also, Wiles R (1990) *Advocacy: Including the Excluded.* Annual Report, West Lambeth Health Authority, Directorate of Public Health, 42–4.

2 Private communication, 20 July 1994. I have taken the opportunity to add this definition to my original text in the hope that it will be useful to the reader.

This article has not previously been published. It gives the text of a speech delivered to the NAHAT conference on Patient Representation at Kensington Town Hall London on 11 October 1993.

19

The Patient's Charter:

a matter of life and death

'Outcomes' – what works, and how do we get it? – has suddenly become a busy word in the NHS. Is it the spark that can finally bring the Patient's Charter alive in the mind of the public?

It is a word that offers vision to justify the struggle over the NHS reforms and to deliver the basic values of the NHS. It has the potential to unite the staff (who generally still dislike the NHS changes), managers (who engage with the process but hardly with quality), doctors (still seen as a vested interest camouflaged by medical mystery as a national interest) and the users of services, who want the best and want to know what that might be and where to find it.

Mrs Bottomley promised an expanded and revised Patient's Charter in January 1995,[1] but is this to trundle along shuffling incremental gains on hospital food, hospital security, dentistry and pharmacy opening hours – all in the penultimate draft – or will it tackle the hard issues of clinical competence, clinical practice, and how we make a real difference to who lives and dies. The Patient's Charter now needs to set tough standards which open up medical practice to scrutiny and comparison on performance.

This would build on what has already been achieved in treating patients as human beings. It has to tackle which doctors lose more patients than others, and why there is such a remarkable divergence between surgeons who are effective and those who are positively dangerous. No English NHS Trust board is tackling this. The unscrutinized expenditure of £260m on clinical audit is not publicly and clearly changing clinical practice. Hospital doctors' sharing of £104m per annum distinction awards is not linked by management to targeted local improvement on outcomes.

The NHS is still not driven by informed choice for patients. This can surely only be delivered by a market driven by knowledge, so that GPs and patients can select which medical team and which hospital by comparing statistics on outcomes.

If there *is* to be a new focus for the Patient's Charter, if it is to come alive in the minds of the public and the staff, it will take political will, a shift in mind sets, and a focus on the management of the performance that matters. For telling the public about outcomes and naming names will make nakedly explicit the realities of public service accountability voiced, but *sotto voce*, in the language of the Charter. We will cease to shelve as 'too difficult' the life or death issues. We will need to extend the principle of facing the customer and asking to be judged, with the insistence on the current scrutiny of outcomes to discover what actually goes on. We can then make progress, too, on improvement – targeted, measured and compared – linked to performance-related pay. This is to shift from a softer trust in 'best endeavours' to Golden Guarantees which put management on the hook and not patients.

The focus on named individuals is vital. For better outcomes are about documenting current processes, subjecting *individual* performance to continuous scrutiny, and ensuring that relationships between processes and ultimate outcomes enhance health status. There is a coherent list of 'quick hits' to hand which would get at individual clinical performance, process management and hard numbers which the public could understand. They would get us to the heart of individual attainments.[2]

First, specialization. Professor John Yates, the NHS expert on hospital performance, has shown that surgeons who operate on at least 50 breast cancer patients a year have better skills and lower complication rates than those who operate on a few only. Deaths of breast cancer patients after surgery vary between hospitals sixfold. Yates' study of 128 surgical teams – one in ten of those in England demonstrates that death rates following all types of surgery vary from one percent to six percent.[3] The Patient's Charter should require all hospitals to publish how many procedures each doctor undertakes each year.

Second, accreditation. We know that changes in clinical practice in response to changes in scientific knowledge are extremely patchy. Most obviously, the gaps in training of those conducting keyhole surgery remain a cause of public anxiety. It should be a Charter standard that every doctor must attain a new certificate of competence every five years.[4]

Third, making sure that patient experience and values shifts services. This can be done using a document which has hospital doctors' fingerprints all over it. The Patient Satisfaction Audit recently established by the Royal College of Surgeons of England and Wales (and so far only supported by eight hospitals), should be a Charter standard on which purchasers require *all* hospitals to involve *all* consultants.[5]

These new Charter standards would create a dual framework of accreditation of people, places and procedures, both at the professional level; and at the level of patients' experience.

There are other measures which could be embedded in the Charter immediately, to give a good picture of individual clinical and team performance and generate targeted improvement, by doctors and general management:

- the time taken from an ambulance arriving at the door of A&E to the patient arriving in the operating theatre
- the levels of secondary infection, unexpected patient recall, repair rates, variations in wound management, length of patient stay, associated with the work of named individual clinicians.

These innovations in Charter standards would open up to scrutiny huge and known variations in practice and results which are unexpected and unacceptable. Better clinical effectiveness is the alternative to measuring the NHS being busy being busy. One policy objective is thus to identify and celebrate 'Dr Up-To-Date', and to discover and re-educate 'Dr Deadwood'. It is also a challenge to GPs, who cannot be exempt from performance measurement.

Notes

1 See the final published version *The Patient's Charter & You*. Department of Health, January 1995.

2 See Devlin BH (1994) Morbidity and Mortality Data. *Viewpoint,* AT&T Istel, 13–16, and his article (1994) 'Prime Cuts in the Body Politic'. *The Guardian,* Society Section, 14 December 1994.

3 See John Yates, op.cit.

4 See my article in *Hospital Doctor,* op.cit.

5 See Meredith P, Wood C (1994) *Patient Satisfaction With Surgical Services: Report of the Development of an Audit Instrument (1991–1993).* Royal College of Surgeons, London.

A shorter version of this piece appeared in *The Guardian*, Society section, 7 December 1994.

20

The 'Brixton' effect:

does the Charter empower patients?

The Citizen's and the Patient's Charter are the inspiration of one man: John Major. Since 1991 they have been focused on the central goal of service quality, but paradoxically, and perhaps understandably, they are only now beginning to confront measures of real quality, and take us beyond the language of rights to the realities of our own psychology.

The Patient's Charter reflects the Prime Minister's background, temperament and his definition of Conservatism. These are the source of its strengths, and of some of its hesitancies. The Patient's Charter is his alternative to privatization, and also to the idea that the only way to deliver improvements is to give the NHS more money. Instead, the challenge is to *think,* to look outwards not inwards, to see with new eyes, to implement change. But does it give patients power to understand what quality is, to help define what it is, and to insist upon it?

The Charter is an administrative solution to the cultural problems of power, provider attitude and the absence of a sense of provider jeopardy encouraged by half a century of patient passivity and individual powerlessness.[1] These cultural difficulties may or may not respond to administrative treatment alone. We need now to test whether or not our services are being measured by the public; whether we give them sanctions to make sure we deliver. This has to be the key test of Chief Executives: that they know the services wanted by the public; that they are close to the customer; that their principal concern is to seek out customers views, complaints and suggestions; that they *know* the services being delivered by their Trusts.

In the public sector the nature of services provided is still not determined by the market. So good service depends on attitude, on organizational support, and on management consciously focused on the customer. We are asked to shift from judgements based on organizational or professional standards alone to customer standards. It is interesting to ask if this is what we look for when we select our Chief Executives, if it is how we find and promote our heroines and heroes. Ask, too, what can you get sacked for in the NHS.

For John Major, by temperament a conciliator, not a mobilizer, the Charter is the consequence of his experience both as a local Councillor and as an ordinary person frustrated and patronized by public services. It is his answer to the question of how can the ordinary person with no social or cultural power and no expectation of being taken seriously hit back, and get a better service.[2]

The Charter marries the concept of consumerism and customer-driven markets with the provision of those services which, in John Major's view, are a fundamental obligation of the State and must remain public services. It is about learning to be open. We must make sure there is no gap between what we say we are doing and what we are actually doing. And also, of course, that what we are doing is what people want anyway.

We need then to be sure that the answers are enforced in changing management processes, with patients' influence brought to bear in a much more structured, and structural, way, not just tinkering at the margins.

The excitement of the public service changes is that they open up the enclosed organization. Here, the key tests are the attitude of staff, the speed of service, the extent of consumer choice and reference, coverage, discrimination of need and effectiveness. The Patient's Charter provides customers with statements about the standards of service, encourages them to evaluate the service by that standard, and says that this is how management will be measured. We need to think more now about how customers use the services, how they evaluate the services, what they want, and whether the Charter standards cover this.

This means that methods of work need to be designed to meet customer needs rather than organizational needs. The Charter has started to appraise what we do, with staff appraised for the quality of their service: their helpfulness, their listening skills, their support. Senior management is realizing that they cannot be isolated by the organizational hierarchy. We are realizing, too, that what the public wants has to be emphasized at the start of the budget process and at the start of policy planning.

As we think about how to develop the Charter, lists of extra promises are only part of it – and perhaps the least important part. Three things matter much more. First, our psychological states, our expectations of what patients can contribute, and our demands upon ourselves. Second, how we think about completely restructuring management roles, orchestrating these and co-ordinating these so that they focus unambiguously on the patient's experience. Third, how we help the staff to deliver change for themselves and liberate the knowledge they have but are not helped to use.

We are still very internally focused; for example, we still believe that going about 'our' business is what is important, not going about 'their' business. Is that what determines how and where we invest 'our' resources? There are fragmented efforts being made for change: patient advocacy;

user groups; better complaints systems; Patient-Focused Care pilots. However executive directors remain boxed in to old-style role definitions, on Boards that are too homogeneous. We need to bring together the clinical and the non-clinical aspects of relationships, to regroup functions and budgets to focus on the patient as a whole person. If we fundamentally believe in greater public influence over the system, we need to bring together all our fragmented efforts in the person of a powerful executive director who invests in developing advocacy skills in Trusts and in the community and orchestrates all our efforts: Charter action, advocacy, literature, complaints. Too often these efforts are contradictory and competitive. this person could be called the Patient Information Director (probably not Communication Director – seen as a 'whitewash' manager?).[3]

This perspective needs to define budgets and staffing, training and management development and shared learning. We need to change the reasons for why a manager is selected and promoted.

We need to use the Charter to change our policies and practices in several ways. Consumer audit needs to be integrated with organizational, nursing and medical audit. We need more thought on what we can learn from patients, and to reconsider the social contexts in which we learn from them. Patients need to help design policies, facilities and practice, as well as programmes in cultural and disability awareness. We began to do this at Brighton by commissioning patients to evaluate our services. Some of the best work is being done in the field of mental health, where they are far ahead of the acute sector. Here, it is only possible to work effectively if professionals listen to what clients say. The necessity to be open with clients leads to finding challenging new ways forward. Working and interacting with people in home settings is where the individual client in any case has more power. They are tackling such problems as inadequacies regarding Community Psychiatric Nursing coverage; the availability and support of people experiencing withdrawal from tranquillizers; more suitable accommodation for people leaving long-stay hospital care; counselling at the outset of problems to help limit their severity. These all challenge us to address our reluctance to talk clearly about the extent to which users are to have the power in taking significant decisions.[4]

We need to look at our own psychology. We need to look at who we want at the top. We need to re-engineer the organization. We need to think about whether or not the user should be at the top.

It is clear that the management style and traditions of public service have been inimical to patient power, to the demands of the competitive market place, and to a frame of mind that gives priority to empathizing with the values of the user of services. If we really had to change our service to accommodate what patients said they wanted, we would have to empower our managers with data to enable a market to function driven by knowledge. Inevitably, there would be challenges to clinical practice and to unexpected, unexplained and unacceptable variations in outcomes. It is much open to question whether acute care could cope. It is clear, however, that the streetwise patient may be the key to better primary care, and it could cope (although Alan Maynard is right to insist that we must evaluate it).

The Charter does not yet tackle clinical quality, nor does it give patients power to chose. Patients cannot yet turn to the Performance League Tables to find out which doctor, which hospital and which procedure to accept. Yet it is trite, tempting and misleading to underestimate what the Charter has achieved; despite the fact that it has focused on relatively 'soft' quality measures. It has shown the service that it must expect, indeed ask, to be judged by external, explicit, published and comparative performance standards. It is obliging scrutiny and the analysis of process, from which ultimately better outcomes will derive. It is mobilizing consumer expectations. It is focused on measurement and performance. It is obliging medical professionals to produce *their* alternatives for what should be measured to test quality.[5] It should extend wherever NHS money is spent – in Social Services and to private sector providers.

Sanctions exercised by patients are still missing. Political management of competition, too, has restricted the impact on quality of the internal market. The fact that a contractual relationship exists between purchaser and provider does not by itself transform these political realities. Indeed, purchasing has been managed (as, realistically, we should have expected) to influence and reflect political reality. The Charter is one of several instruments which are nevertheless importing the best of private sector practice to improve performance: audit, local pay, information on performance, better complaint processes, and the core idea of the citizen as an individual consumer of public services which prompts a new relationship between the client and the provider.

How do we engage the unique knowledge and experience of the user? How do we get both staff and users to help us develop the Charter, to get into it the things that matter to them, so that both staff and users say 'That's it! That's what we want! That will really make the difference.' For staff this means being given the power to deliver what works, and in ways acceptable to patients. We must recognize and address the serious difficulty, that many in the service struggle with a sense of discomfort and dissonance about the Patient's Charter. They see it as a set of external constraints, which fell on them from above, and many argue that it addresses the wrong things.[6] Some users, too, who want a guarantee of kindness, mutual understanding, and the transfer of power and control over what happens to them, appear to feel that the Charter is insufficient. Anecdotally, I have heard the assertion that patients can be 'Chartered' but they cannot be given sanctions and power over effectiveness and acceptability.

All this is only really worthwhile if it improves effectiveness. This gets us to ask fundamental questions about clinical practice and effectiveness. All of our data about diagnosis and treatment must be interrogated along the axis of effectiveness, and guide purchasing. A key issue is how can the Charter be moved on to this territory?

How can the Charter tackle the hard issues of clinical competence, clinical practice and how we make a real difference to who lives and dies? The Patient's Charter now needs to set tough standards which open up medical practice to scrutiny and comparison on performance. We need to empower the public to challenge what happens to them clinically, and to show the public how to use that power when it comes, as my former colleague Bec Hanley has argued.

This would build on what has already been achieved in treating patients as human beings. It has to tackle which doctors lose more patients than others, and why there is such a remarkable divergence between surgeons who are effective and those who are positively dangerous – a serious problem, discussed again in an important new book *The Incompetent Doctor* by Marilynn M Rosenthal, is why doctors do little about this.[7] No English NHS Trust board is tackling this. The unscrutinized expenditure of £260m on clinical audit is not publicly and clearly changing clinical practice. Hospital doctors' sharing of £104m per annum distinction awards is not linked by management to targeted local improvement on outcomes.

The focus on named individuals is vital. For better outcomes are about documenting current processes, subjecting *individual* performance to continuous scrutiny, and ensuring that relationships between processes and ultimate outcomes enhance health status. There is a coherent list of 'quick hits' to hand which would get at individual clinical performance, process management and hard numbers which the public could understand. They would get us to the heart of individual attainments.[8]

The challenge of how to give patients power is perennially puzzling. 'Social marketeers' argue that there can be no genuine user power without the prospect of user exit and market signals. Ultimately, unhappy users need to be able to walk away to an alternative service. Unsatisfactory providers need to be improved or replaced.[9]

The justification for patient power must be not only that he and she who pays for it should be in control, but that an informed and empowered patient can contribute uniquely and fundamentally to the management of their own care: to prevention, to better lifestyle, and to cure in a continuous programme of targeted improvement.

The notion of sanctions is surely fundamental to efficiency and choice, as is incentive. Otherwise, 'empowerment' limited to better literature may be a rhetorical device, a substitute for real analysis and real levers which would give power with regard to the individual treatment available to individual service users. Better literature counts, of course, especially if it both describes a condition clearly and then innovatively offers an assessment of risks, benefits, choices and outcomes open to a patient as the shared decision-maker.

The inertia of social institutions, the power of vested interest is in the way. It prevents the introduction of sanctions. It hinders our ability to focus clearly on the conviction that it is how we manage the choices open to the individual that really matters.

We should be careful not to accept too little. We should be careful not to accept that patients *are* being empowered merely because devices are in place which assert that they empower patients. Patient advocacy, patient feedback groups, patient audit, the Patient's Charter, surveys and workshops clearly offer potential. However, we need to be sure that they are based on real knowledge, on real patients' values, on real patients' experience. We need, too, to be sure that local management has the willpower, the empathy and the flair to make them work. And they need to be tied into incentive and sanction.

Equally, if patients have no sanctions, empowerment will be 'a technique' and it will be insufficient to empower patients. Many managers see too much change around them already, and despairingly remember Wilde's aphorism 'There is nothing old under the sun'.

I have recently proposed two tangible initiatives : first, to convert CHCs into Community Outcomes Councils; second, to develop GP fund holding into patient fund holding and with providers publishing both reliable prices and outcomes data. This would be the clearest possible statement that patients are legitimate players in the system. There is a third initiative that is essential. We need to involve the user in the training of doctors right at the beginning. Most junior doctors' first experience of meeting a patient is when they are asked to dissect a cadaver. They need patients' knowledge and experience to be the focus of their training as well as having clinical knowledge at the core of their work.

The voucher may prove essential. To the public the word 'empower-ment' is meaningless, but everyone understands money. The one thing that would spark public imagination is if the money really did follow the patient, for choice is an individual action, not an aggregate idea. Money, too, may represent what people want much better than 'representatives' can do. Indeed, we should keep in mind Arthur Seldon's formulation here 'The ballot-box says "Look! Benefits galore! All free!" The market says "All our goods are priced. Tax shown separately."'

No-one should doubt that it is power around money that could change the system we have. If it were exerted, the NHS information deficit would have to be addressed. As it is, our present system positively disempowers patients. The patient has little or no power to affect anything in financial terms, nor to influence what is provided. Is this not why many Chief Executives never feel it necessary to meet them? Is this not why in late 1994 there were only eight NHS hospitals supporting the Royal College of

Surgeons' Patient Satisfaction Survey? Is this not why Community Health Council budgets are at the £50 000 level?

What is the future of care? The importance of non-hospital care will increase dramatically. The goals of health care will move away from an emphasis on cure, towards the management of chronic conditions. There will be an increasing appreciation that improvements in primary care are the only locale for the prevention and limitation of disease. It is not only that we need to take a patient-centred approach to quality. It is not only that an approach to quality must be more comprehensive. The fundamental and axiomatic point is that to such an agenda the informed, empowered patient is an essential partner in effective, appropriate, timely, safe and acceptable health care. Clearly, in primary care we can accommodate the streetwise patient. It is going to be much more difficult in secondary care.

The Prime Minister began with attitudes. In addition to cost and clinical effectiveness, this is the pivot of it all. The revolution that is most required is a revolution in feeling, in humanity, in humaneness – honestly driving management commitment. It is this revolution on which the NHS reforms have been muted and on which patients still have minimal leverage despite the achievements of the Patient's Charter and the Performance League Tables. We need to construct the instruments of patient partnership, power and sanction so that the voice that the Patient's Charter has begun to express becomes so insistent that it can only be absorbed by change. It has got to hurt if you do not do it. It has got to mean something if you do it well.

In the presence of these challenges management has responsibilities as well as authority, not least for empathy and intellectual mobility. For the whole future story and the potential of patient power is there to read. The service could let it be, but it will be required to quicken, to focus and to understand why as well as how.

This is not about different structures, or the continuing clutter of 'strategies' and 'initiatives', or about local managers 'ticking the box' and going on as before. It is about our psychological states, perspectives, and the expectations we have of ourselves. It is about how each of us is going to respond, to make a breakthrough, to give our actions *definition* in terms of the patients' values and power. If you like, management needs the perspective of the artist, not only of the engineer. For this is from where empathy is derived, as well as movement. This is where we *participate* in experience, through identification and empathy.

Clearly, a manager cannot be expected to cut off his/her leg to achieve empathy with an amputee, but it is not impossible dramatically to improve our ability to see the service from the patient's point of view. One consultant in a diabetic unit wanted nurses to know what diabetics have to endure every day. He asked nurses to inject themselves in the stomach with sterile water. It is not unknown for a Trust Chairman to visit his own hospital in a wheelchair.

Yet, from the system we see around us, we see how *unpractised,* how *unpassionate,* how lacking in resources and knowledge, management has been asked to be at involving patients; and at how great is the change that is required in psychological states. It is clear, too, how little shape and form there is in existing NHS systems which is at all appropriate to the objective of passing power to patients.

It was Sun Tzu who spoke of a blind musician who could hear the footsteps of a mosquito.[10] Managers, unlike the sightless musician, (as one unusual literary critic has put it) 'need to embark on the painful, frustrating, sometimes excruciating business of discerning the difference between looking and really paying attention – *really* looking.'[11] **This is the crux of the whole matter.** This is the test of the value of any initiative posing as empowerment.

Patients are the beginning. Managers must get themselves back to the beginning. There is a huge change required. They need, as this literary critic has put it in the context of the artist and the muse, 'to look in a mirror of their own making, to see themselves all written backwards.'[12] It is no good talking of empowering patients if the service expects to stay living and working in its existing patterns. Courage and daring is essential, and these will not be easy for those who elected to be consecrated in collectivist security, and who came into the NHS system under the old rules.

The best health care depends on the patient.

- We need to learn from the unique knowledge that patients have of themselves and of us.

- We need the patient to take more responsibility for lifestyle.

- We need the patient to help us assess the quality of health care and the outcome of treatment.

- We need to educate the patient about the real distinction between the effectiveness of health care and the demand for it – the work on shared decision making using interactive video-discs where the call for services has fallen.[13]

- We need to educate expectations, meet genuine need, and manage potentially overwhelming demand.

- We must put out of place, put out of taste, old attitudes. New and old values have to be expressed in practice. Ideas gain their impact in action. We must put in place, and keep up to pace, imagination and empathy, to give reality to choice, incentive, and effectiveness. Unless the organizational conditions exist which favour power over service for the public, all that can and will be done is to alter presentation. If we encourage patients to speak up for change but very little change actually happens, they may fall silent, or find more challenging ways to speak.

Meanwhile, the Oxford political philosopher John Gray offers this comment on our notion that we know best, 'Nobody knows if the most advantageous form of health care is obtained from medical producers, from a travel agent or by renouncing work on the night-shift'.[14]

Notes

1   The background is assessed with exceptional insight in Kavanagh D, Seldon A (eds)(1994) *The Major Effect.* Macmillan, London, and I have drawn on this framework here.

2   Kavanagh and Seldon, op.cit. See also for context Kavanagh D (1990) *Thatcherism and British Politics, the End of Consensus?* 2nd edn. Oxford University Press, Oxford.

3   I owe my understanding of these issues to Pauline Sinkins, and I have drawn here on exchanges between us when we were colleagues at Brighton.

4   On these points see Chamberlain A (1993) Working Towards User-Led Services Through A Mental Health Forum. *Community Health Action, 27,* Spring, 6–9; Sheppard B (1994) *Looking Back – Moving Forward: Developing Elderly Care Rehabilitation and the Nurse's Role Within It,* and *Listening To Patients,* both Brighton Nursing Development Unit, Brighton; Wiltshire Community Care User Involvement Network, op.cit.; Spear S (1994) *The Future of Services for People Whose Lives are Affected by Drug Use.* Report of SEARCH Conference on 10 October, Derby; *Mental Health Services in Pembrokeshire: 'Challenging Preconceived Ideas.* Pembrokeshire HA, Haverfordwest, February 1995; also, Rigge M (1991) Listen and Learn. *The Health Service Journal,* London, 30 May, p.8; and the blockbuster and indispensible report, Hogg C (1994) *Beyond The Patient's Charter: Working With Users.* Health Rights (Brixton!), London. Users need to take part in our major conferences. It was not until 23 June 1994 that a patient (Mr Simon Taylor) was for the first time invited to address NAHAT's Annual Conference.

5   See my article (1994) A Chance to Turn the Tables. *The Health Service Journal,* London, 4 August, p.17.

6   Hilary Pepler, Chief Executive of North Mersey Community NHS Trust, in her address 'Quality And Community Services' to the conference on *The Patient's Charter and Quality,* London, 11 May 1995, ably reviewed the anthropology of dissent. the difficulties she reported from her observations included: figures easily massaged; no ownership of data by doctors, who do not check figures and are dissociated from returns; managerial box-ticking passive – no cultural shift; standards not about hard effectiveness/quality issues; key people unengaged – so not responsible for changing practices; a 'Toryism', and opposed on that basis; acute focused – yet most good patient

work re-engineering services is in community and mental health; paradoxically, difficult to apply the Charter at a time of crisis in the service; irrelevant to culture in which we live unless basic structure of housing in place; no user evaluation of the Charter; not based on staff or patient preferences; not focused on continuum of care/too fragmented; no targets for challenging work – e.g. containment of behaviour which is not responsive to treatment; central monitoring leaves little local scope for a focus on local pressures; GP practice key site – initially omitted; process of Charter development disempowering/did not build relationships; does not contribute to support staff who want to meet the patient need for time to be devoted to them, to ensure continuity of advice and the reassurance that gives; no impact on duplication in the system, nor on need for joint working with Social Services to ensure the same standards are applied there; unhelpful to development of a learning culture not based on blame; PR exercise. See also Bec Hanley, address on 'Clinical Issues', commenting on patient perspectives, at the same conference.

7   Rosenthal MM (1995) *The Incompetent Doctor, Behind Closed Doors.* Open University Press, Buckingham.

8   See 'The Patient's Charter: a matter of life and death', which precedes this chapter.

9   See 'From "Voice" To Sanction' in this book (p.41).

10   Sun Tzu, *The Art Of War.* Hodder & Stoughton, London, paperback edition, 1981.

11   Sue Roe, in Roe S, Sellers S, Ward Jouve N, Roberts M (1994) *The Semi-Transparent Envelope. Women Writing – Feminism and Fiction.* Marion Boyars, London/New York, p.65.

12   Roe, op.cit.

13   Adam Darkins, op.cit. The videodisc programmes really empower patients; their implication for practice on empowerment now requires major British investment.

14   Gray J (1993) *Beyond the New Right, Markets, Government and the Common Environment.* Routledge, London and New York.

This chapter was prepared as the keynote presentation to the conference arranged by Laing & Buisson: *'Patient's Charter – Milestone or Millstone? Patient's Charter and Quality',* London, 11 May 1995. I have added the notes.

The NHS staff

Vladimir   Well? What do we do?
Estragon   Don't let's do anything. It's safer.
Vladimir   Let's wait and see what he says.
Estragon   Who?
Vladimir   Godot.
Estragon   Good idea.
Vladimir   Let's wait till we know exactly how we stand.
Estragon   On the other hand it might be better to strike the iron before it freezes.

Samuel Beckett, *Waiting For Godot* (1955)

Do not wait for the cavalry:

or, what is a Chief Executive for?

What *is* a Chief Executive *for*?

The job of the NHS Trust Chief Executive is to reduce their own importance, and to help the customer in every possible way, by encouraging everyone to define all that they do in terms of what patients say they want.

This calls for the twin premium of both leadership and management, but they are different. The good manager places faith and emphasis on systems and structures. These are shifting sands, as they should be. The leader is intuitive, unconventional, outside systems, inspirational – even colourful. Such a creature is indeed an unusual bird in the NHS, both in the Chief Executive's and in the Chairman's parking space. Yet the old-style Chief Executive needs to become a leader. For leadership has to be shown, and then transferred outwards – especially to managers of clinical teams, where otherwise elusive gains can be made. Leadership is not something that can be uniquely confined to the Chief Executive, nor can it be a private icon. The effective organization is decentralized, and leaders must be developed at every level.

Where are we going to find these leaders? We do not know how to make entrepreneurs – it is not a penny in a slot process. Research suggests that the best leaders have a broad mix of jobs and responsibilities early in their careers, and that they retain a sense of childlike wonder. It may be that we need turnover amongst Chief Executives, to ensure that flair and leadership are rewarded and mere number counting more sensibly valued. Those in the strategic units, the clinical directorates, who need to show the leadership, need support, status, incentive, and reward. For it is at this level that the management skills need to be developed and the leadership empowered. Here, too, we can liberate staff knowledge down below; they know what needs doing but are not freed to act.

Insistently and unavoidably, IT (combining computers and telecommunications) will ensure that the Chief Executive will become less valued as the keeper of systems and structures, but more as the keyholder of leadership opportunities. As the Harvard professor Shoshana Zuboff shows in his book *In the Age of the Smart Machine*, IT does not automate companies, it 'informates' them.[1] It provides workers with access to the information that empowers them to think and to make the decisions they were not able to make before. This changes power relations, the distribution of authority, access to responsibility and the potential of co-operation and partnership in teams. Thus, the 'informated' organization cannot only protect its competitive advantage, it can change its potential.

In Zuboff's world (and yours), top management can no longer sustain a monopoly on information. Indeed, middle managers, whose role was to access and distribute information, vanish. It is at the frontline, where business managers and clinicians are located with patients, that information is accessed and where decision-making is required. Decision-making becomes an *ad hoc* process, actioned by the most appropriate people on the spot. This will not commonly be the Chief Executive.

An NHS Trust seeking to add more value through team-building, will define its strategy in large part in terms of its IT development. Too many NHS Trusts talk mission statement, critical success factors and strategy but stare bleakly into an IT gulf. Information directors are not implementers. Chief Executives talk about truly superior service. If leadership and information access is given to those at the service frontier, it can happen. That is probably the only purpose for which it is worth paying a Chief Executive salary.

The NHS is rarely free of the sound of gunfire. Currently, it is open season on Trust Chief Executives. The highest earners must have felt armour-plated to the tune of up to £100 000 pa. Clearly, we do need executive management, for the NHS needs to manage the £112m it spends every day, even if there is now a hairline crack in the moral ascendency of some Chief Executives.[2] The inflation of Chief Executive salaries has inflated status, and this conceals the fact that many remain marginal to the real management process, which is to shift leadership and knowledge to where it improves service and adds competitive advantage.[3]

The focus on salaries wrongly emphasizes the importance of Trust Chief Executives and of supply-side leadership, too. It diverts attention from the difficult truth that their job is to reduce their own importance.

This is not a synthetic question, nor one linked to politics. The job to be done is to ensure that the service pivots on informed choice for patients in a more developed market driven by knowledge and incentive. This will require very significant changes in NHS management and in the paramount role of the Chief Executive.

Inertia has so far concealed the necessity. The experience of four years of reform indeed suggests that the NHS does not change unless it has absolutely no choice. Top-down political fiat, the visible (ministerial) hand, can shift it, but only so far. The workings of Adam Smith's invisible hand, the incipient social market, will be needed to get the reform job done by government acting as a catalyst for more incentive, competition, and competitively tendered service from public and private providers. Leadership at the middle level is the only model for success.

The prompt is the GP (working alongside the more informed patient) who counts. It is here that we need momentum – not merely a new *modus vivendi* with local clinical colleagues – and development, with the patient as fund holder.

Here is the chance to conduct a daily referendum in a social market on what best care is, where and how to get it. Here is the chance to stop talking about 'reform' and 'structure' and to get as close as possible to a proper market in which individual case decisions on individual days mediate the system and change it. No-one, by-the-by, talks all the time about Marks & Spencer or Sainsbury's being 'reformed'. Individual consumer decisions change them, develop them, and improve them every day. Users do not go to a bad service purely because it is local.

GPs and informed patients in an effective social market will build up a radical front behind local 'effectiveness'. Collaborative consensus, convenience and old patterns of control will not survive.

Provider Trusts will need a much better-educated workforce, efficient technology and capital management, a flexible workforce with much less demarcation and much less division of labour. This agenda will change the balance between managers in the boardroom and managers running the operation. This is where we will see the changed answers to the question 'what is a Chief Executive for?'.

At the macro-level the objective is to sweep away obstacles to better market transactions so the NHS can work much closer to its full capacity, more effectively, and to a lower cost-base.

At the micro-level this requires the efficiency of capital goods and of labour, major gains in the speed and quality of processes, IT investment at ward level and a significant enhancement of the profile and the power of the business manager leading specialist teams in the clinical speciality.

The majority of NHS Chief Executives came in under the old pre-1990 rules. Then, as Matthew Symonds notes in *The Culture of Anxiety: the Middle Class Crisis*[4], they were only 'exposed to competition of the politest kind'. The new rules say that the spending increases of the late 1980s and early 1990s will clearly be unsustainable, yet cost and demand pressures will grow. Executive work and the will to manage will be required for executive salaries. A tradition of administrative progress will be replaced by one of novelty and transformation.

Yet the NHS has only just begun the process of a modern search for efficiencies in its own management structures. Here, as in the wider economy, a white-collar salariat sustains whole functions which are inefficient and which have been made obsolete in flatter, slimmer, focused structures. As good IT yields efficiencies, cost-savings, and access to faster information flows, the consequences include a large query over much of what we now call management.

The necessity to improve the speed and quality of processes means computer investment and many fewer managers. Ward level IT will change both the site and the pace of management. It will produce less standardized, more customer-focused services. It will generate flexibility in working practices, reduce labour costs as a proportion of total costs, and decentralize wage bargaining. It will transform, too, the status and mystique of medical practitioners, as computers take over from guesswork. The management roles that are left, at middle, operational level, will be those that can impact on performance. Co-operation and trust can then be given an incentive to build upwards.

At the bottom of the management structure at present we have the first-line managers, who need to be operationally capable. These are the ward sisters, who blend the skills required to manage the care of an individual patient, with team leadership; the supervisors of medical records, and those managing departmental offices. Then we have the business and service managers, 'in charge' of clinical services (and, why should we always have doctors in charge of clinical directorates?). None of these are really thought to matter. Yet they need the IT. They need to manage the productivity gains. They come between the Board and the frontline workers. Although outside the Board, they are the ones that have to make it all happen. The reward, power and status system is not yet equipping them to do so. They are too lowly regarded and too poorly paid, although often more highly educated and more operationally experienced than their Chief Executive. This is a natural crisis point for the organization, and it is where the contrast between the 'school of soft knocks' Chief Executive (collusion, not conflict) and the go-getter MBA-qualified bright spark is daily evident. This is where the test of change – and its disablement with dotted lines round the system, to suit the doctors if not the business plan – is most evident.

If the service is to pivot on patient values, this is where the prestige and clout has to be located. These business and service managers at service level must, too, be supported in their role of building a cadre of first-line managers and clinicians who evidence management skills, market understanding and the flexibility of effective and adaptable multi-disciplinary teams.

It is at speciality level that better outcomes, productivity and communication is delivered. This means people who listen and ask the right questions, with sound business knowledge who can build co-operation and mutual understanding.

The successful delivery of this agenda might just equip existing executive teams to succeed when the entire process of Trust management is market tested. When this comes, bids can be expected from a mixture of private and public management teams. Business managers as a group can be envisaged as breaking into the boardroom to win these contracts. For the requirements will be clinical effectiveness, cost-effectiveness, shifted risk, and the ability to marry the model of thought ('we need to do this') with method and desired result. Leadership!

What is a Chief Executive for? To change the nature of the workforce, to reduce management numbers, to customize specialist services, to increase the efficiency of capital goods, to generate the data for outcomes analysis, to shift the initiative and power of decision to the operational manager – and to reduce the importance and the cost of the Chief Executive.

In addition they need to recall that they are public servants, and not members of a sub-culture. Their major role and justification may not continue to be control, but it will be to work outside their walls to help carry the public with us in supporting change. Not everyone who came in under the old rules will be able to adapt. As this becomes evident we will need the skills within the organization to enable those who have served well to exit with dignity.

None of this is political. Indeed, Chief Executives who are allergic, or even mute, will not be bugled to safety by the Labour cavalry.[5] The frontier has already moved.

Notes

1 Zuboff S (1988) *In the Age of the Smart Machine.* Basic Books, New York.

2 See *The Fitzhugh Directory of NHS Trusts, Financial Information.* 3rd edn, 1995. HCIS, London. Also, see Brindle D (1995) Spending Up £1bn. On NHS Bureaucrats. *The Guardian,* 6 February, and, by the same writer (1995) NHS Spending £78m. On Cars. *The Guardian,* 17 February, commenting on figures released by the Department of Health. The indefatigable Alan Milburn MP has consistently prompted the release of information on the costs and functioning of the new NHS.

3 We are not managing basic processes, for which Chief Executives are also employed. See, Audit Commission report, *The Doctor's Tale,* op.cit. For a positive view of possibilities see Smidt L, Andrews S, Turner S (1995) Bringing Clinicians into Management. *British Journal of Health Care Management,* **1**, (No. 1), 24 March, 24–6.

4 Symonds M (1994) *The Culture of Anxiety:the Middle Class Crisis.* The Social Market Foundation, London.

5   As mandarins and managers hoped prior to the 1992 General Election. See John
    Willman, op.cit.

An initial sketch of this paper appeared in *The Guardian* (Society section), 1
March 1995, under the title selected by a sub-editor 'Time for Fat Cats to Diet'. I
have restored my original title, and expanded the argument. See also, my lecture, Is
the Job Working? The Trident Trust annual conference, Swanwick, Derby, 26
April 1995, forthcoming in conference proceedings, 1995.

22

Designing a new doctor:

making medicine fit for patients

What kind of doctor do we want and need for the future? How should the selection, socialization, training and employment of doctors change to meet future need?

The future of health care is about chronic sickness and community medicine and enhanced patient management of their own care. We need to select and design doctors who will help us achieve this.

We need to debate what is the optimal policy which will give us the most competent General Practitioner, and the complementary clinician. Both need to have been out there and done it.

If we mean what we say about community medicine, I believe it is time that we structured training, incentive and status to reflect that objective. No-one should be appointed as a consultant until they have served a minimum of three years in General Practice. Yet in the profession the doctors who can deliver that are held in least esteem. It is only recently that there has even been a Royal College of General Practitioners. Doctors love status (especially when it is quo); the GP is still viewed by many consultants as the urchin who sends in the coal to the manorial fire.

Power and authority, within the profession and in wider society, is the prerogative of the consultant – hardly affected at all by NHS management, or even much by the GP fund holder. One consequence is that we continue to train consultants in ways which countermand our community messages.

It is perfectly possible to become a consultant without spending any time meeting the hard knocks of General Practice where 80% of health interventions take place. Yet, curiously, the place where most of the work is done, and, probably, most effectively, has the least status. The isolation of the consultant from the stressed reality of GP and patient alike is the cause of intractable problems: arrogance and rudeness, inability to relate and to communicate clearly to 'ordinary' people. All these issues show up in the rising shoals of complaints that we net. Ways to help doctors achieve empathy would have another helpful consequence: they would become better team-players, and the notion that a team to a doctor is 'me and my juniors' would recede.

The GP is the Jack of all trades, yet his trade is not well known to his hospital colleagues. The hospital doctor should be master of one, and that is his disadvantage. Closer working between the two is an outcome devoutly to be wished. This would be a caucus race in which everyone had prizes.

By the time a GP is appointed into practice he is inevitably already at risk of losing touch with hospital advances which, of course, occur rapidly. But there is one advantage that the GP never loses: he cannot hide from patients. The consultant is a past master of transferring problems to the House Officer and Registrar or back to the GP. The GP has to sign the sickness notes and know the family background, psychological, sexual, and social history of the patient.

Each needs to gain from the knowledge of the other. First, for the GP there would be clear benefits from closer working between the GP and the hospital. The GP would be kept in touch, by an integrated programme of training and development requiring time to be spent in the hospital in rotation where they would keep up to date (they *are* up to date there, aren't they?). The pressure on emergencies, caused by them, could be alleviated by them. The results in Brighton showed me that appointing GPs in A&E reduced admissions to beds and curtailed our drug bill. The GP relies on good diagnostic skills, as well as their intuition, empathy and listening skills. They have much to teach the potential consultant. On rotation in hospital, the reciprocal gain would be to maintain their diagnostic knowledge.

Closer mutual understanding between GP and consultant would impact, too, on admissions and referrals, with the improvement of communications prior to admission. Unnecessary admissions would fall. Indeed, if the GP felt the consultant more approachable (and available), home-care supervised both by GP and consultant would improve. In chronic cases, such as in the care of diabetics and asthmatics, lengths of stay would shorten and admissions be avoided.

For the potential consultant, there will be much to learn, not least about themselves. And there is nothing like experience to make you change the way you behave. Knowledge of the common GP experiences – how do I get that SHO to answer his bleeper so that I can get that child admitted? What has happened to Alice Peardrop? Has she been seen? Why haven't I been told? – would generate a very different frame of mind. It is as sure as mutton that working practices would tighten up if consultants had felt the other edge of the blade.

All this is about exposing consultants to the ordinary life problems of patients. We know that for many consultants 'empathy' is a foreign country, infrequently and inconveniently visited. The Audit Commission report *What Seems to be the Matter: Communications Between Hospitals and Patients* (1993) is on few consultant bedside tables, devastating as it is, or because it is.

The arguments based in clinical effectiveness, cost-effectiveness and convenience nicely coincide with the community imperative. Why should the profession resist it?

Well, they want to hurry up to become consultants (and to be followed home by John Yates!) Private work remains a complication, as do merit awards. The first needs to be managed by the employer Trust; the second should be restructured as a system of open peer review which relates performance specifically to local performance improvement targets for effectiveness. Competent performance as a GP should be part of the junior doctor's reward structure.

What would be the impact on careers? This change would temporarily slow down the number of consultants coming through for appointment. Not entirely a bad thing. The answer would be more European-trained doctors, more use of Staff Grades, more analysis of other ways of getting the work done. Such a change would press forward other necessary changes. At worst, patchily, there would be a short-term problem which might impact on waiting lists. The trade-off would be a better product.

Women would surely agree, for, if some careers were slowed down marginally, others would be enabled to happen. We might correct one of our most intractable problems: the continuing shortage of female consultants. The clinical and personal bias that hinders female careers damages patients. We know that in 1980 9.7% of consultants were women, and the 1994/95 target is still a meagre 15%. In key specialities such as obstetrics and gynaecology – essentially, about women and their bodies – 87% of consultants were male in 1990, and the number of female senior registrars (or tomorrow's consultants, maybe) increased by fewer than five a year between 1985 and 1990. Service as a GP as a pre-requisite for a consultant appointment might bring more women forward as consultants. They could plan a family while in GP practice in the full knowledge that they could expect to rotate from SHO to GP, and eventually to consultant, in an extended and enriched training.

This structure would, too, give both taxpayer and trainee other gains. It would help young doctors make sure they are making the right choices. It is an expensive diversion when a doctor trains through to registrar level and then 'drops out' (as hospital doctors say, so revealingly) to become a GP. Applications to medical school (which are falling) might increase, too, if the prospect of a career reinforced by GP practice offered a more satisfying life.

We need to increase the supply of medical graduates, in part to increase competition and choice. We also need changes in the profile of skills and expertise available if we are to meet the need for a rapid service shift towards primary care in all its forms.

If doctors, too, are to accept their responsibility both to manage and be managed, there are other things to do. There is a separate case for the temporary outplacement of NHS managers and doctors into industry (which itself would bring into hospitals unsocialized and questioning skilled people, albeit on a temporary basis). Both managers and doctors should expect a five-year review of their management skills and their personal development. Management courses are, of course, all about *personal* development (as well as acquisition of knowledge and skills) which is the area where many doctors need most help. We need, too, to think about the problem that doctors (who do not respect other peoples expertise unless they too are doctors) may return from management courses newly equipped to be unmanageable. The shared, and sharing experience, of residential training may be an important element in change. Block release of managers and doctors together to study for MBAs is another change, but not for another day. The family commitments of women doctors and managers would be a challenge that must be met by the service.

It would be an impressive (but at present unthinkable?) achievement if NHS doctor-managers and manager-doctors were to be head-hunted as Chief Executives by major national and international companies. So, too, NHS Trust and purchaser Chief Executives, who might be replaced as vacancies occur through head-hunting by incoming top managers from blue-chip companies themselves seeking career development.

The clinical skills of doctors should in any case be subject to a five year re-examination, which could coincide with their five year rolling contract. An effective consultant, who does what works, is, of course, important. The dismay of boredom, from pursuing a single-track career for so long, might be diluted by diversity. They might, too, be more effective as doctors, as colleagues, and as people if they got there five years later at 40, but had a richer life experience. For the issue for consultant and GP – and *always* for patients – is not how the race is run, but what you gather on the way. If we took more notice of the journey (and if doctors changed railway carriages regularly), we might have a much more effective health care service.

And that is the terminus of all our journeys.

Note

The ideas in this chapter were first sketched in a speech called 'What Seems to be the Trouble, Doctor?', to an IHSM Yorkshire/Northern Region conference, Bradford, 1 April 1995, and in 'Training Should be More Diverse', *Healthcare Management*, 7 May 1995.

23

Managing the future:

or, fire down below

Why put a Chairman 'in charge' of an NHS Trust, or a big Health Authority, who knows nothing about the Health Service?

This question is prompted by the NHS Executive briefing issued on Valentines Day, on the new appointments procedures for NEDs. This guidance states 'Sifting will be based on merit against agreed criteria to ensure that the right people in terms of qualifications and experience will be appointed'.[1] As we struggle to make the link between patient preference and all that we do, it is clear that there is room for discussion about these criteria, and what counts as appropriate experience and point of view.

Perhaps there is much too much emphasis on NEDs, their training and development. Indeed, they may be more effective if they are pushed back, not forwards. When they become too involved many go native, talk like doctors, and, therefore, fail to offer the benefits of independence and patient perspective for which they were chosen. We should *maximize* their involvement to 20 days, not minimize it. Indeed, the future lies not with NEDs, nor even with prominent Chief Executives, but with a generation of young managers now looking for leadership. It is they who can, and should, deliver the cultural changes which are essential if the Health Service is to be generally responsive to patients, and if it is actually to have the will to manage.

It is clear that this new young generation is arriving. During the past six months I have met many young managers in different parts of the country. The new material for the next decade is clearly knowledgeable, committed and understands the dilemmas of public policy. Most clearly, they want to be motivated by seeing their Chief Executive confronting problems at specialty level. They do, too, look to their Chief Executive to bring young managers forward in the system. Essentially they look to see issues resolved at specialty level, which is the only place to do it.

They have the spark, the energy, the optimism and the patient focus. They are knocking on the boardroom doors, and many are of a high intellectual calibre and educational attainment.

This 'Third-in-line Mafia' want to be prepared when asked, and they appreciate the need to think about how to function at Board level, and how to help deliver change and a better service outside the Board as operational managers. The shrewdest among them are aware, too, of the risk of making their bosses nervous!

I have been fascinated by the questions young managers raise for discussion, when they have an opportunity to meet an NED. First, it is striking that they feel that it is a major weakness that Boards remain isolated from the organizational tier below – as one researcher, Dr Adrian Turrell of the University of Nottingham, has recently emphasized.[2] They seek to prompt Boards to ensure that the organization understands what the Board is about, the performance it seeks and why, but many have suggested to me that Boards are not responding. They have raised, too, operational questions which I had not heard Board members raise: for example, 'Why can't patients go directly to a Consultant, rather than to a GP?'.

It has several times been put to me that the role of the Chairman is not understood, 'Why put a Chairman in charge of an NHS Trust, who knows nothing about health issues?', I have been asked. Here are the 14 main questions that young managers have raised with me recently. I have collected the questions they said they would put to their Chairman or to an NED, if they had an opportunity. The questions come from business managers, associate directors of HR, locality purchasers, operational planners, nursing managers, communications and mental health service managers and some young GPs.

- What have you and your Board done to improve patient care that would not have happened without you?.

- As Chairman, what would you consider a resigning issue?

- How many people have been sacked for poor performance, and were any of them doctors?

- If you sat down for lunch in the staff canteen, how many staff would you recognize and would they recognize and speak to you?

- Who do you consider to be the shareholder in your organization, and how do the NEDs represent their interests?

- What actions do you take to verify that the information you receive is accurate and appropriate?

- What measures do you use to evaluate your own individual performance?

- Why do you not publish improvement targets for each individual clinical discipline, and tie these to the performance contracts of the Chairman, Chief Executive and top clinical staff?[3]

- How would you reconstitute your Board to enable it to make a greater contribution to the effectiveness of your organization?

- How would you like to select NEDs in the future (and what happens in reality)?

- What was the last *specific* thing you changed which meant that a patient had a better experience? And who are the patient's advocates on your Board?

- How do you ensure that the views of all staff are engaged in the management process?

- What difficult issues, such as the apparent non-fulfilment of their NHS contract by some Consultants, are not being managed by the Chief Executive, and why?

- If a good Chief Executive can run a Trust well for a salary of £60 000, what is the justification for someone in a comparable NHS Trust to be paid much more? What should the NEDs do about this?[4]

In conducting seminars and in the consulting I have been doing, I have asked colleagues to reflect on another cluster of questions. Here they are.

- Where do Chairmen get their information, and how does the avoidance of knowledge pass up the chain to the top?

- Is the Chairman's main job to be reappointed?

- Are Chairmen managed down the phoneline or down the purchasing line?

- Is it a gain or a loss if the Chairman and Chief Executive 'think as one'?

- Is it okay if the Chief Executive is 'happy' with his Chairman?

- Who manages the Chairman?

- Who manages the Board Agenda?

- How can Chairmen use 'opening remarks' and 'any other business' at NHS Boards to best advantage?

- Do some NEDs avoid information, as they know they are supposed to be responsible for it?

- Do NEDs really shape the organizational vision that underpins strategy, and is it really credible to argue that they form strategy?

- How do we monitor the performance of NEDs and Chairmen?

- How do NEDs monitor the performance of the Chairman?

- How does the Board monitor its own performance?

- Would the Health Organization run perfectly well without NEDs?

When did *your* Board last ask a series of questions of this kind? What would happen if you compared the answers with what middle managers would produce? Is it a requirement to ask questions of this kind and to answer them, just as it is to advance managers who can deliver answers? If we do, we will sustain the NHS in two contexts: first, its place in the nation; and, second, its meaning for the individual. Meanwhile, the historical process has a nasty habit of not stopping.

Managers who still believe that change will go away will be discomforted by the notion that there are many young managers who hope that it will not. Boards who do not want to know, may be in for some electrifying surprises.

Notes

1 NHS Executive, *Appointment of Chairmen and Non-Executive Directors to NHS Authorities and Trusts – Guidance on Appointment Procedures.* Leeds, February 1995.

2 See Adrian Turrell, op.cit.

3 Echoes of Brighton!

4 See *The Fitzhugh Directory Of NHS Trusts*, op.cit.; Brindle D (1995) Salaries of Health Chiefs 'could pay 11,000 nurses'. *The Guardian,* February, and Durham M (1995) Hospital Chief Costs the NHS £150 000 a Year. *The Observer,* 1 January.

This is a new and previously unpublished piece.

24

Games our mothers
never taught us how to play

What are the new opportunities for our patients and staff that come into focus as we learn more about the working relations of men and women in the NHS? What is it about our existing culture, rules, and styles of work, which we discover as we look for different ways of seeing, hearing, and feeling? What are the radical options and priorities, and how can a District make progress?

How can men and women act together to change the culture that damages both men and women, to deliver more responsive services and to work with new triggers like the NHS Career Development Register For Women, to help us study the actual inside operations of the system? How can this help us insist – *insist* – upon changes to improve the services where, how, and when they want them, not least to reduce the clear bias against women in our medical services?[1]

First, I need to call on your imagination. See in your mind's eye your copy of the *Health Service Journal.* Imagine the following job advertisement (written in code, of course, like rather too many NHS job advertisements).

What does all this signal? It encapsulates many private codes and it sets many rabbits running. In the long alphabet of required cultural changes in the NHS its encoded messages severely challenge us.

First, to ensure that we genuinely give opportunity to all at all levels; valuing all a woman does, at work and at home. Second, to say that women who have managed a home should not only see this as a proper qualification, but boast about it on their CVs and be valued for it. Third, to change the way men think about how they work. Fourth, to revisit our so-called 'objective' and 'rational' definitions of 'best candidate', 'authentic career path', and the suspicious word 'qualified', which is both an adjective and often a euphemism – usually for a detail of the male anatomy. If we do all this, the emphasis on career continuity will take a knock, as should our prevailing methods of advertising, selection, work habits and promotion.

Manager Wanted

Essential qualifications completely open with people, to assist their informed choices. Patient-centred. Believer in the value and possibility of change, actually delivered. Able to manage conflicting demands and dilemmas. Sense of humour. Team builder. Able to manage money. Warm personality. Modern management style – a facilitator, not a controller. Creative communicator in ordinary English.

Conditions fast-track development; family friendly parenting policies; interview by psychometric approach; senior managers closely accountable for actually implementing patient-centred policies.

Would especially suit person over 35 with proven management skills tested in management of a home, children, or elderly dependants. Male returners who have sat in out-patients regularly with three hungry, screaming children (and shared parenting over period of years) also considered.

Apply New Culture NHS Trust, Caroline Langridge Avenue, Richmond House, New Town.

'Striving for equal opportunities at every level'.[2]

We are committed, or are supposed to be committed, to serve patients better by redesigning services to give patients what they want, where and when they want it. We are supposed to be committed to motivate, to inspire confidence, to value all our staff. We are supposed to want to manage everyone in a way that is motivating to *them*, so that we endorse staff values and release the extra 10% – the willing smiles. By valuing them, we help them value patients.

It is not only women on the staff who need more women to come forward into senior posts. It is patients who need more women to come forward, so that we put in place and endorse compellingly different ways of thinking how to respond better to the patients experience. We need to give more women real power and help them see the career track; to make it work in their own way as well as helping them see what is it that works for men. This needs to happen without them becoming men. Yet our selection processes still limit and exclude many women who are highly educated, dedicated, competent and with the necessary professional qualifications, together with the enabling and intuitive skills traditionally and perhaps patronizingly dubbed 'female'.

For this, essentially, we need a revolution of ideas in which both men and women believe. To develop a new blend of the best of male and of female abilities, as proven by examination (objective?), in a new management style. This needs to be innovative; neither male-macho nor feminist-triumphalist. To help us genuinely treat every patient as a unique individual, we need more true friendship, more mutual caring, more sharing at work.

We are, all of us, involved in this. We are in a compelling situation, for the NHS is suddenly catching up with social reality, with what has been happening in women's minds, and in patients' minds too. There *has* been a great deal of unsystematic advance, yet in many work situations these cultural issues remain unresolved, and often unarticulated. As we seek to move forward we are fortunate in our national leadership, which is in itself an inspiration. We see powerful role models, yet none is a bully, none a token, none a triumphalist. Instead, Caroline Langridge and others are calm, strong, competent, reassuring, communicating, facilitating.

There is, however, a genuine gap between what is possible and what is being achieved locally, although the new statistics given by Baroness Cumberlege (which show more women in management) are very encouraging.[3] But there are still problems of culture, not least in how men change men, and my image persists of the beautiful moth in the jar, vainly beating its wings against the glass. We are all in the jar, male and female. It is labelled male culture. The problems are cultural and cognitive, observational, and programmatic. If the first measure is in the numbers, the challenge is in cultural change, in identifying new destinations (new ways of seeing, feeling and thinking) which can only be reached by men and women acting together.

One word about individuals. We should beware of treating concepts like 'cultural change' and 'organizational change' either as dialectical or as McKinsey structural abstractions. We are talking about real flesh and blood people trying to live real once-only lives, and they and our patients are hurt by cultural sexism and the organization of work that reflects it. So managers who can contribute to change – and if they cannot, why are they employed? – need to keep a real face in their minds eye, like the young nurse (in this case female) who is deeply committed to her profession, who loves her partner, who knows they cannot survive without two incomes, who wants children, who knows she has got to work but who wants to work differently for patients. Her stress, dilemmas, anxieties are *our* job – on her behalf, on behalf of the organization, on behalf of the patient.

Equally, Chairmen and Chief Executives should not wait for 'the service' to change 'the culture'. this is the *individual* responsibility of each of us. The problems are not 'nobody's fault' or 'somebody else's fault'. They are ours. Each of us, at our own desks, in our own working practices, in our own assumptions, in our expectations of ourselves, of our colleagues, and of patients. We each need to see how we can redesign jobs, working methods, approved styles, rewards, selection and promotion. Men will not inevitably vote for this, like cats voting for tin-openers (in Christopher Filde's delicious phrase).[4] Yet, as Margaret Vissard says in her new book, *The Rituals of Dinner*, we all seek to be a diner, not a dish.[5] Women are not seeking a special dispensation. Men should not seek – stooping – to make changes 'to help the poor women', but to embrace new ways of seeing to improve their own lives as well as to improve services, while shifting their relations both with colleagues and with their own work. They do not need Julia Kristeva[6] or Mary Daly[7] on their bedside table for them to agree to that.

Equally, women should not think blaming men for the culture they were born into will work as a strategy for persuasive change, nor that men will disappear through a politically correct trapdoor, for they clearly will not. Instead, the effective operation of the new and dynamic internal market which brings greater choice is a better bet than sexual tribal warfare. The bonds of change are strongest when they are put in place by willing co-operation. The practical discussion this requires does, however, ask of men that they think, observe, query, and reflect much more about their own situation – all this under an insistent central spotlight, which the new *Register* in part represents.

I am a relative newcomer to the NHS, but much of this has been going on successfully in liberal, capitalist, private companies like mine, few of which make much room for the socialist and collectivist thoughtlessness which guides large numbers of NHS managers. My own companies had such family friendly policies like encouraging the employment of married women from 10:00 am to 3:30 pm in school term only (with some paid holiday, too) 22 years ago. Male roles were queried, too. I am proud to say that my deputy Chairman and finance director was a woman, as was half of the main board. None of my senior female colleagues were seen as surrogate wives at work; although I see this assumption around me in the NHS.

So I am not a ticketholder on a bandwagon, nor a subversive incendiary, but a tribune from the Keep Calm Party – an enthusiast, a pragmatist, and arguing the ecumenical doctrine that men and women must act together to reach these goals of cultural change. Jointly and severally they need to share an understanding of the games your mother and mine taught us how to play. Its rules are understood by men from an early age: how to see the track ahead; who counts; approved ways of working; how to foresee consequences, with an understanding of how and why the game works and how to live with its consequences.

We have gone a long way (but not far enough) in encouraging women to come back to work, to keep their hands in, to participate, but generally only at lower levels. We are not yet welcoming, reinforcing, or adopting for ourselves female ways of working with patients. We have not yet, in real numbers, seen women go forward beyond essential, but basic and low level jobs, into positions of influence, of power, and of management leadership, despite the fact that there *are* very visible, distinguished and successful women like those here on the platform today. We hear a great deal about flexible working. This helps meet the first need in encouraging women to stay with us or come back to us but it does not and will not necessarily *ensure* the second need is fulfilled. That is, that men change and that we transform management to transform what happens to patients.

Only cultural and organizational redesign is likely to do that. This would help us change everywhere: lower down, where the service is actually delivered, but also at the top where our true values are symbolized. As we bump up against the limits of what we can achieve by providing necessary better facilities (such as creches), we will, I believe, find ourselves looking hard at the radical options, to *ensure* that we deliver the patient-centred service.

The core of the radical option for cultural change seems to me to be encapsulated in three things.

- In working practices, management style, and in what we reward.
- In the need to treat childcare as a parenting issue, not as a 'woman's issue'. Within present cash limits even we must make maternity care leave much better, and not only for women.
- In encouraging a blending of the best of male and female styles, and rewarding equally those who demonstrate the blend.

The impact on the structure of work and on pay structures will, inevitably, be substantial, difficult and complex. It may not come swiftly, but I believe it must inevitably come. Let us look at these areas.

First, the working practices and management style we reward. Take just one thing, performance review, who is ranked highly? Is it the male achiever, hacking it, cutting it? Or is it the personal facilitator, the team-builder, the builder of corporate success? Who *should* be most highly ranked? We need to synchronize the structure of reward with our policies for working to build the healing environment, by celebrating facilitators, by bringing them to the top. Notice that some male managers think that if they listen to these ideas ('women's ideas'), Grace Jones will suddenly come bursting through the wall.[8] It should not be like that, but we have to find ways to help them change. It is about opening up in *both* sexes the human skills of intuition, of team-building, of the ability really to listen (*really to listen, not merely wait to spot a chance to speak*), and to build negotiating skills in women and men so that people-centred qualities are the core values. Crucially, the ultimate issue is about what we judge is good health care, and how we manage it better. So change on 'women issues' is not a fashionable bolt-on. It is a key strategic shift.

Second, in the enquiry about the radical option for cultural change, is child care as a parenting issue. Men face the certainty that they will not get pregnant, women that they might. This is a critical unknown in women's lives, and is a fundamental factor in stopping women seeing the clear career track. For men, it is not a problem. When declared a father they assume more support, not less. Much of our organizational culture and our working practices starts with that idea. Most of the changes needed are about addressing, finding, introducing and auditing the alternatives to it.

In a sense, men can hide in success, but who pays the price of that success? Men do. Women do. Children do. Patients do. Each in a different way, but there is a price for each. And it is women who, almost exclusively, have to balance the demands of family and job – and, incidentally, whose heart attack and stress rates are going up.

Men pay a different price; for example, a senior editor in my publishing firm said to me ten years ago, at 7:30 pm one evening (when I should not have been there, either!), 'I'm not going home yet. The children are still up.' Men exchange closeness and 'being there' for seniority and power. In industry, many become strangers to their families, and, when they are made redundant, what have they got? Those years never come back.

Third, the radical option is all this stuff about new ways of seeing, feeling and thinking. The patient's experience, the 'invisible hospital', really believing in *guaranteeing* that we do it right first time, every time. To encourage the best of male and female skills, we surely need a mutual transfer of skills and styles, and the abandonment of the inappropriate (which include only working in the office, and the obsession with long hours). To deliver the patients agenda, we do need a sense of direction. Let me beg some questions – feet on the ground, male if you like. Intuitive, enabling management, less emphasis on 'control', female, if you like. Each of us needs the other. Patients need us both.

If we are to deliver the care that we hope to make effective, and that patients should have, we must turn women's abilities outwards, not inwards. Women, motivated by their value systems, often hide them at work. That problem has got to be recognized by the system, and space created. We need a big drive from the centre to get these issues embedded in contracts, and to think how we can manage changed processes down the purchaser chain. So, is not the big issue that of how do we switch our cultural outlooks to think in detail about what clinical quality and the management of the patient's experience means for patients and how we reshape roles at work to improve the experience of our service? Reshaping roles at work is an immense challenge, and it will affect men and women both at work *and at home*, where many of these issues and stresses arise in an intensified form. Men will see much that they have worked for challenged, both at work and at home. Advantages and comforts threatened/paradigms queried which have served male interest at work and at home. It is clear that it will not be easy to be heard, yet NHS boards need to develop action plans to address and overcome a status quo which hinders the best patient care, and we should keep in mind the words of the New York critic Erving Goffmann 'Infractions make news.'[9]

This conference is evidence of the new surge of energy and the search for creative innovation – and cultural understanding, as well as self-knowledge – released by the NHS reforms. Yet change has hardly begun to seep into the critically influential sub-cultures of the professionals, into which cultural burglars like me find it so hard to intrude. We have only just begun to move an organization that was made by and for men; one in which any woman needs great confidence and persistent support if she is to seek to shape it. This is especially so for those women driven by intrinsic satisfactions and not mainly by power, fame, or money.

The NHS is not a tin toy wound up by extreme theory. It needs ideas that work, which will help us now to start to shift the culture, but it must test and think about ideas that are offered to it with a different definition of what that 'work' is to be. The practical issues for Chairmen and for Chief Executives is to embrace the radical options I have described, and only then to take refuge in the practicalities by asking 'What works? Where do I put the effort?'

My understanding of my role as Chairman at Brighton is that we need an action plan focused on real outputs defined as changed working structures and changed mentalities. Inspector Morse says 'I always try solving problems by starting at the end, never the beginning'.[10] We know where we want to get to, at least, I do! Morse, like us, has the job of seeing the statue in the marble. What is possible, what achievable, when? The first imperative is to map the territory, see what is reliably known, and look hard at daily reality while also getting the world's work done. We need to raise expectations and then actually invest in implementing change. Actualité requires audit and then action. Like us, you may discover a paper mountain of existing policies, most of them unknown to most staff. Like us, you may find one person who tells you that the pre-retirement course they were offered was the only training opportunity given to them during their years of employment. So we need levers in our hands, levers linked to real wires, not only policies and plans, but action and outputs. Outputs, too, defined as changes in structure to deliver changes in culture.

What can an individual District try to achieve? In Brighton we have commenced the cartography. We have had the active support of Dame Wendy Mitchell from SE Thames Regional Health Authority, from my non-executive colleague Mrs Dagmar Gann whose skills and commitment have made the project credible and possible, from our Nursing Research Co-ordinator Barbara Sheppard[11], and from some previously covert enthusiasts. In Brighton we have appointed Anne-Marie O'Donnell as our New Opportunities Officer. We held an open public meeting attended by 180 staff, then set up 17 working groups all led by women with a co-ordinating Women's Forum (to be followed by a Men's Forum).[12]

The Women's Forum co-chairman Mrs Gann has written to the eleven consultant directors, and instead of saying 'Do it!' she said 'Please tell us how *you* can help us to deliver our goals'. We have two replies so far. Good going! The other consultant managers perhaps treat the request in their hands with some surprise, like being caught buying *Hello* magazine. It was a reasonable request, and I do not think management can accept that doctors in their employ should expect to deal with such a request by ignoring it. But we will encourage replies and co-operation. We do not want to drop a rose petal down the Grand Canyon and wait for the echo. We want real movement and change.

To that end, our first job is a total audit of our practices. We want to discover why, on specifics and in departmental detail, existing policies work or do not work. We want to uncover dilemmas, and to help contribute to better practice. For policies put on walls like mallard ducks do not deliver change. It takes pick and shovel work; for example, if we can convert middle managers (who often view a new initiative as yet another stick to beat them with), we can achieve real changes. If we can show them that family-friendly changes achieve staff stability and save substantial sums, we can sell this to the whole organization. We can then release the time, money and experience of trainers to do other work. We can stop the demoralization which feeds high turnover and comes from it.

I think the way forward is in two complementary programmes of action. First, to give women what they tell us they want and need: to help them work and cope in a system still clearly designed mainly for men who have supporting partners at home. Second, to set off and persist on the long project to understand and to change the prevailing behavioural rules and incentives and the male model of our culture. We need a set of priorities in asking what outputs could a District sensibly seek to attain. Let me focus on three priorities, among many.

First, the doctors. We have recently appointed two new female consultants, and want to make a serious contribution to bringing forward more women into top medical positions. We want to understand why this is such a difficult area. We know a lot already, of course. In my view, the present positioning of the national leaders of the medical bodies is inadequate. Political leadership has to persuade them that the consultant goal has to be worked for, that we are looking for urgent manifestations of change, and that local management has to have the authority to get it. 'Champions' are essential. One, Dr Meg Price (consultant dermatologist at Brighton) has set up a support network for women doctors in Brighton, and serves on our Women's Forum which is looking at why women in Brighton are in trouble in bringing more women into consultancy. One shift has been our active support for the career-break registrar – we have recently appointed three women into these career-break positions – admittedly relatively easy to do since it does not hurt financially. However, if we are to encourage women candidates to plan ahead, we should create a register of likely future vacancies: for example, even if tenure is unchanged, we know the retirement dates for all our present consultants. We could project ahead and say we hope to appoint women to these vacancies.

Second, an audit of family-friendly practice. What *are* our policies? Who knows of them, and how? Are the opportunities we offer helpful? Are they taken up? Do they work? For example, on job-sharing, we are preparing a specific piece of fieldwork, focusing on line-managers as pivots. What are the real barriers to implementing the job-share policy? Why is it not done? Why is it so difficult? We will be asking managers about their needs to fulfil their roles. How could we help them to implement the policy? We expect this to produce practical advice 'This is why it is not done.' This is to address the reality that the policies exist, but are not much implemented. It offers a creative opportunity for training and change by inhabiting reality, and by involving managers in identifying the benefits and the costs of policies that should be in place. This should help lever open the door behind which informal and unofficial reality functions, where attitudes affecting women's progress and limiting changes in male mind-sets are embedded.[13]

Third, how decisions are really made. We are designing a substantial research project to dig deeply into the informal politics of the organization, to make the rules of the game much more transparent.

We urgently need to open out discussion about this 'Yes Minister' area, which is the real source of the frustration of many women's hopes. This is about the implicit and explicit levers of male culture, which we need to dissect and discuss.[14] It is about structures, atmospheres, codes, invisible walls, unspoken ideas and understandings: about who is a player and who a spectator; about who decides who attends which meeting; who gets which papers (and how early); which policy issues come to the fore[15]; which reports are circulated; whether meetings are at a late hour, or in the pub over a pint[16]; what is decided on the steps of the hospital, in twos and threes; which executives really have power[17]; which committees matter, and which are merely ego; and who fixes them in advance.

This is to open out where the real decisions are taken, and how. This is about the real games that some of our mothers never taught us how to play. About how alliances are formed, managed, manipulated; how deals are done, networks built and relied upon; how protegée systems function; about who gossips with who and why; about cohorts and coat-tails; about how procedures can be useful traps to slow, divert, and ignore decisions. Unminuted lobbying; unreported caucuses; implied codes; deals in car parks – with the pretence (central to all politics) that no-one is in fact politicking. This is about approved styles, language, method. The rules people take for granted, never think about, well-worn statements about what is the done thing. How *is* power used and how are decisions really made in an organization? The games our mothers taught some of us how to play.

We are working at Brighton on a major attitudinal survey, to help transform the organization by increasing understanding, by making it more open, and by seeking to challenge the assumptions and methods of the old power structures. We are targeting 2000 staff – about half of our total workforce. This survey will complement the SE Thames RHA survey.

You are all individuals. I hesitate to comment on your personal action plan, but we must not lose the pass by allowing there to be any force in the argument that good women candidates do not come forward, or do not exist. The redesign of our work and the cultural changes of which I have spoken is all essential, but each of us, too, needs to rely on ourselves. We must be prepared to do it ourselves; believe in ourselves; encourage one another to come forward; take the training chances; join the Springboard Programmes; build confidence and contacts.

The *Register* is, in part, about visibility. If you ask what are the key contributory factors to being spotted and promoted, what are the key areas of personal development, these are confidence, contacts, communication and visibility. Training experts say that what picks you out in a field is personality and image where all are equally qualified: exposure, networking, being seen and known. The Springboard Project addresses it. Visibility is 60% of the answer to promotion.

Patients and the service need people to be promoted who are working with the patient-centred issues, and who embrace the radical options set out in this paper, spot issues and work-up new areas. Look at service needs – there are lots around: for example, how are GPs and Health Authorities to work together for The Health of the Nation targets? How can we embed quality? How make purchasing bite? How optimally manage the market? How manage the GP fundholder? How manage the non fund holder? How ensure training in a provider environment? How assess and deliver consumer choice? Who will take part in pilot projects, serve on

Management Executive, IHSM, NAHAT, King's Fund, or Trust Federation study groups and write up the reports in the HSJ?

Even if more women want to work in different and in separate ways — and patients need them to do so — there is no need to feel unease about the tactics for visibility. It is a critical imperative that good, qualified women come forward to lead the service in new ways, with men and women working together in a genuine new partnership for health. Opportunity 2000[18] is firmly in the mainstream of NHS strategic development, and chimes with the Patient's Charter in letter and in spirit.

We all have a huge professional agenda, but someone has to link the present with the future, and shape it.

Why not you?

Notes

1 There is no specialism called Womens' Health. Yet women are the largest users of the NHS, the largest employment group, and the main communicators about health to other family members. There is a bias based on male values which shows that women are not well served by modern medicine, even where modern medicine itself can be shown to be doing a good job. There is neglect in some areas and over-intrusive and harmful treatment in others. British women receive fewer investigations than men and less treatment for the same condition in men: for example, they are less likely to be offered kidney dialysis or a transplant; have a longer wait than men for heart pace-makers; get half as many heart operations as men with the same condition; seek help for heart problems later than men and are taken less seriously by a gender-biased profession when they do. Womens' abdominal operations outnumber all others, many of them ineffective or unnecessary. For breast cancer, Britain's treatment and success record is the worst in the world. For stress, women are over-medicated and prescribed twice as many mood-altering drugs as men. Only now, under heavy pressures for change, are we seeing women advancing as senior doctors. In 1980 less than 10% of consultants were women and for 1994/95 the target for women consultants was still only 15%. In key specialisms like obstetrics and gynaecology in 1990 87% of these consultants were male and the number of female senior registrars increased by fewer than five a year between 1985 and 1990. Women doctors are generally excluded from the controlling hierarchy of the General Medical Council, the Royal Colleges, and the British Medical Association. Their influence on positions of power and on major research is suppressed by cultural attitudes which regard women as inferior in medicine. Women doctors generally earn less than men, do less interesting work and abandon the profession more readily. For an extended discussion from the patient's point of view, see Spiers J, Lilley R (1995) *How to be a Street-wise Patient.* (In press.)

2 Caroline Langridge is, of course, the very effective founding Head of The NHS Women's Unit and an experienced Health Service manager. Richmond House is the Headquarters of the Department of Health at 79 Whitehall.

3 Baroness Cumberlege CBE, Parliamentary Under Secretary for Health in the House of Lords, 1992–; previously, Chairman of Brighton Health Authority, of NW Thames Regional Health Authority, and of NAHAT. Keynote speaker at the same conference where this paper was first delivered.

4 Quarried from one of Christopher Filde's 'City And Suburban' columns in *The Spectator*, but I cannot locate which.

5 Vissard M (1992) *The Rituals of Dinner, the Origins, Evolution, Eccentricities, and Meaning of Table Manners.* Viking, London, p.4.

6 Juliet Kristeva, French feminist, deconstructionist icon; ultra PC; theorist of cultural politics and author of *Desire in Language, a Semiotic Approach to Literature and Art.* Editions du Seuil, Paris, 1977; English translation, Columbia University Press, New York, 1980. The body of work most accessible via Toril Moi (ed.) (1986) *The Kristeva Reader,* Blackwell, Oxford.

7 Mary Daly, American feminist author of *Gyn/Ecology, the Meta Ethics of Radical Feminism.* Beacon Press, Boston, 1979, and *Pure Lust, Elemental Feminist Philosophy.* Beacon Press, Boston, 1984. Both published in the UK by The Women's Press (owned by a man, Naim Atallah). These books, even with my frame of mind, seem loopily serious, and seriously loopy.

8 Grace Jones, the devastatingly threatening black American model/singer/actress/photograph.

9 Quoted by Vissard, op.cit., p. 75.

10 Colin Dexter (1991) The Jewel That Was Ours. Macmillan, London, p. 180.

11 Barbara Sheppard, Research Co-ordinator, Brighton Nursing Development Unit and subsequently for the Brighton 'Listening To Patients' project was in the vanguard of support for my work at Brighton. See her important report on the role of the nurse in the rehabilitation of elderly people on patient-centred principles, *Looking Back – Moving Forward, Developing Elderly Care Rehabilitation and the Nurse's Role Within It.* Brighton Nursing Development Unit, Brighton, 1994. Also, her report focusing on the patient's views and the powerful impact which they had on the organization and practice of the Unit, *Listening to Patients: an Action Research Project.* Brighton Nursing Development Unit, Brighton, 1994. Barbara Sheppard also enabled colleagues to appreciate that many Patient-Focused Care projects are constructed with a cost focus and have to shift to a patient focus by including patients in their design and audit.

12 As it turned out, the Men's Forum was never set up, and the changes in the structure of men's jobs and working practices was not ultimately an agenda that even an activist non-executive Chairman was able to achieve. Some men from the middle ranks did contribute to the Women's Forum. Brighton won a SE Thames RHA award for its family-friendly policies in February 1993, but a survey at the same time showed how much still needed to be done. See *Brighton Health Care Bulletin*, No.279, April 1993.

13   Some advances in job-sharing followed and the Domino Consultancy were commissioned to produce both descriptive literature for our 'Flexible Partners Initiative' and 'How to do it' management guides which were of a very high standard, working with an outstanding and newly recruited Communications Manager (Pauline Sinkins) – in my view, it was essential to bring in people who would be patients' champions and who genuinely believed in this. Mrs Dagmar Gann, an NED with long service with Brighton Health Authority helped set the terms of the debate with a report to the Board in February 1992. She was sorely missed when ruled out on grounds of birthdate as a possible NED for the Trust.

14   During the period from September 1992 when this speech was made and my departure from Brighton in September 1994, the organization made no progress in unlocking these very firmly locked doors.

15   It is the Trust Chairman's responsibility to shape and control the agenda for the Board meeting, and if more did so we would make more progress (or less!). It is very difficult, however, for the non-executive outsider to discover what other meetings are going on, what they are supposed to achieve, and why those that are minuted appear to be attended by almost every executive director. My proposal that Brighton should close half of all committees and see what (if anything) happens next was regarded by the Chief Executive as entertainingly eccentric. Yet in my view it would have released substantial time and money for patient care, with nil impact on managing anything else that mattered.

16   The location of pre-Board discussion in Brighton was thought by some to be The Sudeley Arms, near The Royal Sussex County Hospital. When I referred one unresolved question to 'The Sudeley Arms Executive Sub-Committee' at the end of one boardroom discussion there were knowing glances. There is, too, the serious point that women (and some men) who had family responsibilities were not always able to be part of this 'social' group; some observers believed that this limited career opportunities.

17   It is interesting to ask how appropriate is the membership of NHS Trust Boards, and to compare who should really matter with who does. For the cultural change we need, the HR Director and the Director of Nursing should be critical. But how many really throw weight at Board meetings, or go on to become Chief Executives? Does the medical director represent medicine (that is, patients) or medics, and what if they are reliant for their private work on colleagues who they are being asked to manage? Where are the political doctors and the clinical directors – certainly, not at the Board. We know that the great majority of our problems concern communication. Lamentably, communication directors are not required to be main Board appointments, which is idiotic. This is where the battle is being lost, in provider units. This key function is not being resourced, nor backed psychologically by Chief Executives, nor by Chairmen. Nor is there anyone whose principal role is to co-ordinate all the initiatives which seek to improve our focus on patient values.

18   See *Women in the NHS – good practice handbook.* NHS Women's Unit, Department of Health, London 1991; *Women in the NHS – An implementation guide to Opportunity 2000.* Department of Health, London, 1992. The initiative was launched by Business in the Community.

This paper originated as an address to the National Conference of Women Managers in the NHS to launch the *NHS Career Development Register For Women,* in London, 29 September 1992. At the time it was given, discussion of transformational management was not well developed in the NHS, and both the position of women and the inappropriate working practices of men, were not taken seriously at Board level in local NHS units. A shorter version of the paper was published as 'Role Up, Role Up' in the *Health Service Journal,* 30 September, 1993, pp. 18-19. It is chastening to appreciate that the NHS has still been ahead of most Whitehall departments in opening out opportunities for women, for which Virginia Bottomley MP has been given insufficient credit. I am indebted to Caroline Langridge and Louise Churcher for a number of discussions on the issues sketched in this paper. Where I fall into pot-holes, they are of my own making. In preparing this paper for publication here I have retained the structure of the original, clarified a number of points which seemed too compressed, and discarded some rhetorical flourishes appropriate only to the theatrical needs of a large conference speech. The notes seek to report some subsequent events, or non-events, but I have not diluted the original (which stands in its own moment of time) by rewriting it to take full account of subsequent developments.

Index